INDIA AND SOUTH EAST ASIA

INDIA AND SOUTH EAST ASIA

States, Borders and Culture

Edited by
Arpita Basu Roy
Subhadeep Bhattacharya

Maulana Abul Kalam Azad Institute of Asian Studies, Kolkata

SHIPRA

The views expressed in this volume are of individual contributors and do not represent the viewpoint of the editors or the Council.

Rs, 750; US$ 37.50

ISBN: 978-81-7541-792-2

First Published in India in 2015

India and South East Asia: States, Borders and Culture

Published by:
SHIPRA PUBLICATIONS
LG 18-19, Pankaj Central Market, I.P. Ext.
Patparganj, Delhi-110092
Tel: 91-11-2223 5152, 2223 6152
E-mail: info@shiprapublication.com
www.shiprapublication.com

"Indian civilization took root especially in the countries of south-east Asia and the evidence for this can be found all over the place to-day."

Pandit Jawaharlal Nehru

Discovery of India

Acknowledgments

The editors are indebted to Maulana Abul Kalam Azad Institute of Asian Studies, Kolkata and the Vietnam Academy of Social Sciences, Hanoi for collaborating on different academic ventures including this one. The editors wish to acknowledge the support and encouragement received from the Director of Maulana Abul Kalam Azad Institute of Asian Studies (MAKAIAS), Dr. Sreeradha Datta in this regard. Prof. Ngo Xuan Binh, Director-General, Institute for Indian and Southwest Asian Studies, Vietnam Academy of Social Sciences, Hanoi has been particularly co-operative and enthusiastic about the volume. The volume is an outcome of a Roundtable entitled "States, Border, Religion in Southeast Asia" held in October 2013 when a delegation from VASS which included Professor Binh visited MAKAIAS. The editors are also extremely thankful to all the contributors for their valuable contribution to this volume.

Contents

Introduction

India's relations with Southeast Asia passed through many vicissitudes. Close cultural interaction of India with Southeast Asia began from prehistoric times and continued until the beginning of colonial rule. The term 'southeast' bears an important connotation in the context of the identity of this region—a region which is '*south*' of China and '*east*' of India. The region was considered by the anthropologists and historians of Europe as a far away region in Asia sandwiched between the two rich civilizations of India and China. Archaeological excavations are also a testimony to the interaction between the regions. The rich native culture of Southeast Asia got enriched further after coming in contact with her two big neighbours whose civilizational touch gave a new shape to the civilization of Southeast Asia. The nationalist historians of India called Southeast Asia as the 'Greater India' in the early twentieth century referring to the ancient contacts that India had with the region impacting the socio-cultural constructions in Southeast Asia in the early times of her history. Pandit Jawaharlal Nehru, in his famous book *Discovery of India*, refers to the rich contact India had with Southeast Asian lands of *Suvarnabhumi* (Sanskrit term meaning Land of Gold) and *Javadwipa* (Java) and the rest of Southeast Asia in ancient time.

Apart from movement of people, racial and linguistic affinity, there were also trading relations. Along with traders, *brahmans* (priests) from India came to Southeast Asia, who acquainted the local elite with Indian rituals, scriptures, and literature. They became counsellors in the affairs of the courts and provided political support to the rulers by giving them a sort of investiture and genealogical list, which legitimized the position of rulers. Indian elements like Sanskrit language, the Hindu-Buddhist cults, *Dharmashastras*, and the Indian concept of royalty became essential features of the early states of Southeast Asia. The Indian impact on the ancient kingdoms of Funan and Champa in Indo-China and that on the maritime kingdoms of Sri Vijaya and Majapahit is reminisced by the historians while the Indian imprints on the Boro Budur, Ankor Tham and Ankor Vat temples are the witness of this historical connection. The common people were influenced by Indian cultural elements as Indian deities became popular and the stories of the epics like Ramayana and Mahabharata were indigenised. Nobel Laureate Rabindranath Tagore, while writing his travelogue about his visit to the Siam (present day Thailand), Bali and Java, wrote about these deep connections. Thus in the whole gamut of Indo-Southeast Asian relations, both Indians and Southeast Asians played an active role.

Such ancient connections acted as the foundation of the India-Southeast Asia relations in the post colonial period. Pandit Nehru shaped his government's policy towards Southeast Asia by bolstering the anti-colonial movements in Indo-China and Indonesia. The Indian independence movement provided a stimulant to the anti-colonial struggle in Southeast Asia. Southeast Asian leaders, such as Sukarno, Norodom Sihanouk, Aung San, and Ho Chi Minh admired Indian personalities like Mahatma Gandhi, Rabindranath Tagore, and Jawaharlal Nehru. Many Southeast Asians also attended the sessions of the Indian National Congress and met Indian leaders. In the framework of the freedom struggle, the Indian leaders mooted the concept of Asianism and emphasized the spiritualism of Asia over materialistic west. They called upon a common Asian identity in opposition to the West.

Nehru convened the Asian Relations Conference in New Delhi in March 1947, even before his country formally achieved independence from the British bondage, to discuss the future of the Asia still languishing under the European colonial shackles and his contribution in Indonesian independence struggle is acclaimed world over. India whole-heartedly supported the liberation movements of Vietnam and rest of Indo-China since she always stood for anti colonialism.

Throughout the Cold War period India's engagement with Southeast Asia became stronger and closer. Such friendship crystallized further in the post Cold War period when India became a partner of ASEAN dialogue process and eventually became the part of the bigger East Asian platform, the East Asia Forum. Southeast Asia, on the other hand, also welcomed India's gradual involvement in the regional geo politics with the approach of the new millennium. The emerging India as an economic and political power was acknowledged by Southeast Asian nations who welcomed the 'Look East' policy of India. Today, India wants to 'Act East'. The new government in New Delhi gives immense importance to India's neighbours in the east and wants to strengthen India's engagement with them in every way.

Any discussion on India-Southeast Asia relations will remain incomplete without referring to the eternal friendship between India and Vietnam. India championed Vietnam's liberation war and even became part of the UN commission on Indo-China. India advocated Vietnam's case in the international field and insisted on the liberation of Vietnam from the French colonial rule. Later, during the Vietnam War for unification of the divided territory, India extended her support for the struggling liberators. Not only the government, even the Indian mass displayed their solidarity with the fighters of Vietnam by organizing mass demonstrations condemning the atrocities committed against them. India tried her best to help Vietnam emerge as a self-reliant country during the initial period of united Vietnam. Today, Vietnam is a valuable partner of India in Southeast Asia, the partnership is based on the eternal friendship cultivated by both sides for long.

The current volume covers different issues and perspectives of India and Southeast Asia ranging from discussions on the historical importance of the region to comparative studies on states. Issues like borders, security, disputes are analysed alongside issues like religion, culture and traditions. Some retrospective essays also attempt to question lost opportunities in Indian foreign policy and prescribe how India should look at the region. India's connection and engagement with the region has therefore been analysed and re-imagined by both Indian and Southeast Asian scholars and analysts. An interesting feature of this book is that it is an attempt by scholars in Kolkata and Hanoi to put their ideas and research on states, borders and religion of the region together. The collection of essays has been enlisted under three categories: States and Borders, Tradition and Culture and India and Vietnam. The last section interestingly covers Indian Studies in Vietnam and Vietnam Studies in India with a focus on bilateral relations.

States and Borders

States in Southeast Asia are multi-ethnic where nations are nascent; the problems of ethnicity and nation-building are typical. Myanmar and Indonesia are ethnically diverse societies. In his paper on *Ethno-Religious Diversity and National Unity: A Comparative Study of Indonesia and Myanmar*, Rabindra Sen draws a comparison between the ethno-political set up between Myanmar and Indonesia. The paper here discusses the similarities as well as differences of the socio-political characteristics of the two countries in details like the ethnic and religious plurality and the political history of colonial domination, military dictatorship as well as the nation building challenges. It also makes comparative study of the ethnic struggle for autonomy experienced by the two Southeast Asian countries. It suggests that the post Suharto Indonesia's democratization and lifting of restrictions can be a lesson for Myanmar which is also on its way of post-junta changes which is of course, according to the author, very challenging. The paper acknowledges that both Indonesia and Myanmar have a lot of issues to address in their process of nation building. However, in the context of Myanmar, it says that democracy and regional autonomy are important for the progress of the country.

State(s) in international politics have struggled to devise mechanisms that would ensure a minimum amount of protection against the use of force. The effort to combine forces that act as a protective shield for individual states evolved into collective security. In her paper on *The Security Community Experience in Southeast Asia: Lessons for South Asia,* Ishani Naskar analyses the feasibility of the growth of the South Asian Security Community by making a detailed study of the experiences in building the Security Community in Southeast Asia. The paper makes an elaborate study of the regionalization of Southeast Asia in the form of ASEAN and ASEAN Regional Forum (ARF) and studies the feasibility of the growth of Security Community in the region with reference to the constructivist as well as realist views on the issue. With reference to the Southeast Asian experience, the paper analyzes whether South Asian Association for Regional Cooperation (SAARC) can act in founding a Security Community in South Asia in which, the paper insists, India should play a bigger role adhering to the Gujral Doctrine. The paper argues that Security Community whether in Southeast Asia or South Asia will not be easy to achieve but the difference between the two regions is that while in Southeast Asia the process has already begun, South Asia may not be prepared for it at all.

Border disputes form the bone of contention between several states in the region and the South China Sea dispute is an important subject of the current East Asian geo politics. Subhadeep Bhattacharya in his paper on *The Maritime Border Dispute of South China Sea: Factors Impeding Solution* primarily focuses on the nature of the dispute and argues that the dispute is no longer a simple clash of sovereignty but is the source of assertiveness of the emerging powers active in the East Asian scene, including the extra regional powers. It says that the dispute has many shades. In the one hand when the dispute centres around the question of economic prosperity of the claimants, on the other hand the issue of geo strategic calculations and over all the strong nationalistic zeal produced by the internal pressure groups with a sprinkle of historical references, also play important role. Thus, the paper argues that the South China Sea dispute is difficult to resolve with so many competing interests working.

Tradition and Culture

The history of insular Southeast Asia can be established in its maritime history where the written and oral accounts include the maritime trade, both internal and international, as well as the life and culture of the maritime kingdoms and their spiritual life. In the paper *Re-imagining Insular Southeast Asia through Traditional Works*, Huynh Thanh Loan has attempted to discuss how the historical writings and chronologies have helped in shaping the history of insular Southeast Asia, including the cultural life of the region. And this history is available in many forms, in written or verbal accounts and in the inscriptions engraved on the monuments. Even the myths, chronicles and legends play their part in the writing of the history. The paper discusses the history of the political life of the insular Southeast Asian kingdoms like their courts, the relation between the kings, queens and the priests who played important role in these ancient kingdoms of Southeast Asia.

Such writings also narrate the history of the states and their maritime activities and the gradual development of cultural cross connections with different parts of the region and beyond via maritime activities. It refers to the old literatures of the region to understand the characteristics of the old kingdoms. It cites the example of the ancient Javanese literatures like the Javanese *Ramayana kakawin,* composed in the ninth century, which gives the character of the ancient Javanese kingdoms. The paper refers to the tenth century Javanese version of *Mahabharata* in this context. Talking about the Hindu Brahminical influence on the local creativities and rituals of Southeast Asia, the author mentions about the Hindu ceremonies in Indonesian courts called royal consecration or *abhiṣeka* and funerary rites called *śrāddha*, the Indian way of life for higher classes like the *āśramas* and also about the worship of royal ancestors. Apart from Hinduism, the author refers to the influence of Buddhism in the maritime Southeast Asia. It mentions how Buddhism spread in Java, Nusa Tenggara, and east Borneo under the patronage of the Sailendra Kings. It mentions about the famous Borobudur Temples in this context. The author also refers to the historical evidence about the maritime trade of the coastal regions of Southeast Asia and the shaping of the polities of the region on the basis of the trade. The paper although admits at the end that no accurate chronology can be drawn from the available information yet these inscriptions and the myths give some idea about the life of the ancient people of maritime Southeast Asia.

Hinduism and Buddhism are the two pillars which connect India with Southeast Asia. It is interesting to note that the people of Southeast Asia show their immense respect towards these two religions. For example, in countries like Myanmar, they are indebted to the Hindu teachers who taught not only History, English, law, philosophy, etc., but even Myanmar language, to the people of Myanmar. In her paper entitled *Understanding of Buddhism-Hinduism and Promotion of Indian Studies in India and Abroad: The Missed Opportunity in Indian Foreign Policy,* Swapna Bhattacharya (Chakraborti) mainly focuses on the soft power potentials of India latent in her centuries old cultural relations with her neighbours in Southeast Asia, especially Myanmar, which the foreign policy makers have not properly utilized. The paper insists that India could gain the position in Asia that China has gained lately if the cultural relations potentials are exploited by India. The paper here focuses on the educational potentials that India can exploit to strengthen her connections with Southeast Asian countries. It argues that in the colonial period the Universities of Calcutta, Bombay and Benares were very popular across Asia. So was Visva Bharati University, founded by Tagore. But during the Second World War, when Indology, especially the theology of Hinduism and Buddhism, was taught even in war-torn Germany, India gradually lost the opportunity to promote such studies abroad. The paper insists that Indian students should be equipped with proper texts and reference books at the university level since these students of today will become future policy makers.

Nguyen Ngoc Quynh's paper on the *Some Features of Tantrism in Vietnam* deals with *Tantrism*, an important aspect of Vietnamese Buddhism. It says that the Vietnamese are accustomed with Tantrism since the tenth century AD. It discusses in details the character of Tantrism in Vietnam, how it became popular in the country and who its scholars were. The paper suggests that an Indian Brahmin from South India took Tantrism to Vietnam. The paper discusses the practices of Tantrism in Vietnam today. It says that today Tantrism is attracting many Buddhist and non-Buddhist followers since 'it can meet people's spiritual needs in current social conditions in Vietnam, and help people to solve problems in their life'. The paper says that there are many sects of Tantrism and there are many methods to teach Tantrism. It mentions the major uses or methods in Vietnam to learn Tantrism. In conclusion, the paper informs that Tantrism lacks official transmission and that it does not develop systematically but appears only in some pagodas where monks are knowledgeable about it.

India and Vietnam

Traditional friendship between India and Vietnam, support of both countries towards their respective national struggles, the historical trade relations that existed between India and Vietnam and the strong cultural links between the two sides are exemplary. Tridib Chakraborti in his paper entitled *India and Vietnam: The Historical Strategic Friendship in Asian Domain* discusses in details the present India-Vietnam strategic relations with reference to the past. It refers to the friendship that developed between the two countries in the post-colonial period. It referred to the Indian support to Vietnam's liberation struggle and Prime

Minister Nehru's relation with Vietnamese leader Ho Chi Minh. The paper suggests that India and Vietnam experienced convergence of strategic interest even during the Cold War period which helped India develop close relations with Hanoi. It mentions about the economic aid provided by India to Vietnam during the Cold war period which shows how India was involved as a donor country in Southeast Asia during that time. The paper vividly describes the evolution of Indo-Vietnam relations since the post-Cold War period which gradually took a definite strategic shape with the rise of China as the new century approached. The paper here argues that the developing Indo-Vietnam closeness has both the economic as well as strategic connotation in the context of China's naval empowerment and growing assertiveness, especially in the South China Sea region. It opines that to counter China's South Asia policy of encircling India and to involve more in Southeast Asian affairs, New Delhi is developing close relation with Vietnam who also shares similar apprehension about the Chinese rise. Indo-Vietnam relation is important, according to the paper, to promote India's strategic interests in the maritime domain and Vietnam's pursuit for engaging reliable international stakeholders in the region.

Discussing the reasons behind the expansion of the Indo-Vietnam economic cooperation, Ngo Xuan Binh and Ngo Minh Duc writes about *Vietnam-India Economic Relations from a geopolitical perspective*. They put forward the internal as well as external factors that have helped in making the cooperation possible. The paper discusses the factors that promote the economic bonding between India and Vietnam, their characteristics and their prospects. Discussing the internal factors of both countries promoting the trade relations, the paper mentions the traditional friendship of the two countries referring to support of the both countries towards their respective national struggles. Next they mention the historical trade relations that existed between India and Vietnam which developed strong cultural links between the two sides. The paper also talks about the geo-political location of Vietnam which has helped in the strengthening of the India-Vietnam relations. It mentions Vietnam as the bridge between Indian Ocean and the Asia Pacific region which gives Vietnam political advantages in Southeast Asia. It refers to the India's Look East Policy with special reference to ASEAN and says that 'India regarded Vietnam as a "springboard" to expand relations with ASEAN countries and then reach out off the region and far beyond'. It also refers to the China factor in India's East Asia policy. Discussing the external reasons strengthening India-Vietnam relations, the paper mentions the growing importance of ASEAN of which Vietnam is an important member and the China factor influencing India-Vietnam relations. The paper also discussed the current shape of the Indo-Vietnam trade and investments, tourism and the initiatives of both sides to promote tourism sector and the prospects of the Indo-Vietnam economic relations citing the guidelines of the Joint Declaration of the two countries.

Two papers reflect Indian Studies in Vietnam, with one being a comparative study. Nguyen Thi Ngoc's paper on *Urban Environmental Pollution in India and Vietnam: A Comparative Study* makes a comparative analysis of the environmental pollution in the urban areas of India and Vietnam which is a major problem throughout the globe today, especially in the fast growing economies. It takes up two major areas which are more vulnerable to pollution, water and air. At the same time, it discusses about the municipal solid wastes as a major contributor in the environmental pollution. Assessing the comparative study of India and Vietnam in the context of water pollution in the urban areas, the paper depicts a more serious picture of India but also warns Vietnam about the situation. Similar situation is depicted about the air pollution in the urban areas of both the countries but here also, the author suggests, India's case is more serious. The paper concludes that both India and Vietnam face serious environmental pollution in the urban areas which will be a big threat to the future.

In the other paper, Le Thi Hang Nga attempts to discuss a very interesting and complex issue of the relation between India's iron lady, the former Prime Minister Indira Gandhi and religion. Heading a secular party, the Congress, Indira Gandhi's viewpoint about religion has not been very widely discussed or even known for that matter. The paper entitled *Appraisal of Indira Gandhi's Religiosity: A Vietnamese Perspective* however, at the outset, refers to the book of the leader's biographer Pupul Jayakar, who was a close associate of Indira Gandhi, as the source of his inspiration. It explores this issue with reference to Indira Gandhi's relation with J. Krishnamurti, a philosopher of her time and discusses the issue by dividing his paper under three categories—by discussing the overall issue of religiosity and spirituality, Indira Gandhi's family's views about religion and finally, Indira Gandhi's religiosity. The argument in the paper is that Indira Gandhi was spiritual but not religious "in its narrow sense". In support of the argument, it discusses how the secular views of his father and India's first Prime Minister, Jawaharlal Nehru, had influenced the thinking of Indira Gandhi in the initial days. However, it writes how secular Indira turned to the religious philosopher J. Krishnamurti during the concluding phase of her political career when she was passing through critical time. Indira Gandhi's mode of spirituality is discussed by the author at length where she refers to her views on death. What comes out of the paper is the urge of this iron lady of India, brought up in a Westernized family with secular thoughts and practices and groomed under a secular father-come-leader, to take refuge in the spiritual world during the 'depressing time' of her life.

It must be understood that the Indian engagement with the Southeast Asian region extends beyond recent conceptualisations to periods when connectivity was defined not just in strategic terms but also cultural terms. It is undeniable that India views the region as a crucial partner today and there are vital concerns that both regions share. But contemporary concerns should not overshadow the broader issues that have been important to both regions through the ages.

BIBLIOGRAPHY

Tarling, Nicholas (ed.), *Cambridge History of Southeast Asia,* Vol. 1 & 2, Cambridge University Press, 1999.

Hall, D.G.E., *A History of Southeast Asia,* Palgrave McMillan, 1981.

Nehru, Jawaharlal, *Discovery of India*, Oxford University Press, Delhi, 1985.

Thien Ton That, *India and Southeast Asia: 1947-1960*, Librairie Droz Geneva, 1963.

Majumdar, R.C., *Ancient Indian Colonization in Southeast Asia*, Maharaja Sayajirao Gaaekwad Honoraruim Lecture 1953-54, http://www.sabrizain.org/malaya/library/indiancolonization.pdf.

Majumdar Ashish Kumar, *Southeast Asia in India's Foreign Policy: Study of India's Relations with Southeast Asian Countries from 1962-82,* Noya Prakash, 1982.

Ayub, Mohammad, *India and Southeast Asia: Indian Perceptions and Policies*, Routledge, 1990.

Nanda, Prakash, *Rediscovering India: Evolution of India's Look East Policy,* Lancer Publishers and Distributors, 2003.

States and Borders

1
Ethno-Religious Diversity and National Unity

A Comparative Study of Indonesia and Myanmar

Rabindra Sen

Introduction

Given the extent of ethno-religious diversity witnessed in Southeast Asia, it is appropriate to begin with the following observation by Leo Suryadinata:

> ' ...in multiethnic Southeast Asia where nations are still in the making, the problems of ethnicity and nation-building have never been out of sight.... However, with intensive globalization and the revival of ethnicity, the problems become more salient than before' (Suryadinata, 2007:162).

The above observation is especially important for two of Asia's most ethnically diverse countries the present study focuses on. Both Indonesia and Myanmar are particularly important in studies relating to ethno-religious diversity and nation-building. Indonesia's special importance lies in its extraordinary geographical, linguistic, ethnic and social heterogeneity. Politics in poly-ethnic Indonesia has been dominated by the Javanese ethnic group. This dominance has given rise to grievances and ill-feelings in the Outer Islands of the sprawling archipelago. In the late 1990s and the early part of this century, the ethnic stirrings became even more marked, threatening to tear apart the Indonesian national fabric. Not surprisingly, the dominant task of the ruling elite in Indonesia has long been that of holding the country together. Myanmar too has a genuine ethnic and religious plurality. About one half of Myanmar is comprised of territory traditionally occupied by ethnic minorities. Although Theravada Buddhism of the Burman majority is shared by the Rakhine and most Shans and Karens, Myanmar has a sizeable community of Christians, Hindus and Muslims (Matthews, 2001). Frequently feeling marginalised, the ethnic and religious minorities find no comfort living in a State largely defined by the cultural and political priorities of an overbearing majority (Matthews, 2001). Needless to say, there is deep distrust of the central authorities among most ethnic minorities.

Given the striking similarities in historical experiences, it would only be natural to draw parallels between the two countries. It would indeed be interesting to study the implications of ethno-religious diversity for the nation-building process in both the countries. Also pertinent is the question as to whether and how far the problem of separatism or the fight for autonomy in Indonesia and Myanmar is explicable in terms of the fault lines mentioned above. Most importantly, the purpose of the present paper is to see how much Indonesia has to offer in terms of tackling the challenges to nation-building as Myanmar progresses on the path of reform[1]. The change in Indonesia in the post-Suharto era—and though late in coming—also in Myanmar, has been the subject of much discussion and debate. Quite naturally, a comparison of the two countries would help us understand the nature and importance of the changes and their implications for national unity.

Similarities and Differences

Indonesia and Myanmar are similar in more ways than one. Besides having a genuine ethnic plurality, the religious plurality in both the countries also deserves due attention. Both have their dominant ethnic groups—the Javanese in Indonesia, though not constituting a majority of the total population, and the Burmans in Myanmar, accounting for around sixty per cent of the population—and also their dominant religions—Islam in Indonesia and Buddhism in Myanmar. It would, however, be wrong to think that the experiences of the two countries have been identical. While the Indonesian nationalist movement, as

Jacques Bertrand has pointed out, rallied groups from different parts of the archipelago, in Myanmar, or what was then known as Burma, the independence movement was mostly an enterprise of the Burman majority (Kuhn, 2013). Compared to Indonesia, Myanmar has used the dominant religion for bolstering its legitimacy. In Indonesia, on the other hand, Sukarno and other leaders had to be firm in dealing with demands for adherence to orthodox Islam and for transforming Indonesia into an Islamic state. The fear was, and has always been, that succumbing to such pressures would have a potentially disastrous impact on the unity of the Indonesian nation (Sen, 2014: 235). Turning to the similarities once again, it is important to note that neither the British nor the Dutch had done anything to foster a sense of ethnic harmony or national unity. While in Myanmar, the colonial power had used divide-and-rule tactics successfully and cultivated Christian minorities such as the Karens as a hedge against the Burmans[2] (Kuhn, 2013), the Dutch use of the Ambonese in the colonial army in Indonesia had planted the seeds of future ethnic conflict (Suryadinata, 1976: 211-12).

In the immediate aftermath of colonial rule, sharing the same vision of 'unity in diversity', both Sukarno and Aung San sought to bring heterogeneous peoples under a banner of national unity (Ghoshal, 2013). In both Myanmar and Indonesia, the military had played a prominent part in the achievement of independence. Also, in both the countries, the multi-ethnic composition of the army gave way to majority Burman and Javanese domination (Ghoshal, 2013). In the post-Suharto period, the growth of democratic institutions accelerated the military's "return to the barracks." But down to the present day the military continues to wield a strong influence (Vatikiotis, 2014). In Myanmar, in spite of changes setting in, the levers of power continue to be in the hands of the military, which retains sweeping emergency powers and extensive control over state budgets. The Constitution reserves one-quarter of parliamentary seats for the military, which has control over vital sectors of the economy, such as energy and international trade (Kuhn, 2013).

Ethno-Religious Strife and Separatist Movements/Autonomy Demands

Indonesia has been plagued by the problem of separatism right from independence. Several separatist movements grew bolder in Indonesia after the ouster of President Suharto in May 1998. In Papua, a low-level insurgency has continued to simmer. Myanmar too has been ravaged by civil war between the Burman-dominated central government and the country's ethnic minorities since independence from Great Britain in 1948. The history of Myanmar in terms of the insurgency problem, roots of which go far into the past, is one of failed ceasefires (Lintner, 2012). A long-standing ceasefire between the government and the Kachin Independence Organization, for example, broke down in 2011 over issues of ethnic and political rights. Fighting has also continued in north-central Shan State, despite a ceasefire agreement signed with the government. Both the struggles have cast a shadow over the government's largely successful peace drive so far in other insurgency-afflicted areas of the country (McCartan, 2012).

Since both the countries have been affected by ethnic and religious violence and outbreaks of civil unrest, the important question is whether and to what extent ethnic diversity has fuelled the eruptions. More importantly, has it been the root cause? The answer is that it may not have been always so, or even in most cases. It is important not to be carried away by the ethnic overtones of domestic conflagrations to conclude that these are invariably rooted in ethnicity (Sen, 2014: 242). The problem may basically be economic as was the case in Tasikmalaya, which exploded in violence in December 1996 (McBeth and Cohen, 1997: 14-15). Or, it may well be a political crisis eventually taking on an ethnic and communal colour.

Economic issues, which were important also in the past, have been at the centre of Indonesian politics and largely explain much of what has happened in the country. Conflicts between different ethnic groups are likely to occur especially when competition for resources and position is accelerated (Suparlan, 1979: 71). This phenomenon is also observed in the social relationship between the Chinese and the local Indonesian ethnic groups. It is interesting to note that the potential for widespread anti-Chinese conflicts is great in areas where economic activities are dominated by the Chinese. The same explanation also applies to the gruesome violence erupting from time to time between the native Dayak people and the migrant Maduranese on the island of Borneo. Separatism, which has plagued Indonesia since the early days of independence, is the manifestation of a historical problem dating from the colonial period. And here too, ethnicity is not the only, or perhaps not even the primary, cause (Sen, 2014: 244).

Transformation in Indonesia: Lessons for Myanmar

After the end of the Suharto era and almost a decade of political paralysis, economic crisis and ethno-religious strife, the change in Indonesia has truly been phenomenal. As Ben Otto and Andreas Ismar put it, "What we're seeing is extraordinary" (Otto and Ismar 2013). Among the notable examples of the remarkable change in Indonesia are a freer press boosting public demands for better governance and accountability, and the government's decision to lift restrictions on political parties (Kuhn, 2013). Quite obviously, Myanmar needs to take cognizance of the changes occurring in Indonesia as lessons, as it itself undergoes the process of transformation, notwithstanding the doubts and uncertainties which still persist[3].

Various measures have been adopted in Indonesia to promote national integration and cope with the challenges and threats to the continued existence of the nation-state[4]. Indonesia is fortunate not to have been saddled with a language problem. From the pre-independence period, the importance of *Bahasa Indonesia*, the national language, as a cohesive force is particularly worth stressing. (Sen, 2014: 235-236). The importance of *Bahasa Indonesia* as a unifying element has been and will continue to be strongly felt in Indonesia. The teaching of *Pancasila*, the philosophical basis of the Indonesian state is also noteworthy in this connection (Budhisantoso, 1996). The third principle of *Pancasila* which embodies the concept of nationalism is particularly important and relevant. *Pancasila* nationalism demands that Indonesians avoid feelings of superiority on grounds of ethnicity, ancestry and colour of the skin (*Indonesia,* 1997:40). Political parties in Indonesia all have to swear to abide by the state *Pancasila* ideology, which recognizes all the main religions. Also, given the still strong position of the military in Indonesia in spite of the emphasis on democratic governance and steps taken in this regard, it will not be out of place to refer to a doctrine, which stresses loyalty to the central authority and is intended to unify the multi-ethnic military. Under the doctrine, the military personnel swear their allegiance not to the ethnic groups they belong to but to the Indonesian nation (Suryadinata, 1976: 228).

Given the nature and extent of diversity in Indonesia and Myanmar, and the fact that both are unitary states, an especially important question is whether decentralization is likely to promote or endanger unity and territorial integrity. Opinion is bound to vary on this question. Nevertheless, what is important is that the big policy change in Indonesia in the form of a bold and ambitious decentralization programme after the fall of Suharto was perhaps based on the conviction that decentralization, democratic governance and national integrity are closely intertwined. Regional autonomy as a matter of fact was a cherished aim of Indonesia's reform movement (*Economist,* 2001). Critics of the decentralization scheme of course feared it might jeopardise national unity. Under the scheme, quite a few new provinces and over 100 new regencies have been established, some of them based on ethnic identities. Jakarta responded to demands for local autonomy by devolving authority over nearly half of government spending to local governments. After a quarter-century-long insurgency in westernmost Aceh province, Jakarta even made it a special administrative region and empowered it to legislate Shariah, or Islamic law (Kuhn, 2013). Local elections have been held peacefully, giving real meaning to local autonomy (Vatikiotis, 2014). The outcome of Indonesia's 'big bang' decentralization, though not an unqualified success, has, as Marcus Mietzner has argued, been remarkably good taking into consideration Indonesia's history and the conditions prevailing in the country when the programme was launched (McCulloch, 2011). Today, Indonesia is no longer a country where all important matters are decided in Jakarta as was the case for more than three decades of Suharto's New Order when Indonesia was one of the most centralized states in the world (McCulloch, 2011). Each district now has its own directly elected mayor or district head, as well as an elected parliament (McCulloch, 2011). This should undoubtedly be considered as one of the most significant and welcome changes brought about by decentralization.[5]

Myanmar has not yet succeeded in evolving a mechanism—such as federalism—for bringing in the minorities under the Union. As a result, large parts of Myanmar's border areas remain under rebel control (Kuhn, 2013). Is federalism really the answer? Will there be a second Panglong?[6] Notwithstanding its deficiencies, the 1947 Panglong Agreement clearly constituted an historic achievement. However, the assassination of Aung San shortly before independence, immediately compromised the agreement. Aung San's successor, Prime Minster U Nu had neither the vision nor the capacity needed to carry forward the ethnic accord and infant federalism (Kuhn, 2013).

Will Myanmar with its traditionally highly centralized polity and what some describe as 'garrison nationalism', embrace the notion of federalism? The problem with federalism is that it is not part of the traditional cultural or political language. Any suggestion, therefore, that Western-style federalism is Myanmar's political answer to ethnic pluralism is simplistic. In this context, it must be kept in mind that barring one or two minor fringe groups (e.g. the Arakan Independence Alliance), Myanmar's minorities are not agitating to break away from the State. Their objectives rather are simply more regional autonomy and better representation. Herein lies the importance of the Indonesian decentralisation programme as a lesson for Myanmar for addressing local and regional grievances. Needless to say, ethnicity is the key to the success of Myanmar reform. But the question is how to resolve the issue in view of the irreconcilable differences. Constitutional reform is a must. As Shan leader Sai Wansai has argued, as long as the core problem—the highly controversial 2008 Constitution—is not addressed, 'it is hard to imagine that the ethnic conflicts within Myanmar could be resolved anytime soon.' (Lintner, 2012) But the procedure is highly complicated (Lintner, 2012).

In her first statement as an elected parliamentarian, Myanmar opposition leader Daw Aung San Suu Kyi chose to highlight the plight of ethnic minorities, underscoring the issue's rising importance in domestic politics. Indeed, ethnic conflict resolution is crucial for stability and security, without which economic development and democratic processes cannot be strengthened and sustained. Suu Kyi's speech was delivered amid the ongoing fighting between the government and ethnic insurgents in northern Shan and Kachin States and communal strife in the western Rakhine State. It also underscored the need for the government to reach durable political solutions with ethnic minority groups or risk the unraveling of democratic and economic reforms. Invoking the 'Panglong spirit' Suu Kyi implicitly connected it to the agreement signed between her father, independence hero General Aung San, and ethnic Kachin, Shan and Chin representatives.[7] For ethnic minority leaders, the Panglong Agreement was thus viewed positively as a step towards federalism. Suu Kyi noted that the 'spirit' of that agreement was 'based on equality and mutual respect'(McCartan, 2012).[8] President Thein Sein also said, 'In implementing political and economic reforms, easing of ethnic conflicts needs to be considered. Only when such reforms are carried out, will national reconciliation be achieved and ethnic conflicts ended.' (McCartan, 2012) A notable difference, however, is that while Thein Sein's speech indicated that reconciliation with the ethnic groups will result from political and economic reforms, Suu Kyi's statement emphasized the importance of achieving political solutions to ethnic problems as a stepping stone to countrywide political and economic development (McCartan, 2012).

Aung Min, Vice-Chairman of the Union Peacemaking Working Committee—entrusted with the responsibility of negotiating with ethnic political organizations, has recently hinted that the government may be willing to consider discussion of the creation of a federal system. Aung Min has said, 'The guidelines are not carved in stone. We can discuss and amend them as necessary. Right now, we are working hard to hold a Panglong-like political dialogue before the end of 2014.' (McCartan. 2012). His statement was interpreted by some as a reversal of the government's previous refusals to discuss federalism, a new Panglong-style conference, or engage with more than one ethnic group at a time for discussions on politics, self-government or autonomy issues. It also represented an apparent change from the government's earlier rigid stance that all political settlements should be worked out in parliament, a body currently dominated by the military and the Burman majority. This has given new hope to some ethnic leaders that while a federal union is unlikely to materialise in the immediate term, it could be achievable in the long-term. Thein Sein's government may be genuinely keen to reach political settlements with ethnic-based insurgent organizations, but there are still many hardliners in the military believing that they can crush their resistance through military means (McCartan, 2012). Whether Thein Sein's and Suu Kyi's calls will result in real reconciliation, however, continues to depend on the military top brass.

Ongoing Concerns and Tasks Ahead

Ethnic and religious tensions have not been uncommon in Indonesia. But the vast archipelago was wracked by such tensions so much after Suharto was forced to relinquish power, that the very existence of Indonesia as a united nation-state was doubted. Although conditions improved a great deal during Yudhoyono's presidency, it would be wrong to think that uncertainties and undercurrents of instability have ceased to exist. A survey in 2008 in fact showed that even after more than six decades of independence national unity continues to be a cause for concern in Indonesia. The situation in Indonesia thus remains, at least potentially, quite volatile. There still are worries, for example, of creeping extremism. In Myanmar similarly, communal conflict between ethnic Buddhist Rakhines against Muslim Rohingyas in the western Rakhine State, though not an insurgency, is also a cause for concern. The violence between one ethnic minority—allegedly backed by the security forces of the majority government—against another minority group points towards the potential for continued instability in ethnic relations.[8]

Aung San Suu Kyi recognises the importance of ethnic rights and their due participation in the negotiations. There must be mutual recognition of diversity from all parties, followed by equality and mutual respect. 'The essence of the Panglong Spirit is equality and mutual recognition,' said the prominent exiled politician, U Than Htut (Aung Naing Oo, 2002). Needless to say, ethnic peace, as already stressed, is the key to reform in Myanmar. But in view of the irreconcilable differences the question is how to resolve the issue.

Although violence in the Indonesian archipelago has noticeably ebbed since the middle of the last decade, the ethnic clash, as recently as October 2012, in the remote South Lampung district of Sumatra is a reminder of the continuing undercurrents of tension and instability (Osman, 2012). Turning to the situation in Myanmar once again, the assault on the Rohingyas which sparked sectarian violence across the rest of Myanmar now seems to be spreading to other parts of Asia too. A tit-for-tat escalation is going on which, not without reason, is viewed by many in the region with a great deal of concern (*Economist,* 2013).

For Myanmar's reforms to take root, the imperative is to soon move beyond emphasis on the country's central region and begin to address the military's supremacy over the civilian government in the border regions where most ethnic minorities reside. After decades of civil war, democracy and local autonomy represent the best hope for alleviating entrenched poverty and underdevelopment in the ethnic minority regions.

Conclusion

Can we consider the recent developments in Myanmar to have heralded the beginning of a new era of democracy and peace? The answer would to a large extent depend on settlement of an issue yet to be addressed: respect for Myanmar's ethnic and religious diversity. As Matthew J. Walton points out, 'Without attention to continued differential treatment of non-Burmans in many parts of the country as well as the privileged position of Burmans with regard to the national "Myanmar" identity, ethnic reconciliation in Myanmar will remain elusive.' (Walton, 2013:22) There has been a noticeable improvement in the situation in Indonesia after the turbulence witnessed in the late 1990s and the early part of the present century. Indeed, Indonesia is better placed than Myanmar in its efforts to deal with the enormous and diverse challenges—consolidating democracy, addressing regional conflict, and most importantly, regenerating the economy. Democracy in Indonesia, if not already firmly rooted and endowed with resilience, at least seems to be well on the way to becoming so. But Myanmar has a long way to go in this respect.

A decision to reverse the reform process to manage conflicts will only further complicate matters. The economy is undoubtedly the key to stability, particularly because unlike before the 1962 coup, when Myanmar had had one of the highest living standards in Southeast Asia (Ghoshal, 2013), it is now the poorest country in Southeast Asia. There is clear enough evidence to see the economic factor as the root of tension, albeit not exclusively and inevitably. The following instances respectively from Indonesia and Myanmar should suffice. In Indonesia, the Dayaks of Kalimantan and the Papuans are hostile to the newcomers, whom they see as getting favoured treatment and whose new lifestyle is at their own expense (Suter, 2001:24). And in Myanmar, the insurgencies are being fought in part for control of resources, including jade, timber and hydropower, and foreign investment in these resources

(Kuhn, 2013). Insurgency and government counter-insurgency operations continue to wreak havoc in many border areas where much of Myanmar's trade passes and wealth of natural resource lies (McCartan, 2012). Needless to say, increasing unemployment and food shortages will only increase ethnic strains. After all, it should be remembered that national unity can be maintained only on the basis of social justice. Those feeling disadvantaged, underprivileged and discriminated against, cannot simply be expected to embrace unity with the privileged (Djiwandono, 1997: 12). Addressing the grievances of the Outer Islanders in Indonesia and the ethno-religious minorities in Myanmar is thus enormously important. If the national government's development programme fails to satisfy the minority groups, the forces of regionalism and separatism would naturally be strengthened (Suryadinata, 1976: 234).

In conclusion, two points are worth emphasising. First, ethnic diversity in itself would not invariably pose an insurmountable obstacle to nation-building and national unity. Diversity in itself is not—but may become—either an asset or a liability. And second, if after the clearly noticeable change in Indonesia from authoritarian and centralised governance to democracy and decentralisation, doubts can still be raised about the strength of democracy and fears expressed about the possibility of progress being undermined by a troubling trend of religious intolerance and a failure by the leadership to uphold constitutional guarantees of pluralism (Vatikiotis, 2014), in the case of Myanmar, where the process of change has barely begun, the uncertainties and doubts will surely be much stronger. The greatest challenge before both Indonesia and Myanmar in any case is and will continue to be to strive for unity amidst diversity by taking concrete measures to get closer to the desired goal.

NOTES

1. Above all one can go to the extent considering Myanmar's case as exceptional (Matthews 2001).
2. The Karen are still perceived by many as having received 'preferential treatment' from the British.
3. Some would, however, say that the process remains unfinished (Kuhn 2013).
4. For details see (Sen 2014: 235-41).

5. For a discussion of the positive outcomes of the programme, see Bunnell, Miller, Phelps and Taylor 2013.
6. The Panglong Agreement was meant to be the glue to hold the country together. A central weakness of the agreement, however, was the conspicuous absence of the Karen, Karenni, Rakhine (Arakanese) and Mon.
7. That agreement was intended to provide for equality between the country's ethnic Burman-dominated central regions and ethnic minority frontier regions by granting autonomy to peripheral areas. In exchange, the Shan, Kachin and Chin agreed to join what was then known as the Union of Burma (McCartan 2012).
8. But there are question marks over Suu Kyi's stand on the ethnic issue. Her silence on the plight of the Rohingya Muslims, which has not gone unnoticed, may be cited as an example.
9. Naypyidaw views the Rohingya as foreigners and many, including among other ethnic groups in Myanmar, look upon them as illegal immigrants from Bangladesh (McCartan 2012).

REFERENCES

Aung Niang Oo, 2002. "Burmese Politics and the Broken Unity", *The Irrawady*, May 1, http://www2.irrawady.org/opinion_story.php?art_id=2615 (accessed May 25, 2014).

Budhisantoso, S., "National Identity and Development in the Plural Society of Indonesia", 1996 at http://ignca.nic.in/ls_03015.htm (accessed May 11, 2014).

Bunnell, Tim, Miller, Michelle Ann, Phelps, Nicholas A. and Taylor, John, "Urban Development in a Decentralized Indonesia: Two Success Stories?", *Pacific Affairs*, 86(4), 2013, pp. 857-76.

Ghoshal, Baladas, "In Myanmar's transition, shades of Indonesia", *The Hindu*, January 9, 2013 at http://www.thehindu.com/todays-paper/tp-opinion/in-myanmars-transition-shades-of-indonesia/article4288738.ece (accessed May 11, 2014).

Djiwandono, J. Soedjati, "Ethnic/Religious/Cultural Challenge to National Security: The Indonesian Case", *The Indonesian Quarterly* 25(1) 1997: 7-12.

Indonesia 1997: An Official Handbook, Department of Information, Republic of Indonesia (reprinted in India).

Kuhn, Anthony, "As Myanmar Reforms, Indonesia Offers Some Lessons", at http://www.npr.org/blogs/parallels/2013/05/21/185815047/as-myanmar-reforms-indonesnia-offers-some-lessons (accessed May 11, 2014).

Lintner, Bertil, "Failed path to peace in Myanmar", June 2, 2012 http://article.wn.com/view/2012/06/02/Failed_path_to_peace_in_Myanmar/ (accessed May 25, 2014).

Matthews, Bruce, "Ethnic and Religious Diversity: Myanmar's Unfolding Nemesis", February-March 2001, at http://www.iseas.edu.sg/documents/publication/vr32001.pdf (accessed May 11, 2014).

McBeth, John and Cohen, Margot, "Tinderbox", *Far Eastern Economic Review*, January 9, 1997, pp. 14-15.

McCartan, Brian, "Ethnic peace key to Myanmar reform", *Asia Times*, July 28, 2012 at http://www.atimes.com/atimes/Southeast_Asia/NG28Ae01.html (accessed May 25, 2014).

McCulloch, Neil, "The Decentralisation of Indonesia—what happened after the Big Bang?", June 24, 2011 at http://www.globalisationanddevelopment.com/2011/06/decentralisation-of-indonesia-what.html (accessed May 25, 2014).

Osman, Salim. 2012. "Indonesia Facing Ethnic Tension", *Straits Times*, November 12, at www.thejakartaglobe.com/.../indonesia-facing-ethnic-tension/55575- (accessed May 25, 2014).

Otto, Ben and Ismar, Andreas, "In Indonesia, a New Breed of Politician Is on the Rise", *The Wall Street Journal*, October 9, 2013 at http://online.wsj.com/news/articles/SB10001424052702303442004579123080039432594(accessed May 11, 2014).

Sen, Rabindra, Ethnic Diversity and National Unity in Indonesia", in Sanjukta Banerji Bhattacharya and Purusottam Bhattacharya (eds.), *The Asian Problematique in the Twenty-first Century: Random Perspectives*, Progressive Publishers, Kolkata, 2014, pp. 224-54.

Suparlan, Parsudi, "Ethnic Groups of Indonesia", *The Indonesian Quarterly* 7(2), 1979, pp. 53-75.

Suryadinata, Leo, "Ethnicity and National Integration in Indonesia: An Analysis", *Asia Quarterly* (3), 1976, pp. 209-34.

Suryadinata, Leo, *Understanding the Ethnic Chinese in Southeast Asia,* Institute of Southeast Asian Studies, Singapore, 2007.

Suter, Keith, "Indonesia-West Papua Inside or Outside?", *The World Today*, 57(4), 2001, pp. 23-4.

"Talking about a devolution", *The Economist*, January 6, 2001, p. 25.

"Buddhism versus Islam in Asia: Fears of a new religious strife", *The Economist,* July 27-August 2, 2013, pp. 23-24.

"Most Indonesians concerned about national unity", *The Jakarta Post,* September 14, 2008 at http://www.thejakartapost.com/news/2008/09/14/most-indonesians-concerned-about-national-unity.html (accessed May 11, 2014).

Vatikiotis, Michael, "Indonesian Democracy's 'Guiding Hand'", at http://www.nytimes.com/2014/02/22/opinion/indonesian-democracys-guiding-hand.html?_r=0 (accessed May 11, 2014).

Walton, Matthew J., "The 'Wages of Burman-ness': Ethnicity and Burman Privilege in Contemporary Myanmar", *Journal of Contemporary Asia*, 43(1), 2013, pp. 1-27.

2

The Security Community Experience in Southeast Asia

Lessons for South Asia

Ishani Naskar

The search for security of state(s) in international politics has been quite elusive. States have struggled to devise mechanisms that would ensure a minimum amount of protection against the use of force. The effort to combine forces that act as a protective shield for individual states evolved into collective security. Substantively different from an alliance, collective security as a process is defensive and perhaps even a preventive mechanism against the use of force or threat to use force. Collective Security as a strategy for security has also sought to maintain balance of power in international politics and thus have found acceptance in supranational organizations like the League and the UN. Yet collective security does not rule out the use of force in the conduct of inter-state relations. On the contrary collective security is reflective of the fact that international politics is embedded in realistic settings and hardly bereft of conflicts and confrontations.

Collective Security has come of age, but now the search for security is not in responding to critical situations involving use of force or a threat of the same. Instead state(s) in international politics are looking for security that implies the absence of force or threat of force as a tool of inter-state interaction. Such an approach will presume a mean of opinions on what states perceive as challenges to their security and what they feel are way(s) of being secured. At the institutional level search for this approach towards security has manifested through the formation of security communities. The concept of Security Community was conceived in the 1950s by Richard Van Wagenen[1] but was developed by Karl Deutsch. Karl Deutsch studying on the North Atlantic Area, provided a categorization of security communities as amalgamated and pluralistic.[2] The research agenda on security community was furthered by Emanuel Adler and Michael Barnett who viewed such communities as nascent security community to mature ones.[3] Further, scholars have categorized security communities as interstate security communities[4] and comprehensive security communities[5].

Practically the focus on security communities became possible in the post Cold War period with the withdrawal of bloc politics and the decreasing threats of nuclear standoffs. More importantly, the nature of security threats to the states began to change and newer forms security concerns began to emerge mostly non-traditional threats and transnational challenges. These developments are noticeable in the theatres of Cold War politics like Europe and parts of Asia especially Southeast Asia. Southeast Asia has witnessed proxy wars and Cold War alliances. This is a very interesting region which was host to a Cold War alliance, the Southeast Asia Treaty Organisation (SEATO) and yet formed its own regional organization, the Association of Southeast Asian Nations, (ASEAN). For ten years from 1967-1977 both these kind of institutional arrangements which are in a way reflective of two opposite trends (external intervention on one hand and immunity from such interventions on the other) were coexisting in this region. Cold War in Southeast Asia saw the dominance of realism and the predominance of power competition, conflicts and the unrestrained use of force. Yet there is enough evidence that could be put forward to evince that ASEAN was an institution that even during Cold War was seeking to evolve its interest and identity. But it is in the post-Cold War period in particular that ASEAN has begun evolving into a prominent regional grouping gradually consolidating its identity and now directed towards forming a community. It is the purpose of this paper to look at this process of community building with a particular focus on the security community. There is a rich literature on ASEAN Security Community on the possibility of such community in Southeast Asia. Primarily there is an ongoing debate between the Realists and Constructivists, but in addition there are the rationalists who rather cater to an eclectic approach. In discussing the prospects of building a community in Southeast Asia, one must follow trace the evolution of ASEAN into a matured regional formation and get an idea of these theoretical positions attending the debate on the possibility of the Security Community of this region.

Origins of the ASEAN: In Response to Cold War Politics or to Control Regional Politics?

ASEAN was formed in 1967, at a time when the Cold War had already taken control of regional political developments and the Vietnam War was in full swing. Earlier attempts at building regional organisations viz. Association of Southeast Asia (ASA) and the MAPHILINDO were unsuccessful. The reason for their failure to sustain as regional entities was largely due to the internal discord between the member states. ASA established in 1961 and MAPHILINDO established in 1963 suffered due to the lack of the spirit of cohesion and the feeling of region "remained stunted".[6] Perhaps one could conclude that the states of Southeast Asia were not prepared for this kind of a regional affiliation, but one should take into account the real issues that were plaguing the region. The high hopes of having a regional feeling within ASA was challenged by the unavoidable influence of the most dominant state in the region. Indonesia had a telling influence on the prospects and of both these organizations. When the ASA was formed Indonesia was not a part of the Association as Sukarno's theatrical conceptualization of Old Forces versus New Forces kept him away from this grouping dominated by pro-capitalist members of Southeast Asia. In addition, Indonesia's problems in West Irian Jaya and the conflict with the Dutch, was followed by its long confrontation with Malaysia. Indonesia's struggle with Malaysia over Sabah and Sarawak began in the early 1960s and turned into a confrontation since 1963, the year in which MAPHILINDO was established. Thus it was hard call for regional organisations in Southeast Asia to survive successfully without a change in Indonesia's outlook towards international politics and towards its neighbourhood.

It is in context of a changing internal environment with a new Indonesian regime that ended the *konfrontasi*, a new regional organisation was possible. Yet it was the fear of the growing communist aggression and the intimidating role of the region's neighbour China that sent the non-communist states of the region scurrying for security and huddling under the shelter of a regional organisation—ASEAN. In the words of the Indonesian Minister Roeslan Abdulgani, "the commonality of political attitudes and ideological orientations, which were non-communist, among the five member nations of ASEAN has clearly been the uniting factor in ASEAN."[7] Thus ASEAN was an organisation that was established in the context of politics of power and confrontation that conditioned regional inter-state action at that point of time. ASEAN's composition labeled it as a non-communist amalgam rather than a regional organisation. All the states followed the free-market model with pro-western political orientations. In the face of a communist threat their loyalty towards the US was explicit and they received assistance from the superpower. In fact not for once there was a doubt that the entire balance and longevity of the ASEAN were propelled internally by Indonesia and externally by the US. And since Suharto's regime, the relation between Washington and Jakarta was becoming strong.

Focusing on this aspect of the origins of the ASEAN substantiates the realists[8] standpoint that Southeast Asian identity building began under conditions of duress and not from any long well thought plan to form a regional entity steeped in a feeling of oneness. In addition the organisation was established in *response* to a particular political situation marred by conflict and therefore security remained a priority in its agenda though its Bangkok Declaration avoided the word. It was not until 1971, the first agreement in response to the political situation was signed. The Zone of Peace, Freedom and Neutrality Declaration (ZOPFAN) clearly recognized the growing threat of external intervention and reiterated the objectives of the United Nations in abstaining from threat or use of force, settling international disputes peacefully, and refraining from interference in affairs of States. The states clearly mentioned that the members were, "determined to exert initially necessary efforts to secure the recognition of, and respect for, South East Asia as a Zone of Peace, Freedom and Neutrality, free from any form or manner of interference by outside Powers."[9] Yet the Declaration did not emphasise the 'specifics of the necessary efforts' that would ensure the minimization of external influence or external intervention.

The serious situation that evolved since 1975, following the Vietnamese Cambodian War[10] severely jolted the Association because it indicated the continuing predominance of power and force in inter-state relations and the failure of ZOPFAN to bring about *any change* in the power relations in Southeast Asia. It was evident that the ZOPFAN did not affect countries outside ASEAN and therefore the element of insecurity and threat from aggression and communist incursion could not be ruled out. Subsequently the Treaty of Amity and Cooperation, the TAC signed in 1976. TAC formed one of the pillars of the Association. The TAC provided a detailed layout of how to maintain peace and balance of the region. The TAC projects the objective of promoting regional peace, cooperation and resilience based on certain significant principles that reflects how the Association was trying to build up its own immunity against the developments in the Indochina region. Notably unlike the ZOPFAN, the TAC provides for both positive and negative means of cooperation. There was the urge to cooperate in "economic, social, technical, scientific and administrative fields as well as in matters of common ideals and aspirations of international peace and stability in the region and all other matters of common interest."[11] But more important cooperation implied that the Signatories shall, "not in any manner or form participate in any activity which shall constitute a threat to the political and economic stability, sovereignty, or territorial integrity of another High Contracting Party."[12] Further, Signatories shall, "endeavour to strengthen their respective national resilience in their political, economic, socio-cultural as well as security fields in conformity with their respective ideals and aspirations, free from external interference as well as internal subversive activities in order to preserve their respective national identities."[13] Dispute settling mechanisms were also mentioned including the role of a High Council that would settle the contentious issues.

The TAC was a quick yet an appropriate response to the emergent political situation but one could see it as a stepping stone towards establishing a sense of regional oneness. More important, the TAC brought forward the security anxieties of the ASEAN members. Subsequently the TAC reoriented ASEAN's identity from a socio-economic regional grouping to that of a serious regional group that is seeks to address the political security challenges confronting the members collectively. In ordering out the objectives and setting out the principles through the TAC, became a cornerstone document that would provide the Association an ability to take control of regional politics and inter-state affairs and thus immune the members from external interference. One could thus believe that ASEAN during the 1970s made an attempt to evolve from an Association of response to an Association with responsibilities. Particularly so because along with the TAC, the ASEAN Concord signed in the same year was an additional step towards attaining regional cooperation—by providing a framework of cooperation in the field of politics, economics and social activities. The Concord document too underlined the necessity of avoiding force, "Member states, in the spirit of ASEAN solidarity, shall rely exclusively on peaceful processes in the settlement of intra-regional differences".[14] Whether these significant documents could help ASEAN develop an ability to take responsibility of the region and control the politics of the region is always a subject of debate. It will be discussed later.

ASEAN's post-Cold War: Institutionalising the Security Agenda

The post Cold War period raised vital questions about the future security agenda of the ASEAN. Notwithstanding the urge of economic cooperation through the establishment of the ASEAN Free Trade Area (AFTA) in 1992, there were growing concerns regarding the future of the Association which in the early 1990s, was still restricted to the pro-capitalist states (Brunei joined in the 1984). In the post-Soviet Period the US remained the only power to play a vital role in international politics, but with its diminishing presence in Southeast Asia, the ASEAN countries realized that they were not well equipped to engage with, China the only formidable communist power from Cold War days. It was in an attempt to fathom the existing balance of power and address the deriving security calculations that ASEAN found it necessary to establish a politico-security arm of the Association. The ASEAN Regional Forum established in 1994 was only a dialogue forum established in *response* to the emerging balance of power in the region that was underlined by an apprehension of the future role of external powers in this region. Yet the formation of the

ARF, optimists and constructivists would argue, heralded the beginning of an era where ASEAN would take control of the security structure of the Asia Pacific and emerge into a controller rather than respondent to the state-to-state interactions of the members as well the outsiders.[15] The ARF is a dialogue forum that is basically inspired by the ASEAN Way of interaction. The ARF not only seeks to address the security concerns of the member states but also takes account of the external actors and challenges that will affect the balance of this region. Yet the ARF in the immediate post-Cold War period discussed largely traditional security issues. Yet, ASEAN could only react to the military conflict between the disputants in South China Sea, by making a Declaration in 1992, a non obligatory document that makes request to restrain use of force and encourages joint development of the disputed region.[16] This did not impact the growing Chinese intolerance on the South China Sea as clashes continued in the 1990s.[17] Moreover although the ARF mentioned comprehensive security, the ASEAN did not look into the non-traditional security challenges. For instance, ARF took the job of confidence building very seriously but were not ready to prevent or tackle the economic crisis. Consequently, the 1997 Asia economic meltdown brought a large shockwave to the region. However the positive aspect in the establishment of the ARF was that it provided ASEAN a separate forum to discuss security issues at length. It also proved that security was an undying concern for ASEAN and it has never for been able to dissociate itself from the strategic calculations of Southeast Asia.

At the institutional level ASEAN's strength began to change with the induction of new members belonging to the erstwhile communist regime bringing in an element of uncertainty amongst the original members of ASEAN.[18] Yet it was the financial crisis that made ASEAN think anew about its ability to face changing situations and transnational crises. It unleashed a number of high-thinking and high-hoping documents. ASEAN Vision 2020 was the preliminary document of the ASEAN Community Building project where very high goals were mentioned—a Concert of Southeast Asian States, a Partnership and Dynamic Development and the a Community of Caring Societies.[19] The ASEAN Community Plan was proposed in 2003 at the Ninth ASEAN Summit, held at Bali. This Community Plan is another very serious step towards consolidating the identity of the region through the establishment of three communities—economic, security and socio-cultural communities. This was complemented by the ASEAN Concord II signed at Bali, Indonesia in the same year. The process of community building was furthered by the Vientiane Action Programme (VAP) that placed a detailed roadmap towards the establishment of the ASEAN Community at the 10th ASEAN Summit at Vientiane. Elaborate blueprints ensure that this community becomes a reality by 2015; specifically at the 14th ASEAN Summit at Thailand, all the respective blueprints for three separate pillar-communities were conceived that would expected to be achieved by 2015. With the community building project in full swing a serious debate on the feasibility of such a humongous project is also active. In particular a vibrant debate revolves around the feasibility of Security Community in Southeast Asia.

A Security Community for Southeast Asia: To be or Not to be

Before analyzing the prospect of a security community, one must begin from the institutionalized security dialogue forum under the aegis of the ASEAN—the ARF. Though the origins of the ARF can be contextualized in the changing post-Cold War scenario marked by uncertainty and speculation, Constructivists would interpret the establishment of the ARF as an optimistic move that seeks to take control of the security scenario and strike the balance of power in its own favour. A strong advocate of this position Amitav Acharya points out that ARF is not a simple respondent to the emerging security situation in Southeast Asia in the post-Soviet era, but an emergent diplomatic community. Citing from realist scholar Michael Leifer Acharya stresses that the ARF has evolved into an institution of considerable cognizance such that it rules and processes are able to establish rules of the region.[20] Yet there is no getting away from the fact that the ARF in whatever rules it may have evolved, they attempt only to prevent conflicts from escalating, and try to engage powerful actors in a way that their actions do not harm the members of ASEAN and imperil the balance of power of the region. ARF has no actual mechanism that would address ongoing conflicts.

Constructivists stressed the importance of regular interactions, dialogues, communicative networks that reiterate the 'we feeling' of a regional entity[21]. Southeast Asian constructivist scholars like Acharya and Alice D. Ba in addition project the importance of ASEAN norms as having transitionary powers, to change security scenarios and harnessing the balance of favour in ASEAN's own advantage.[22] Norms, values are unique to the Association and are derived from two sources—from the various acts and agreements that have taken place as ASEAN has evolved and also from what is known as the 'ASEAN Way' that have derived from the socio-cultural fabric of the countries of the region. Fundamental acts like the TAC, and the Bali Concords, their provisions have contributed very significant norms like mutual respect for sovereign equality, territorial integrity; non-interference in the affairs of other states; freedom from external interference; pacific settlement of disputes and renunciation from the use of force or the threat of the same. These are the dominating norms that act as guiding light for the members of the Association as well as for external members who are associated with ASEAN either through the ARF, or through bilateral summits or through the ASEAN+3 mechanism, the APT. The other source of ASEAN norms is derived from the cultural similarities and the basic commonalities that characterize inter-state interactions within Southeast Asia. For instance in the case of decision making, Acharya discusses elaborately on the origins of the decision making process that has imbibed the principles of *musyawarah and mufakat,* i.e. consultation and consensus; this largely follows the Indonesian political tradition of decision making. The inclination for non-formal and non-confrontational style of bargaining is clear in ASEAN's negotiating process. In this context Peter Boyce's work on these techniques helps one understand how ASEAN has a preference for informal, unofficial engagements with an eye towards consensus than disagreements and voting.[23] Constructivists reason out that norms can restrain, control and engage dominant powers that affect the political calculations of ASEAN—by engaging Indonesia in regional obligations ASEAN has managed to wean it away from any hegemonic designs. They have had a restraining effect on the regional power. Similarly by involving intimidating neighbours like China, the ARF through the norms and processes typical to this regional association has espoused the constraining effects of multilateral engagements. In course of time this has become a positive effect of normative regionalism.[24]

The Realists see ASEAN and its security affiliate, the ARF conditioned by the existing power politics and act as mere respondents to the existing balance of power. Leifer particularly pins down the point that Southeast Asian security is largely conditioned by the state of relations between the external players primarily the US and China. Leifer has analysed both ASEAN and ARF focusing on their origins and their roles as diplomatic community and security community. He viewed ASEAN as a product of the existing security architecture that developed *within* Southeast Asia. In his words, "ASEAN was established as the institutional fruit of conflict resolution rather than as a vehicle for promoting such resolution in any direct sense."[25] This was possible as he acknowledged through a regime change in Jakarta. He explained, "(t)he judgement of a succeeding military leadership in Jakarta was that the international rehabilitation and economic regeneration of the Republic required a revised outlook and above all a cooperative relationship with regional neighbours, preferably in institutionalized form".[26] ASEAN was directed at post-conflict intra-regional reconciliation within a structure of relations. Such a structure was more normative in nature based on norms and principles directed towards mutual economic development and security. Herein realists see ASEAN as an aspiring security community. A security community as mentioned earlier would presuppose some basic consensus on security perceptions and challenges facing the region. Yet during Vietnam's aggression some states were still more concerned with China's involvement in the conflict than Vietnam's increasing aggressive intentions. Thailand being a frontline state, ASEAN was bound to get involved in the Cambodian crisis. But as a diplomatic community ASEAN's efforts at resolution of the conflict must be seen in light of the actual change in the balance of power in the greater sphere of Cold War politics and the ability of the United Nations to a play a more responsible role. Leifer here observed,

> "(t)he experience of the Cambodian conflict served to demonstrate the limitations of ASEAN's regional security role...ASEAN's involvement as a diplomatic community was buttressed by a distinctive pattern of international alignments. Its participation in a tacit alliance relationship was in

> contradiction to the ideal goal of regional order being managed on an autonomous basis of registered both in the founding Declaration and in the founding Declaration and in the ZOPFAN formula. Ultimately, the Cambodian peace process was ordained and managed by the permanent members of the United Nations Security Council with ASEAN confined to the diplomatic margins."[27]

Thus there are doubts about ASEAN's success as a diplomatic community, yet the constructivists have lauded the role of ASEAN as a diplomatic community. In changed circumstances ASEAN's success as a diplomatic community is further difficult to achieve. The best example would be the South China Sea where ASEAN has failed to develop a solution. Here Leifer feels it essential that the United States need develop an interest in order to seek a resolution of the South China Sea dispute. How could that be achieved in the present ASEAN framework is doubtful. In practical terms a functional cooperation between the US and China at least in the ARF will also be necessary in order to find an acceptable solution to the South China Sea. This is also not forthcoming in the immediate future.

Realists see ARF as a product of post-Soviet uncertainty, a post-Cold War arrangement in the absence of US when was ASEAN left in the lurch to deal with China and new security challenges. Michael Leifer's analysis of ARF clearly projects it as conditioned by the existing balance of power. He describes the ARF as, "an imperfect diplomatic instrument for achieving regional goals in that it seeks to address the problem of power which arises from the anarchical nature of the international society without provision for either collective defence or conventional collective security."[28] He describes the ARF as a forum of diplomatic contact and cushioning and seen as a way of securing a possibly progressive conformity to international norms.[29] At present, ARF faces the problem of being drained out defocused with its rather large membership. It has not only failed to take care of the South China Sea problem, it has not done any commendable job regarding intra-mural tensions within Southeast Asia. Further ARF could not respond to serious non-traditional challenges facing its members like the 1997 Asian economic crisis and were left mute spectators as the region slipped into misery and chaos, political turmoil and ethnic unrest.

The ASEAN Security Community, Constructivists claim, is expected to evolve from the culture of dialogue and interaction that has prevailed over ARF more than a decade. The Security Community constructivists would argue, bears the legacy of norms and values that have dominated both the organs ASEAN and the ARF. But it is here realists like Nicholas Khoo have questioned the very basis of this outlook. Khoo has identified ASEAN as a failing realist institution and one of the major reasons of this failure is Indonesia's inability to provide the right kind of leadership[30]. It has created a leadership vacuum that is taken as an advantage by external powers. On the contrary Indonesia had become a source of several problems—Asian financial crisis, the East Timor problem and the humanitarian crisis and the growing threat of transnational terrorism. ASEAN has failed to respond to these problems either. While constructivists have identified ASEAN as nascent security community, the realists have asked the very premises of the security community—the norms, the values and the collective identity. Khoo has questioned the quality of the norms, their origins and deviations from norms that which is purposely called negative norms. Moreover there are serious problems related to the compliance with the fundamental norms. For instance, how can one explain Indonesia's violation of East Timor's sovereignty in 1975? On the other hand how does ASEAN expect to deal with the *tatamdaw* in Myanmar? Erstwhile Malaysian Prime Minister Mahathir Mohammed had urged ASEAN to consider putting pressure on Myanmar. Thailand had also proposed for flexible engagement in order to deal with the challenging states like Myanmar and to deal with intra-mural issues that have transnational implications. However this was rejected overwhelmingly by members in favour of non-interference because as Haacke explained it would "open up a can of worms that could endanger intramural stability and, in some cases, jeopardize regime security."[31] Instead the states settled for 'enhanced interaction'. On the question of identity and norms, realists also raise the issue of aggregating the components of identity formation. Khoo has questioned, "How does a hetereogenous organization like the ASEAN, whose members differ on a multitude of dimensions, come to develop a common identity?"[32] Moreover in the case of bilateral disputes states have resorted to adjudication and arbitration, the case of Sipidan and Ligitan islands off Sabah, disputed between Indonesia and Malaysia is a case in the point. This is reflective of a tendency to depend on legalistic methods than informal methods. Realists think that the best approach to understand deviation from ASEAN norms is to focus on negative norms that perhaps can explain negative actions within various Southeast Asian states—human rights violations in Myanmar, the thousands of killing during the Khmer Rouge Regime in Cambodia. Most important Constructivists in all their optimism to build a community based on the norms that have been identified by them to be essential and fundamental to ASEAN's identity and oneness, have forgotten very serious challenges prevalent within the states of Southeast Asia and in the region—problem of nation building, the challenges of post-conflict reconstruction, the issue of democracy and human rights, identity based conflicts, nontraditional threats like health hazards, economic meltdowns, environmental disasters, etc. Equally important and unavoidable is the strategic relations between outside powers as much as their relations with the members of ASEAN that will affect the strategic future of Southeast Asia. It is here that realists like Leifer think that ARF has failed to play the role expected of it and is only an institution adjusting itself to the changing power relations of the region. It hardly has any proactive role in controlling the balance of the region.

It is the rationalists who try to take a mid-way approach between two extremes of pessimism and optimism and try to evaluate the state of inter-state interaction that exists between members of ASEAN within the framework of community building. Rationalists and Neo-Liberal Institutionalists stress that the basic security arrangement within Southeast Asia is actually in close resemblance to a regime rather than a community. A security regime is a framework of intestate interaction where certain norms and rules have a regulating effect on their relationships and create a certain degree of security guarantee. Members in the regime interact through norms of behaviour that have a constraining or controlling effect on its members. Yet states are egoistic units who despite their interactions through rules and norms are not entirely 'other regarding' i.e. they do not see their security inextricably attached to those of the others. This is only possible in a mature security community situation. Regime proponents like Robert

Jervis[33] and Allan Collins[34] have explained that in an anarchical system, states respond through self help by aggrandizing military power. A search for security ends up as further insecurity—this is basically security dilemma. Practically a security community is difficult to achieve because of a security dilemma[35]. Rationalists claim that in practice within any security arrangement there is always a minimal chance of defection because every member apprehends defection by the other. In addition war is the last option but it can never be totally ruled out. In the case of ASEAN, Allan Collins[36] emphasizes that the concept of fundamental norms like non-interference had become important to develop immunity against neighbourhood's intervention in domestic affairs. It would encourage nation building without inhibition. Non-interference has strengthened the concept of national sovereignty but hinders the process of community building, security community per se. In order to ensure security compliance big powers, and dialogue partners are needed to abide by the TAC that ensures that the behaviour of ambitious states are restrained and their activities are in consonance with the security priorities of ASEAN. Regional solutions for regional problems as Collins interprets are not particularly for immunity against external intervention because ASEAN does not wish to detach relations from non-ASEAN states. On the other hand bilateral level relations remain intact and bilateral defence agreements remain in place. Collin thinks that regional solutions to regional problems enhance the element of self reliance. Rationalists argue that the serious emphasis placed on rules and norms, makes ASEAN a rule-based community and not so much of a community based on collective identity. The priority of rules makes ASEAN and ARF in close resemblance to a regime than a community. Rationalists however argue that security regimes may mature into security communities in the future. A community feeling should involve a plurality of approach and interaction. Thus the role of civil society groups and Track II institutes are necessary. Rationalists think that non-interference is not indifference; on the contrary community building requires involvement of people interaction. In this context rationalist encourage the ASEAN Socio-Cultural Community. Rationalists are also encouraging of Track II interactions, and recommend the increasing role of ASEAN People's Assembly (APA) in the formation of ASCC. The entire spirit of the rationalists regarding ASEAN Security Community is captured in the observations of Allan Collin:

> "If ASEAN is to become a security community it will need to generate a regional identity among the people of Southeast Asia and give then a stake in the association's development. So long as ASEAN remains a club of for the governing elite then it will remain detached from the general populace and thus unable to create a sense of commonality or 'we-feeling'. The APA and the ASCC are important steps to community building and their existence is a positive sign. ASEAN has only begun the process of creating a security community but the process will be moribund if the ASEAN elite fail to engage with the region's CSO's, and through them, their own people."[37]

The rationalists have projected that ASEAN is at best a security regime and at worse a nascent security community. The point at which they differ from Constructivists is that ASEAN is unlikely to reach the next two stages of security community—ascendant and mature. They differ with Acharya because he thinks that ASEAN is maturing in to a security community. Again, rationalist see the importance of self regarding priorities overpowering the other regarding aspects and no norms have any transformative role in controlling the security scenario in favour of the ASEAN countries. That is a position followed by the realists, but unlike them, Rationalists do not think that there is no hope for security organizations. States function in self-help based anarchical situations filled with known and unknown threats but security institutions are also necessary to enhance inter-state cooperation such that they can face security challenges but rationalists think that this kind of cooperation does not necessarily ensure a security community.

A Security Community for South Asia? Emulate Southeast Asia or should India Show the Way?

South Asia is Southeast Asia's neighbour, with its own regional organization—the South Asian Association for Regional Cooperation

(SAARC). SAARC is a much younger association to ASEAN and has its own history of origin. Unlike ASEAN South Asia did not directly bear the brunt of Cold War conflicts, there is no history of Cold War confrontations as was seen in the Indochina region. Yet South Asia has witnessed non-receding violence beginning from India-Pakistan confrontations, the ethnic turmoil and civil war in Sri Lanka, the democratic upsurge in Nepal and the constant political violence in Bangladesh, Pakistan, and the serious challenges of post conflict reconstruction in Afghanistan. Nothwithstanding the various security challenges, when SAARC was formed in 1985, the organization did not look at the political and security issues of the region because most of them were related to bilateral tensions between the member states and interestingly a major part of the bilateral issues involved India as one of the disputants. Thus India was more concerned that security issues remain outside the purview of SAARC.

Given this brief background of SAARC that is representative of South Asian identity, the question of a security community for this region is timely and essential given the complicated political matrix of inter-state relations in South Asia. One of the most important observations regarding South Asian security is that such issues of the region are closely linked to each other; this is because of their historical trajectories. In addition transnational threats like terrorism, health hazards, and environmental problems all affect entire South Asia. In this context South Asia may be seen as a 'security complex'[38]. One of the most important security challenges that face South Asia is the challenge of nation building that is directly related to the political maturity, future and stability of the states of South Asia. Apart from India, most of the South Asian states—Pakistan, Nepal, Bangladesh, Afghanistan and Sri Lanka have undergone frequent political transitions or face internal socio-political challenges. Even India has her own share of troubles—Kashmir separatist movement, insurgency in the Northeast India, Maoist anti-state activities, ethnic conflicts, terrorism. In addition South Asia is one of the hot beds of nuclear tensions with threats of nuclear standoffs occurring as recent as the Kargil War. Moreover the sensitive relations between the two nuclear states and neighbours, India and Pakistan, have overshadowed all the efforts made by SAARC to enhance inter-state cooperation and hijacked the agenda of South Asian integration.

Given this very complicated political scenario and the overwhelming presence and power asymmetry between the India and the other members of South Asia, it is quite interesting that SAARC has not found it necessary to give security due importance. If any lesson can be derived from ASEAN and ARF, then it is that security issues should be addressed rather than avoided and bilateral sensitivities should not be allowed to come in the way of developing some of form security organization. Keeping in mind the security challenges of the South Asian system, the fundamental norms that have characterized the regional organizations of Southeast Asia, namely the principle of non-interference, regional solution to regional problems, have been included in the SAARC Charter. But the point is that these principles should not only be adopted, they should be implemented to ease the political tensions and implied security connotations in South Asia. In contemporary times cooperation between South Asian states is more probable because of a number of reasons. First, in order to face the forces of globalization, the states ought to cooperate with each other, particular in context of global recession. Second, a number of South Asian states are undergoing democratic transitions—Pakistan, Nepal, Bangladesh and it is the scope and duty of all the other members of South Asia to stand by these states in anticipation that this cooperation will bear rich dividends for the future security scenario of South Asia. Third, with two nuclear states in the region, India and Pakistan, who have a history of animosity and conflicts, it is essential that there must be a common dialogue forum that should discuss ways of achieving and maintaining durable peace. Fourth, with the scourge of terrorism affecting almost all the states of South Asia especially India, Pakistan and Afghanistan there is a pressure from the international community especially the US to address the issue of cross border terrorism across the states of South Asia. This is a very serious issue that needs to be addressed immediately and in a cooperative manner. In this context it is a fair possibility that China shall also cooperate in this effort. It is possible because notwithstanding the various points of tension in the trilateral relations between India, Pakistan and China there do not seem to be any immediate threat of a war or armed confrontation between these countries.

Yet practically the most important condition for a successful security community for South Asia is that the apprehensions about India's motives and policies must be addressed by India herself. It demands a minimal amount of what Peter Jones describes as 'strategic altruism' implying that India takes a softer and more accommodating stance towards the cause of South Asian security.[39] There are considerable reasons why Indian leadership matters. Adler and Barnett to begin with have agreed that the future and success of a security community may depend on the ability of strong states in the community to give positive leadership.[40] India's leadership as a formidable power in South Asia has been undeniable but till date there have been elements of suspicion and apprehension about India's moves towards her neighbours. India is reaching global heights with her economy having taken off the economic springboard. She is considered to be a formidable player in international politics. Therefore a precursor to India's role in the global stage is how she reiterates her good will towards her neighbours. India is also interacting with major powers, outsiders, who are expected to play a telling role in the future in South Asia. The US and China are the major powers who will matter in the future, the India-US civilian nuclear deal is only reflective of the future course of relationship between the two states. It is also extremely important that India steadily work her relations with China because although China is just an observer in SAARC, China's activities have a direct impact on the strategic future of the region. In order to carve an impressive role India must help expand the spirit of democracy without negative bearings, India's relative success as a democratic state provides her with the scope to provide leadership in this region. Another field where India may seek collaboration with neighbours and from perhaps outsiders is the case of terrorism, the SAARC Declaration on Terrorism is a good example of cooperation on transnational challenges.[41] Much of India's involvement will depend on her attitude to South Asia. The Gujral Doctrine was a good starting point that argued that there could be reciprocal relations on security issues of South Asia. The Gujral Doctrine called for a generous Indian approach to the neighbours, if they were ready to respect India's security concerns.[42]

There has not been much serious thought in the direction of security institutions in South Asia perhaps because of the amount of apprehension and suspicion about neighbours and their motives. In that case a good starting point would be discussion forums that could include security specialists and scholars of South Asia who could create the background for greater cooperation at the official level. Track II interactions are essential components towards successful community building. A security dialogue forum for South Asia could be a good starting point which could encourage frank informal discussions on the impending and emerging security threats in South Asia.

Conclusion

Security Community whether in Southeast Asia or South Asia will not be an easy to achieve but the difference between the two regions is that while in Southeast Asia the process has already begun, South Asia may not be prepared for it at all. Here it is also important to mention that the building of Security Communities in Europe may not be the same in Asia, especially in both these regions. ASEAN and ARF as explained by the realists have always devised new rules, regulations and mechanism to improvise their association in response to external developments either attended by crisis or by uncertainty. For instance, ASEAN was created in the post *konfrontasi* period as a post conflict regional reconciliation effort, the TAC was signed only in response to the neighbourhood war between Cambodia and Vietnam, the ARF was established in response to the retrenchment of US forces in Southeast Asia, the Community Plan was launched in response to the Asian economic crisis. Yet ASEAN has proven that there is no way a regional organisation can survive by diminishing or avoiding the security element. SAARC is yet to accept this reality and take a step forward. In fact SAARC could take a step forward and establish a politico-security arm before any major security challenge impairs normal state-to-state relations within South Asia. In this context, India's role ought to be exemplary and responsible in instilling a sense of confidence within her neighbours about her non aggressive intentions. A plausible starting point could be interactions between academics and strategic experts—a sustained dialogue process would go a long way in dislodging a lot of apprehensions among the neighbours of South Asia, particularly the fears revolving around India. More important, it will be a conspicuous stepping stone towards evolving a sense of South Asian identity.

NOTES

1. Richard W. Van Wagenen, *Political Community and the North Atlantic Area*, Princeton, N.J., Princeton University Press, 1957. Also read, Wagenen, *Research in International Organisation Field: Some Notes on a Possible Focus*, Center for Research on World Political Institutions, Princeton University 1952.
2. Karl Deutsch, *et al.*, *Political community and the North Atlantic area; international organization in the light of historical experience,* Princeton, N.J.: Princeton University Press, 1957.
3. Emanuel Adler and Michael Barnett, *Security Communities*, Cambridge University Press, 1998, pp. 413-441.
4. Raimo Vāyrynen, "Stable Peace through Security Communities? Steps Towards Theory Building", *Occasional Paper # 18:OP: 3*, The Joan B. Kroc Institute For International Peace Studies.
5. Andrej Tusicisny, "Security Communities and Their Values: Taking Masses Seriously", *International Political Science Review,* Vol. 28, No. 4, 2007, pp. 427.
6. Peter Lyon, *War and Peace in South East Asia*, London, Oxford University Press, 1969, pp. 95-96.
7. Roeslan Abdulgani, *Nationalism, Regionalism and Security: Problems in Southeast Asia,* New Delhi, Banyan Publications, 1986, p. 42
8. A large amount of realist literature is available, some very prominent ones include, Michael Leifer, "The ASEAN Regional Forum: Extending ASEAN's Model of Regional Security", *Adelphi Paper,* 302, Oxford, Oxford University, 1996. Press; Nicholas Khoo, "Constructing Southeast Asian Security: the Pitfalls of Imagining a Security Community and the Temptations of Orthodoxy", *Cambridge Review of International Affairs*, Vol.17, Number 1, April 2004, pp. 137-153; David Jones and Michael L.R. Smith, "ASEAN's Imitation Community", *Orbis*, Vol. 46, No.1, Winter 2002, pp. 93-109.
9. See, *Zone of Peace Freedom and Neutrality Declaration*, Malaysia, November 27, 1971.
10. To get an idea of the Vietnam-Cambodia conflict, read, Noam Chomsky, *At War with Asia*, Library of Congress, 2005.

11. *Op cit.* no. 9
12. *Ibid.*
13. *Ibid.*
14. *Declaration of the ASEAN Concord, Denpasar, Bali,* February 24, 1976.
15. Amitav Acharya, "Do Norms and identity matter? Community and Power in Southeast Asia's Regional Order," *The Pacific Review*, Vol. 18, no. 1, March 2005, pp. 95-118.
16. See, *Declaration on the South China Sea*, Manila, Philippines, 1992.
17. Clashes between China and Philippines in 1995, 1996-1998, between Taiwan and Vietnam in 1995 and the Philippines and Vietnam in 1998.
18. Vietnam joined in 1995, Laos and Myanmar in 1997 and Cambodia in 1999.
19. *ASEAN Vision 2020*, Kuala Lumpur December 17, 1997.
20. Michael Leifer, "ASEAN's Search for a Regional Order", *Faculty Lecture* No. 12, Faculty of Arts and Social Sciences, Singapore, National University of Singapore.
21. Karl Deutsch *et al*, *Political Community and the North Atlantic Area*, Princeton University Press, 1957, p. 36.
22. Amitav Acharya, *Op. cit.* no. 15. p. 112-113, Alice D. Ba, "On norms, rule breaking and security communities: a constructivist response", *International Relations of the Asia-Pacific*, Vol. 5, 2005, pp. 255-266.
23. Peter Boyce, "The Machinery in Southeast Asian Regional Diplomacy", in LauTeik Soon (ed), *New Directions in the International Relations of Southeast Asia: Global Powers and Southeast Asia*, Singapore, Singapore University Press, 1973, p. 175.
24. Amitav Acharya, *op. cit.*, no. 15, p. 113.
25. Michael Leifer, "The ASEAN Peace Process: A Category Mistake", in Chin Kin Wah and Leo Suryadinata (ed), *Michael Leifer Selected Works on Southeast Asia*, Singapore, ISEAS, 2005, p. 121.
26. *Ibid.*
27. *Ibid.*, p. 129.
28. Michael Leifer, "The Merits of Multilateralism" in Wah and Suryadinata (ed), *op. cit.*, no. 25, p. 156.
29. Leifer, "Regional Solutions to Regional Problems", in *Ibid.*, p.150.
30. Nicholas Khoo, "Constructing Southeast Asian Security: The Pitfalls of Imagining a Security Community and the Temptations of Orthodoxy", *Cambridge Review of International Affairs*, Vol. 17, Number 1, April 2004.
31. Jurgen Haacke, "Enhanced interaction" with Myanmar and the project of a security community: is ASEAN refining or breaking with its diplomatic and security culture?, *Contemporary Southeast Asia*, Vol. 27, no. 5, August

2005, pp. 188-216, available at, http://findarticles.com/p/articles/mi_hb6479/is_2_27/ai_n29211995/.

32. *Ibid.*, p. 148.
33. Robert Jervis, "Cooperation under the Security Dilemma", *World Politics*, Vol. 30, no. 1, pp. 167-214.
34. Allan Collins, *Security and Southeast Asia: Domestic, Regional and Global Issues*, Boulder Co: Lynne Rienner, 2003.
35. Allan Collins, *The Security Dilemmas of Southeast Asia*, Basingstoke, Macmillan, 2000.
36. Allan Collins, "Forming a Security Community: Lessons from ASEAN", *International Relations of the Asia Pacific*, Vol. 7, 2007, pp. 203-225.
37. *Ibid.*, p. 222.
38. The concept of a "security complex" is defined by Barry Buzan as "a group of states whose primary security concerns link together sufficiently closely that their national securities cannot realistically be considered apart from one another", Barry Buzan, *People, States and Fear: An Agenda for International Security Studies in the Post Cold War Era,* Lynnie Reiner, London 1991, p. 90.
39. Peter Jones, "South Asia: Is a Regional Security Community Possible", *South Asian Survey*, Vol. 15, No. 2, 2008, p. 189.
40. Emanuel Adler, Michael Barnett, *Security Communities*, Cambridge University Press, 1998, p. 52.
41. SAARC Declaration on Terrorism was on February 28, 2009 at Colombo.
42. *The Hindu,* February 9, 2003.

REFERENCES

Abdulgani, Roeslan *Nationalism, Regionalism and Security: Problems in Southeast Asia,* New Delhi, Banyan Publications, 1986.

Adler, Emanuel and Michael Barnett, *Security Communities*, Cambridge University Press, 1998.

Allan Collins, *Security and Southeast Asia: Domestic, Regional and Global Issues*, Boulder CO: Lynne Rienner, 2003.

Chomsky, Noam, At War With Asia, Library of Congress, 2005.

Deutsch, Karl *et al.*, *Political Community and the North Atlantic Area: International Organization in the Light of Historical Experience,* Princeton, N.J.: Princeton University Press, 1957.

Emanuel Adler, Michael Barnett, *Security Communities*, Cambridge University Press, 1998.

Leifer, Michael "The ASEAN Regional Forum: Extending ASEAN's Model of Regional Security", *Adelphi Paper,* 302, Oxford, Oxford University Press, 1996.

Lyon Peter, *War and Peace in South East Asia*, London, Oxford University Press, 1969.

Soon, Lau Teik (ed.), *New Directions in the International Relations of Southeast Asia: Global Powers and Southeast Asia*, Singapore, Singapore University Press, 1973.

The Security Dilemmas of Southeast Asia, Basingstoke, Macmillan, 2000.

Wagenen, Richard W. Van, *Political Community and the North Atlantic Area*, Princeton, N.J., Princeton University Press, 1957, *Research in International Organisation Field: Some Notes on a Possible Focus*, Center for Research on World Political Institutions, Princeton University 1952.

Wah, Chin Kin and Leo Suryadinata (ed), *Michael Leifer Selected Works on Southeast Asia*, Singapore, ISEAS, 2005.

3
The Maritime Border Dispute of South China Sea

Factors Impeding Solution

Subhadeep Bhattacharya

The economic boom in East Asia, especially Southeast Asia, in the latter half of the last century, was seen as the sign of the rise of new Asia, vibrant with economic potentiality. It was prophesied that the new century will be the century of Asia. Undoubtedly, East Asia has come a long distance and from the zone of coercion, during the Second World War and later throughout the Cold War period, the region has become the zone of cohesion with the foundation of several regional organizations, led by ASEAN (Association of South East Asian Nations), which are working hard to maintain the ambiance of peace and tranquility in the region. However, the East Asian unity is not well established since the inter-state disputes over territorial claims are the ominous signs of East Asia turning into another zone of conflict in future. The root of this tension lies in the history and the geography of East Asia. The rise of China, the biggest and the strongest neighbour of East Asia, and the history of her tensed relations with her East Asian neighbours, along with her assertive posture over the maritime disputes in her neighbourhood, in East China Sea and South China Sea, all are creating an ambiance of tension in the region.

The South China Sea dispute is fast becoming the latest source of conflict in East Asia. China, the rapidly developing economies of Southeast Asia along with their complicated relationship with China, the intriguing role of the ASEAN and the re-engagement of the US with East Asian geopolitics; are all making the South China Sea issue most intricate. The ASEAN seems to be a divided house in this context, while the history of the region, coupled with inter-state relations often triggers a strong zeal of nationalism which sometimes impede any solution to the dispute. Also, the response to the dispute varies from party to party. The South China Sea dispute has gone beyond simple disagreement over territorial limits and has become a part of wider geopolitics of East Asia which currently revolves around the 'China factor'. This paper takes up the case of Vietnam, the Philippines and Malaysia, apart from China, as case study.

The importance of the South China Sea lies in the huge concentration of oil, natural gas, hydrocarbon and other natural resources as well as its strategic locations connecting the Indian and Pacific Oceans. The US presence and China's emerging naval policy along with the hunger for the resources and the growing demand for freedom of navigation in the region by the extra regional powers like the US, India and Japan, have made the situation critical. The latest addition to the dispute is the Chinese declaration of the 'Air Defence Identification Zone' (ADIZ) in the East China Sea. This declaration, although targeted against Japan, has been perceived as an ominous signal by weaker parties to the disputes in the South China Sea. China's Defense Ministry's announcement said that it will "establish other air defense identification zones at an appropriate time after completing preparations".[1] This declaration of China has added to the wariness about its intention among her neighbours while it is the reflection of the Chinese ambition to reform the geopolitics of the region which is in vogue since the end of the Second World War.

The South China Sea, a semi enclosed sea, of around 3.5 million square kilometres wide, extending from the Singapore Strait in the east to the Taiwan Strait, forms the geo-strategic core of the Southeast Asia. The area has the strategic sea lanes of communication between Indian and the Pacific Oceans. The discovery of promising off-shore oil and gas reserves, together with one of the richest fishing grounds in the world has added to the dispute. The South China Sea is important maritime route since one-third of the world's ships transits the route between Europe and the Middle East to East Asia.[2] It is also important because it is rich in fisheries resources and it is believed that there are huge oil and gas reserves beneath its seabed. According to a Chinese report, the South China Sea could hold as much as 213 billion barrels of oil, which is equivalent of 80 per cent of Saudi Arabia's known reserves. In a separate BP (British Petroleum) estimate, the entire region may also contain 2 quadrillion cubic feet of natural gas, which is more than five times the known natural gas reserves of North America.[3] Thus, both strategically and economically, the South China Sea region is very important for the littoral states, which is fostering a sovereignty dispute.

The Nature of the Dispute

Until 1970s, nobody questioned about 400 plus rocks, reefs and islands that are scattered within an 800,000 square kilometre area of South China Sea belong to whom. In the seventies, the region became a target for exploration of multinational oil companies. Also there was gradual codification of international maritime law. In the meantime, to extend control over sea bed resources, neighbouring states in the area started coming into verbal conflict and even sporadic military confrontations over sovereignty, jurisdiction and arms control efforts in the South China Sea started taking place.[4] At present, Vietnam occupies more than twenty islets or rocks, China occupies eight, Taiwan one, the Philippines eight and Malaysia, three to six, scattered in the disputed water body.[5]

The claims can be divided into historical claims of discovery and occupation claims that rest on the extension of sovereign jurisdiction under interpretations of the provisions of the United Convention on the Law of the Sea (UNCLOS III) (1982).[6] The Spratlys and the Paracels are claimed by Vietnam China and Taiwan. Their claims are mainly based on historical grounds, that is on prior discovery and occupation. The Philippines and Malaysia support their claims (on Spratly archipelago) referring to the international law, which includes the natural prolongation of the continental shelf provision.[7] The strategic importance of South China Sea has resulted in a number of overlapping claims.

China's claim over the South China Sea is a part of her plot to reunify areas regarded as part of China and to consolidate her borders. China claims all of the more than two hundred islands, reefs and shoals in the South China Sea which are into four groups, the *Dongsha* islands (Pratas) in the northeast, the *Xisha Islands* (Paracel Islands) in the west, nearby the *Paracels* in the east and southeast, *Zhongsha* (the Macclesfield Bank) and *Huangyan* (Scarborough Shoal), and the *Nasha* (Spratly) islands in the south. China bases its claims of sovereignty over the islands 'since very ancient time' following the discovery, development and continuous administration and jurisdiction of China that proved that "South China Sea islands have always been part of China's territory" and that "the Chinese people have indisputable sovereignty".[8]

The '*nine-dash lines*' mark the boundary of the Chinese claims in the South China Sea. Modern China has shown areas within the nine-dashed line as part of Chinese territory since 1914.[9] These lines originated after the Second World War. Following Japanese defeat, China realized the significance of the maritime power.[10] Kuomintang (Nationalist) government of 1947 published an official map of the archipelagoes of South China Sea. Here, eleven interrupted lines were drawn to mark the boundary of the islands, islets, reefs, banks and adjacent waters over which China exercised sovereignty.[11] After 1949 the People's Republic of China tailored the map with nine dashes to exhibit its claims. But the map did not draw much interest until reports of oil and mineral reserves and the treasures of the seabed surfaced in 1970s.[12] So, it is seen that initially the Chinese interest in the South China Sea was to project the maritime power of the country since the Second World War had established the significance of maritime supremacy. It is to be remembered that the eastern waters are the only maritime opening for the Chinese. The economic importance came later.

Besides historical reasons, there are other reasons which prompted China to exert its demand to control the South China Sea. On economic terms, this area presumably stores billions of tons of off shore oil and gas, mineral resources like iron, copper, manganese. When growing discrepancy surfaced between China's energy demand and supply, particularly after 1984, China turned increasingly to offshore areas, including the South China Sea.[13] Politically speaking Taiwan remains central to China. Control of Taiwan ensures control of Taiwan Straits which connects the southern with eastern and northern regions of China. Claims over the entire South China Sea strengthen the Chinese assertion that Taiwan belongs to the Chinese territory.[14] Strategically, South China Sea is located between the sea routes of the northern-southern as well as eastern-western bound maritime passage. Thus Chinese control of the South China Sea is important ensuring protection to China's merchant fleet.[15] Fourthly, denying control of the region to any adversaries is a major security priority of China.[16] Fifthly, China's all special economic zones, which include three open cities and two open areas, border South China Sea. They were strategically important for China's coastal development project and this has boosted the use of South China Sea as a major channel for China's expanding trade. Lastly, due to population expansion in the country, China considers South China Sea islands can provide *lebensraum* (survival space) for the Chinese people.[17]

On the other hand, Vietnam claimed that she has been using the Paracel (*Hong Sa* in Vietnamese) and Spratly (*Truong Sa* in Vietnamese) archipelagoes for centuries and they are under the effective and continuous administration of Vietnam. Court documents during the reign of King Le Thanh Tong (1460-1497) suggest that both Spratly and Paracel archipelagoes were considered to be Vietnamese territories. Vietnamese exercise of sovereignty over the Paracels was mentioned in the 1630s, like in Journal of Batavia which reported that the Vietnamese helped Dutch merchant boats that got stranded there. Vietnam's claims were documented regularly in the 17th century. Vietnamese maps from that area show both groups of islands as part of Vietnamese territory under the administration of the Binh Son district of Quang Nghia prefecture while there are items of evidence like maps and administrative records supporting the view that Vietnam exercised sovereignty over Spratlys in the 19th century.[18] Vietnam's claim in these islands is mainly based on national security as well as living natural resources in the sea.

The Philippines' claim is the largest in the Spratlys which are grouped together as an administrative district of Palawan province.[19] The Philippines claims the islets (and not the Spratly Island itself) since the islets are adjacent to the main Philippine islands, and the region is vital to the country's security and economic survival, while the islets were *less nullius* or 'abandoned' after the Second World War, some of which are occupied by the Philippines which gives it title either through 'discovery' or 'prescriptive acquisition'.[20] The *res nullius* claim of the islets is based on the 'discovery' or 'occupation' of the Spratlys by a Filipino businessman and Lawyer, Tomas Cloma in 1947 who publicized his claims in 1956 asserting 'protectorates' over the islets, named them 'Kalaya' an or 'freedom land' as the Chair of the Supreme Council. In 1974, Cloma handed over Kalaya'an to the Philippine government. In 1971 and again in 1978, President Ferdinand Marcos formally announced "Kalaya'an Island Group' as part of the Philippines.[21] Therefore, Philippines' claims over Spratly islands are not historical in character, but an inheritance from its citizen. By that count, the Philippines' claim is unique.

Malaysia also raised its stakes in the South China Sea's territorial game. Out of twelve islands that Malaysia claims, she occupies six, in some sense. There are two legal bases behind Malaysia's claims, continental shelf extension, which derives from Geneva Conventions of 1958 regarding territorial waters and continental shelf boundaries which Malaysia signed in 1960, and discovery or occupation.[22] Therefore, Malaysia's claims are legal in character and not historical unlike Vietnam's or China's case.

The obvious result of these claims and counter-claims in the South China Sea was war and the first territorial war took place in latter half of the last century. This was the time when Chinese assertiveness over the issue was visible.

The Maritime Border Dispute: Regional Initiatives to Resolve the Crisis

Up to 1975, the ASEAN did not involve itself in any issues related to political matters. In 1976, it, for the first time, had taken the Treaty of Amity and Cooperation (TAC) as a principle for its independent existence. So, the five ASEAN members did not take any stand related to the South China Sea dispute since the security matters remained outside the purview of its original charter because this region at that time was much disturbed on account of the Vietnam War.

Until 1995, ASEAN did not take any position on South China Sea. But a series of unilateral actions by China since 1992 culminating to Mischief Reef incident, forced ASEAN to rethink its ignorant posture. On March 18, 1995, the ASEAN, for the first time, issued a statement calling for parties concerned to comply with the Manila Declaration (which emphasized sovereignty of the claimants and asked for peaceful resolution of the dispute) on the South China Sea.[23] ASEAN, as part of its strategy to deal with the South China Sea problem, involved China into multilateral groups like ASEAN Regional Forum (ARF). But the differences continued among the ASEAN countries regarding their individual policy towards China. ASEAN failed to take cohesive stand on China since not all of its members are claimants in the dispute. However, ASEAN countries emphasized that Chinese actions were a blow to the building of mutual trust between ASEAN and China which pushed the Association towards USA and Japan.[24] The Philippines and Malaysia proposed a 'regional code' for security, economic aspects of Spratly dispute at the July 1999 ASEAN Foreign Ministers' meeting, in Singapore which was finally accepted in East Asia Summit in Manila in November, 1999.[25] China signed the Code in 2002.

Renewed South China Sea Conflict in the New Millennium

In recent years, the South China Sea issue has once again created severe power struggle among the claimants. As China gets stronger, the issue seems to be veering towards serious conflicts. Today, other claimants in the dispute are also growing economically and militarily, along with China, and the dispute is governing the geopolitical calculations of the Southeast Asian region. The emerging US-Vietnam and US-Philippines rapport is the product of the South China Sea feud. There are many factors which are making the resolution of the dispute more and more difficult.

To begin with, China's military *preparedness* and the reciprocal actions of other claimants are making the situation very critical. Over the past several years, the PLAN (People's Liberation Army Navy) has stretched out its presence in the South China Sea. The Chinese Navy has increased the rate of its 'presence missions' in the area by both surface and sub-surface vessels. These visits are boosted by establishment of a major naval base at Sanya in Hainan Island (in South China Sea) in 2007 which is prepared with underground facilities for submarines and piers capable of accommodating a mix of sub surface and large surface vessels, including amphibious landing ships and aircraft carriers, satellite images indicate. China has also expanded her facilities on the Paracels (especially Woody Islands) and in the Spratlys.[26] Although PLAN's modernization mission is Taiwan centric, modern warships are versatile platforms can perform a variety of missions, including those in South China Sea. According to Chinese media, the PLA regularly conducts integrated exercises over the South China Sea and that the size and sophistication of these exercises increased since 2010.[27] These developments are part of the naval policy of China in the 21st century. One who rules the water, rules the world. China is seriously following this Mahanian doctrine. China's prime concern is to defend her interests in the adjacent waters. China is investing heavily to strengthen her navy, mainly to counter the US dominance and the Taiwan headache and also to bring the South China Sea within her naval strategy ambit.

Vietnam is the forerunner in challenging China in the South China Sea. The Chinese objections have impeded the ventures of the foreign oil corporations like British Petroleum and Exxon Mobil forcing them to suspend their joint development ventures with Vietnamese companies. The regular harassments of the Vietnamese fishermen at the hands of the Chinese patrol boats become major point of dispute. Also the passage of Chinese legislation in 2007 extending maritime jurisdiction of Hainan Island over the Spratlys and the Paracel triggered anti-China protests in Hanoi and Ho Chi Minh City.[28] Two of Vietnam's most lucrative maritime industries are offshore energy and fisheries resources, which China, as Vietnam alleges, is seeking to curtail. The Defence White Paper of Vietnam, 2009 reads: "*Concerning the disputes over sovereignty, sovereign rights and jurisdiction over the territories in the East Sea (South China Sea), the complicated developments so far have seriously affected many activities and the maritime economic development of Vietnam.*"[29] This shows the economic importance South China Sea holds for Vietnam.

With China modernizing her military, Vietnam embarked on a similar mission. The country's defence budget has increased over the years, from $910 million in 2003 to $1.327 billion in 2008 and she is modernizing her navy and air force with the help of foreign, mainly Russian made, advanced military hardware.[30] Vietnam's 2012 defence budget was $3.3 billion in current terms.[31] The Vietnamese Navy has gained the maximum from the increased budget expenses which is prepared to promote Vietnamese claims in the 'East Sea' and to control the waters and the islands there, to counter any challenge to the country's sovereignty claims in the disputed waters and to uphold her national interests at the sea. Certainly in one hand Vietnam wants to consolidate her presence in the disputed water to uphold her sovereignty claims and on the other, she is preparing herself to face any adverse situation, especially with China in mind.

Currently, the Philippines is most the vocal claimant against the Chinese 'expansionist' policy in the South China Sea (*West Philippine Sea* in Filipino version). In July, 2013, Manila referred the South China Sea dispute to the UN Tribunal leading to the Chinese voicing their displeasure. The Philippines traditionally relied on the US-Philippines mutual defence pact signed in August 1951, for her security. Such a defence arrangement, with a temporary loss of significance in the early 1990s with the end of Cold War, got revamped in the post 9/11 era and particularly with the re-surfacing of the South China Sea dispute. With the assistance of the US, the Philippines has devised a Capability Upgrade Programme (CUP) to improve the operational capabilities of its armed forces. After doubling it defence budget to $2.4 billion, the Filipino Government allotted $118 billion further in September 2011, as part of its Capability Up-gradation programme (CUP) to strengthen its armed forces in the context of the South China Sea dispute.[32] The government allotted $970 million which was meant for the weapons procurement projects which were inspired by the developments in the neighbourhood like the rise of China and military modernization missions of her other neighbours.[33]

Although the US is the prime source of security to the Philippines, Manila is not fully relying on Washington for defence procurements since the latter is not inclined to pursue an openly hostile policy towards Beijing. Thus, in order to develop a minimum credible defence system vis-à-vis China, the Philippines is looking for other sources. According to media reports, the Philippine military wants to procure surface-to-air missiles (SAM) and multiple-launch rocket systems (MLRS) from two Israeli defence contractors.[34] Apart from this, Manila is now forging alliance with Japan and Australia. The visit of the Japanese Defence Minister to Manila in early December 2013, after China's declaration of ADIZ, is worth mentioning in this context. In 2012, the Philippine Defence Secretary Voltaire Gazmin met his Japanese counterpart to sign the Statement of 'Intent of the

Greater Defence Cooperation Agreement', a five year pact which provides high level, working level and unit-to-unit military exchanges between the two countries.[35] To facilitate military ties with Australia, the Filipino Senate ratified the Status of Visiting Forces (SOFA), signed with Canberra in July, 2007, in July 2012. Senator, Loren Legarda of the Philippines, clearly linked the pact to the South China Sea conflicts. He said "We are faced by grave dangers and threats not present 15 years ago and the Philippines is at the strategic center of all these realities. A strategic center that has no fulcrum will not be able to realistically wage a sustainable, winning crusade against these regional and global threats."[36] Apart from this, Manila has not forgotten its traditional guarantor. The Philippines has presented the Pentagon with a 'wish list' of new equipments including coastal radar, long range patrol aircraft, strategic sea-lift vessels, off shore boat patrols, naval helicopters etc.[37]

All these preparations are the result of the mistrust and suspicion that exists between China and the Philippines. The military prowess of China is unnerving Manila who is now relying on the powers, big and small, who share her concern about China, although in varying degrees. That Manila is trying hard to establish its position on the South China Sea dispute becomes clear when the Filipino Ambassador to Argentina, Maria Amelita Aquino, presented her country's case at the Argentine Council of International Relations explaining how China's claim of "indisputable sovereignty" over waters and features falls within the Philippines' exclusive economic zone. At the same time the Ambassador iterated Manila's wish to resolve the dispute through dialogue via the ASEAN and through implementation of 2002 Declaration on the Conduct of Parties in the South China Sea, which China also signed.[38] The Philippines put forward a 'Triple Action Plan' at the 47thASEAN Foreign Ministers Meeting held at Nay Pyi Taw, Myanmar in August, 2014 which proposed immediate imposition of a moratorium on activities, like construction of structures that raise tensions in the disputed waters, full and effective implementation of the 2002 Declaration on the Conduct of Parties in the South China Sea and the expeditious conclusion of a code of conduct and international arbitration of the disputes.[39]

While Malaysia's claim in the South China Sea is not much heard of unlike Vietnam and the Philippines, she, in her new defence policy

2010, mentioned the country's key strategic priorities as territorial defence, the defence of South China Sea Economic Exclusion Zone, sea and air lanes between East Malaysia and the Malaysian Peninsular and Malacca and Singapore Straits.[40] The naval and the air assets of Malaysia are largely meant for the defence of its territorial waters and its airspace and also for limited regional power projection.[41] This shows that currently Malaysia cannot afford to be overtly assertive with her South China Sea claims. The navy does not possess any aircraft carrier or destroyers and therefore its blue water capability is limited. Malaysia emphasizes the defence of her immediate sphere of influence in her neighbourhood, largely the South China Sea and the Straits of Malacca which is reflected in her fleets of two Scorpene submarines were commissioned in 2010, eight frigates (of which four are guided missile frigates), four mine warfare/counter measures vessel, one amphibious land ship and approximately 115 land craft.[42] That Malaysia is slowly strengthening her position in the South China Sea region became clear when its defense minister, Hishammuddin Hussein, declared on Oct. 10 (2013) that Malaysia will build a new naval base in the Bintulu Division of Sarawak, only 100 kilometres away from James Shoal, the southernmost point of the disputed Spratly islands.[43]

So, the South China Sea dispute is having an impact on the defence policy of the claimant countries, but the nature of the impact varies. Malaysia's defence policy maintains a very low profile vis-à-vis the South China Sea while Vietnam and the Philippines seem to be very aggressive in their respective defence preparedness. Therefore, the current South China Sea dispute is revolving round the trio-China, Vietnam and the Philippines. However, Malaysia (and even Indonesia for that matter) can play a bigger role in future once Malaysia attains the position to counter China and others with her economy and military taking a bold shape.

The South China Sea dispute is no more limited to the mere differences of opinions and positions of the claimant parties but is gradually becoming an effect of the bigger and more serious causes like the complicated geopolitical ambiance of the Southeast and East Asian region. As China rises, so do her neighbours. Thus, given the eternal tension between China and her neighbours who are wary of Chinese rise, the dispute is motivating the small neighbours of China to prepare for adverse situations. Both sides are the victims of suspicion and jingoism. Moreover, the separate and often conflicting foreign policies of the individual countries is also becoming impediment towards solution of the problem.

The Crisis within ASEAN

The most significant failure of the ASEAN as a regional organization has been its consistent incapacity to resolve the South China Sea crisis. This failure to develop consensus on the peaceful settlement of the dispute became evident with Cambodia's opposition to ASEAN's united stand over the Scarborough Shoal clash between China and the Philippines in 2012. This is a success for China's 'divide and rule' policy which puts 'ASEAN solidarity' to question. Professor Robert Ross once said that the post Cold War bipolar regional structure is characterized by Chinese dominance of mainland East Asia and US dominance of maritime Southeast Asia.[44] Although this was said in a paper written in the late 1990s with reference of China's relation with Myanmar, Cambodia and Vietnam (when Hanoi accepted China's terms of peace in Cambodia), the diplomatic dividend that China currently reaps from her economic involvement in mainland Southeast Asia in the South China Sea context corroborates the prophecy. China's investment in the Greater Mekong Sub Region (GMS) to upgrade the poorer countries like Myanmar, Laos and Cambodia through the Strategic Framework for Next Ten Years of the GMS Programme (2012-2022) and Plan of Action for Trade and Transportation Facilitation, are parts of China's economic diplomacy to advance her interests in Southeast Asia. This is no doubt having an adverse impact on ASEAN's solidarity on the South China Sea issue.

Chinese Assertiveness in South China Sea is an Internal Obligation

China's assertive stand on the South China Sea is sometimes seen as the main cause of the conflicts. The exercises of the Chinese Fleet of the PLA Navy in 2010, the regular clash between the Chinese patrol vessels and the Vietnamese or Filipinos and all other 'aggressive' and 'expansionist' postures of China have put Beijing on the receiving end. However, a close study of China's internal condition will show the obligation of the Chinese government to possess such an aggressive attitude. There are many actors within China who act as pressure groups directing Beijing's policy. The Chinese rejection of Manila's Triple Action plan at the Nay Pyi Taw ASEAN Foreign Ministers' Meeting this year is mention worthy in this context.

On the question of South China Sea, China is an internally divided house. The central government in Beijing is unable to command the South China Sea issue. There are several government actors who play major role in it. These actors include the Bureau of Fisheries Administration, China Marine Surveillance, the local governments, PLAN and the Foreign Ministry. The Bureau, the Marine Surveillance and the local governments have their own commanding forces who actually are involved in clashes.[45] These are termed as 'Chinese expansionist acts'. What is worth mentioning is that the Chinese Navy has not been involved in any of the recent incidents in the disputed water. In 2012, it was the China's Marine Surveillance patrol vessels, along with Fisheries Patrol boats, that clashed with the Filipinos in Scarborough Reef.[46] Similarly since provincial governments have law enforcing forces at their command at the provincial levels, including adjacent waters, this often leads to unfavourable outcomes for the central government when provinces handle relations with neighbouring countries without effective central coordination. Therefore, we see that it is the local law enforcing machinery and not the central government, which is involved, sometimes, without the approval of Beijing, in the skirmishes.

Some of the most potential 'quasi-governmental' actors in the South China Sea policy are the national oil companies of China like the China National Petroleum Corporation (CNPC), China Petrochemical Corporation (Sinopec) and China National Corporation (CNOOC). They want the Chinese central government to fund and approve energy exploitation in the disputed waters since, according to them, such actions would buttress China's sovereignty claims there. So far, Beijing has been unwilling to support them.[47]

Another important aspect of Chinese 'obligation' is the government's playing with the nationalist sentiment. In the case of the South China Sea, it has deliberately imbued maritime disputes with nationalist sentiments.[48] It shows China uses her nationalism to justify her case.

There is also another interpretation of the South China Sea policy. As mentioned earlier, PLAN has so far refrained from engaging in any clash in the disputed waters. Only the law enforcement agencies have so far 'defended Chinese sovereignty' there. To an extent usage of paramilitary forces can be seen as a welcome alternative to military force. While they perform many of the functions of the conventional navy, law enforcing bodies are seen as less threatening.

Compulsions of Other Claimants

Unique historical narratives as well as domestic political and economic situations direct the response of other claimants to Chinese assertiveness. As Beijing's economic and political clout grows, other countries also feel the compulsion to respond to such acts with similar forward stand. However, as we have seen the response of the claimants vary.

Sometimes, history plays its part. The Sino-Vietnam relation narrates the history of Chinese occupation of Vietnamese territory in the ancient period. Even in the late 1970s China invaded Vietnam over Cambodia issue. All these memories are still alive among the Vietnamese. Besides, the sheer presence of such a powerful neighbour is reason enough to lead a small neighbour like Vietnam to be wary. This triggers a strong sense of nationalism. The anti-Chinese grievances are taken advantage of by the political bosses. As a Vietnamese foreign ministry official said, "The two countries are old friends and old enemies".[49] Therefore, the government tries using the common ploy of surrendering the national interests to 'enemy' China.

At the same time, the economic importance of the South China Sea to Vietnam is significant. The bourgeoning economy of Vietnam is hungry of resources. The soaring food price, weakening confidence in the currency and stagnating job market are forcing the government in Hanoi to develop energy resources in the South China Sea to improve Vietnam's economic performance. Also the declining fishing stocks near the shore are forcing Vietnamese fishermen to sail deep into the disputed area, encouraged by the government. Like China, the fishing industry is crucial to Vietnam. Vietnamese fishermen now sail beyond the EEZ of Vietnam off the resource abundant Paracel

Islands. This alleged intrusion often pitches them between the guns of the Chinese patrol vessels.

The current anti China stand of the Philippines is stemming from her Cold War politics which has generated a natural fear of 'rising China'. However, the economic compulsion is also very important in this context. Fishing is important in the Filipino economy as the industry employs close to one—and-a-half million people in the country. In the waters of Palawan, which has plenty of fisheries resources, the Filipino authorities regularly seize Vietnamese and Chinese fishermen.[50] The current South China Sea policy of Manila can be termed as a means to strengthen the country militarily with assistance from China wary countries, especially USA.

Unlike Vietnam and the Philippines, Malaysia prefers cooperation over confrontation. The signing in 2006 of an agreement between Malaysia's national oil and gas corporation, PETRONAS, and China's Shanghai LNG company is an interesting case in reference to Malaysia-China SCS (South China Sea) relations. It implies that cooperation and not confrontation can be an option for the two claimants.[51] Malaysia is not concerned about the Chinese assertiveness in the South China Sea. Defence Minister Hishammuddin Hussein said Malaysia is not worried about how often Chinese ships patrol the areas it claims in the waters, He went to the extent saying "Just because you have enemies, doesn't mean your enemies are my enemies".[52] Thus, Malaysia is not interested in pursuing any hostile strategy towards China unlike the other claimants, at present.

The US Meddling

Apparently, the US is not interested in the South China Sea dispute. The US position regarding the South China Sea has been consistent. Little attention had been paid to the dispute until the 1960s and 1970s, when international oil companies began prospecting in the region. After the fall of the USSR, Washington did not take much interest in the dispute. However, the State Department on May, 1995 stated, referring to the South China Sea dispute, that the US opposes the use of force (to solve the dispute), has interest in maintaining peace and stability in the region, insists on freedom of navigation and takes no position on competing claims.[53] From this it can be construed that the US, even when not taking any side in the dispute, is emphasizing on freedom of navigation which implies freedom from any domination of the regional waters in the South China Sea by any country. By maintaining neutrality, US on the one hand avoided any direct clash with China and on the other refrained from offending any of the ASEAN claimants who are allies of the US. Washington is still maintaining this stand. Recently, the US Secretary of State, John Kerry, in reference to the maritime disputes in East and South China Sea, urged China and other claimants to look for peaceful solutions and not to impede freedom of navigation in disputed waters.[54]

On the other hand, US assistance is vital for the claimants like Vietnam and the Philippines. When Manila is relying on its traditional security relations with the US, Vietnam is capitalizing on US wariness about 'rising China'. The US is also using this tension to justify her presence the Asia-Pacific region. Although Washington avoids any direct clash with Beijing, it is both its obligation and necessity to remain on the scene. The withdrawal of the US will force her partners to compromise with China, making the latter powerful in the region while that will question America's reliability as security guarantor. Both make US intervention in the East Asian disputes unavoidable. Also, it is vital for the American economy that navigation through the South China Sea remains free, and is definitely not controlled by China. In a way the maritime disputes in China's east is an impediment to China's 'gradual rise'. Even China is also suspicious about the US role in the maritime disputes. After the US Secretary John Kerry, concluded his trip to the Asia Pacific region recently, China's state-run newspaper, *People's Daily,* accused US of 'emboldening its Asian neighbours in claims to the water way', and blamed that Washington's position is assuring the Philippines about her victory in the maritime dispute. It also accused USA of encouraging Vietnam and the Philippines to take 'blatant moves'.[55]

Conclusion

The South China Sea dispute has many shades. On the one hand it is the economic rivalry between the claimants. Each of the claimants has an economic stake in the resources under the Sea and each of the claimants is a growing resource -hungry economy. On the other hand, the ugly historical background is giving birth to strong nationalistic zeal, coupled with the role of internal pressure groups who like to uphold their respective interests in the disputed area. The political bosses sometimes use this jingoism to cater to their internal and external political interests. And also, as the economy of the claimants grows, they wish to strengthen themselves militarily and the disputes supply them with the necessary fodder for acquiring this strength. Therefore, the resolution of the South China Sea dispute becomes complex with so many competing interests at work.

NOTES

1. Richard Javad Heydarian, *ADIZ stirs fears for South China Sea*, Dec 6, 2013, http://www.atimes.com/atimes/Southeast_Asia/SEA-01-061213.html, (accessed on January 4, 2014).
2. Robert Beckman, *Geopolitics, International Law and the South China Sea*, Tokyo Plenary Meeting 2012, http://cil.nus.edu.sg/wp/wp-content/uploads/2012/04/Beckman-Geopolitics-Intl-Law-SCS-Tokyo-21-April-2012-final-rev.pdf (accessed on 15.12.2013).
3. *Great Game in the South China Sea,* The Hanoist, April 17, 2012 http://www.atimes.com/atimes/Southeast_Asia/ND17Ae01.html (accessed on October 22, 2012).
4. Scott Synder, *The South China Sea Dispute: Prospects for Preventive Diplomacy*, United Institute of Peace, Special Report No. 18, www.usip.org/publications/south-china-sea-dispute-prospects_preventive-diplomacy (accessed on September 6, 2012).
5. *Ibid.*
6. Ralf Emmers, 'Maritime Disputes in China Sea: Strategic and Diplomatic Status Quo', in Chong Guan Kwa, John K. Skogan (ed), *Maritime Security in Southeast Asia*, Routledge, Oxon, 2007, p. 51.
7. Tridib Chakraborti, 'The Territorial Claims in South China Sea: Probing Persistent Uncertainties', in Arun Banerji, Purushottam Bhattacharya (eds), *Peoples Republic of China in Fifties: Politics, Economy and Foreign Relations,* New Delhi, Lancer's Book, 2001, p. 174.
8. *Ibid.*, p. 177.
9. *Stirring Up the South China Sea (I),* Asia Report N°223-, International Crisis Group, April 23, 2012, www.crisisgroup.org/~/media/Files/asia/north-east_asia/223-stirring-up-the-south-china-sea-pdf, p. 3 (accessed on October 23, 2013).

10. Krishnan Srinivasan, "Waters of tension off China's shores and beyond", The Telegraph, Calcutta, 28th August, 2012, p. 11.
11. Mark J Valencia, Jon M., Van Dyke, Joel A. Ludwig, *Sharing the Resources of South China Sea*, The Hague, University of Hawaii Press, 1999, p. 24.
12. Krishnan Srinivasan, *op cit.*
13. Tridib Chakraborti, *op cit.*, p. 178.
14. *Ibid.,* p. 179.
15. *Ibid.*
16. *Ibid.*, p. 180.
17. *Ibid.*, p. 180-181.
18. Mark J. Valencia, Jon M., Van Dyke, Joel A. Ludwig, *op. cit.,* p. 30.
19. Tridib Chakraborti, *op cit.*, p. 191.
20. Mark J Valencia, Jon M., Van Dyke, Joel A. Ludwig, *op cit.*, p. 33.
21. *Ibid.*, p. 34.
22. *Ibid.*, p. 36.
23. Cheng Ang, Guan, *The South China Sea dispute re visited*, Institute of Defence and Strategic Studies, Singapore, www.rsis.edu.sg/publications/Working Papers/WP04.pdf, p16 (accessed on September 19, 2012).
24. Tridib Chakraborti, *op cit*, p. 199.
25. *Ibid.*, pp. 199, 200.
26. Ian Storey, *Asia's Changing Balance of Regional Power: Implications for the South China Sea Dispute,* National Bureau of Asian Research, www.nbr.org/publications/element.aspx?id=564 (accessed on September 18, 2012).
27. *Ibid.*
28. *Ibid.*
29. Vietnam National Defence, Hanoi 12, 2009, http://www.isn.ethz.ch/Digital-Library/Publications/Detail/?lng=en&id=155222, p18(accessed on August 14,2013).
30. Ian Storey, *op cit.*
31. Defence Economic Trends in the Asia Pacific, 2013, http://www.defence.gov.au/dio/documents/DET_13.pdf (accessed on August 19, 2014).
32. Military Balance in Southeast Asia, Research Paper 11/79, December 14, 2011, House of Commons Library, www.parliament.uk/briefing-papers/RP-11-79.pdf, p41 (accessed on September 18, 2012).
33. *Ibid.*, p. 44.
34. J. Michael Cole, *Philippines Seeks Air Defense Systems From Israel,* June

18, 2013, http://thediplomat.com/2013/06/philippines-seeks-air-defense-systems-from-israel/(accessed on January 22, 2014).

35. George Amurao, *Philippines arms itself with new pacts,* Aug 2, 2012, http://www.atimes.com/atimes/Southeast_Asia/NH02Ae01.html (accessed on January 22, 2014).
36. Quoted in *Ibid.*
37. Carlyle A. Thayer, *The Rise of China and Maritime Security of Southeast Asia,* www.ide.go.jp/japanese/Publish/Download/Seikaku/120208.html (accessed on January 22,2014)
38. Camille Doila, *In Argentina, Philippines presents position on disputed sea,* August 14, 2014, http://www.philstar.com/headlines/2014/08/14/1357559/argentina-philippines-presents-position-disputed-sea, (accessed on August 20, 2014).
39. Michaela Del Callar, *PHL action plan on sea gains support amid Chinese objection-DFA's Del Rosario,* August 11, 2014, http://www.gmanetwork.com/news/story/374316/news/nation/phl-action-plan-on-sea-row-gains-support-amid-chinese-objection-dfa-s-del-rosario, (accessed on August 20, 2014).
40. Military Balance in Southeast Asia, *op cit.*, pp. 20-21.
41. *Ibid.*, p. 23.
42. *Ibid.*
43. *Malaysia to build naval base in disputed South China Sea*, Oct. 22, 2013, http://www.wantchinatimes.com/news-subclass-cnt.aspx?id=20131022000002&cid=1101(accessed on January 22, 2014).
44. Read Robert Ross, *The Geography of Peace: East Asia in the Twenty-First Century,* http://www.jstor.org/stable/pdfplus/2539295.pdf?acceptTC=true&jpdConfirm=true (accessed on February 25, 2014).
45. See *Stirring Up the South China Sea (I), op cit.*
46. *Ibid.*, p. 9.
47. *Ibid.*, p. 12.
48. *Ibid.*, p. 27.
49. *Stirring Up South China Sea(II), Regional Responses, Asia Report* N°229-24 July, 2012, International Crisis Group, http://www.crisisgroup.org/~/media/Files/asia/north-east-asia/229-stirring-up-the-south-china-sea-ii-regional-responses.pdf, p4 (accessed on September 19, 2012).
50. *Ibid.*, p. 17.
51. Johan Saravanamuttu, 'Malaysia in the New Geopolitics of Southeast Asia', in *The New Geopolitics of Southeast Asia*, LSE Ideas, November, 2012, http://www.lse.ac.uk/ideas/publications/reports/sr015.aspx, (accessed on August 20, 2014), p. 51.

52. Sharon Chen, *Malaysia Splits with ASEAN Claimants on China Sea Threat*, Aug. 29, 2013, http://www.bloomberg.com/news/2013-08-28/malaysia-splits-with-other-asean-claimants-over-china-sea-threat.html (accessed on January 18, 2014).
53. Cheng Ang, Guan, *op cit.*, p. 15.
54. Patrick Boehler, *Jon Kerry outlines US-Asia pivot priorities in major policy address*, South China Morning Post Asia, August 18, 2014, http://www.scmp.com/news/asia/article/1573314/john-kerry-outlines-us-asia-pivot-priorities-major-policy-address (accessed on August 20, 2014).
55. 'China-US Tensions Heat Up Over Disputed Sea', Voice of America, Tibetan, August 13, 2014, http://www.voatibetanenglish.com/content/china-us-tensions-rise-over-south-china-sea/2412277.html (accessed on August 20, 2014).

REFERENCES

Kwa Chong Guan, John K. Skogan (ed), *Maritime Security in Southeast Asia*, Routledge, Oxon, 2007.

Banerji Arun, Purushottam Bhattacharya (eds), *Peoples Republic of China in Fifties: Politics, Economy and Foreign Relations,* New Delhi, Lancer's Book, 2001.

Valencia Mark J., Jon M., Van Dyke, Joel A. Ludwig, *Sharing the Resources of South China Sea*, The Hague, University of Hawaii Press, 1999.

Stirring Up the South China Sea (I), Asia Report No 223, International Crisis Group, April 23, 2012.

Stirring Up South China Sea (II), Regional Responses, Asia Report N°229-24 July, 2012, International Crisis Group.

Raine Sarah, Christian Le Miṟre, *Regional Disorder: The South China Sea Disputes,* Routledge, 2013.

Kivimāki Timo (ed.), War Or Peace in the South China Sea?, NIAS Press, 2002.

Valencia Mark J., *China and the South China Sea Dispute,* Oxford University Press, 1995.

Lo Chin-kin, *China's Policy Towards Territorial Disputes: The Case of South China Sea Islands,* Taylor and Francis, 2004.

Linkages: Tradition and Culture

4
Re-imagining Insular Southeast Asia through Traditional Works

Huỳnh Thanh Loan

The reconstruction of early Southeast Asia should not—and probably cannot—rest so much on recovering the chronology of events or of individual accomplishments, as on reconstructing institutions and their development. To understand Southeast Asia, traditional histories became alluvial sources to explore historical life of this society. The traditional history of a society may be reflected by oral or written literature; or by monuments, inscriptions, stele etc. They can also be heroic myths, legends, chronicles or religious tales. One particular feature of this kind of history is that the stories are products of imagination and retention rather than actual truth. It is a symbol from a rich and vast cultural inheritance.

The geographical salience of this vast archipelago, and the traditional histories in insular Southeast Asia was reflected in its maritime affairs. The written and oral histories included maritime trading activities, internal trade, international trade, maritime kingdoms, spiritual life, etc.

By studying traditional history, to some extent, we can explore the nature of political states, the life in courts, kings, queens and priests, the ritual life, the relationship between states and maritime activities, life of merchants, development of religious movements, or in a broader sense, the interaction between the region and the outside world. This kind of study of tradition became important to nation-states of Southeast Asia. Myths about the nation-states, their longstanding pedigree, a heritage of which its citizens can be proud of, and a glorious past, have been researched meticulously and studiously to benefit scholars and tourists.

In Java, old Javanese literature helped scholars explore the complex nature of the court life, the role of kings and queens, marital relations, and the ideal of royal sovereignty in connection with religious beliefs. It also is a rich source, "especially as it reflects on Java's physical landscape and the society and culture that occupied this space during the pre-1500 era"[1]. One of the important literary sources in Java is old Javanese poetic literature known as *Kakawin* which developed in the era of the Gupta kings (320-600 CE). Patronized by kings and their courts, poets always began by invoking the Gods or God-like persons to bring the work to a successful conclusion. The poem is thus initially a religious invocation, a literary offering to the Divine.[2] It is also 'an essay on royal authority'[3]. According to P.J. Zoetmulder, one feature of the *kakawin* is that, "the world of the old Javanese poet was not located in India but the author appropriated Sanskrit names of persons and places to present a picture of his own country and his own society. These men and women with their Indian names are essentially Javanese, acting like Javanese and living in a Javanese environment."[4]

The *Ramayana kakawin*, which was composed in ninth-century central Java, gives details of Javanese characteristics. Although this Sanskrit version maintains the essential Indic plots as well as the Indian names and places, its content focuses more on the *Ravanavadha*—the slaying of Ravana. It is considered as a poet's model—a complex exploration in and a guide book to—the rules of Sanskrit grammar and rhetoric.[5]

In the tenth century, during the reign of Dharmawangsa Teguth, old Javanese literature was well-developed through recitals of books of *Mahabharata* in Javanese prose. There was also a public reading of the Epics by a trained master of the art. Kenneth R. Hall suggests that in these recitals, *Mahabharata* and *Ramayana*, were recited in Sanskrit and then explained to the audience in Javanese.

In the eleventh century, during the reign of Airlangga, court poets composed the *Arjunawiwaha kakawin* to honour Airlangga's consolidation of authority as king of East Java following years of devastation and chaos. The Arjunawiwaha not only provides a glimpse of the eleventh-century Javanese society and culture, but also reflects the complexity of the political duality in the extended royal family. This *kakawin* highlights the "Marriage of Arjuna", as its author elaborates on the plot of the *Mahabharata parwa*, in which Arjuna is tutored by his charioteer, who is Wisnu[6] (Vishnu)—incarnate. Arjuna's initial quest is not for worldly pleasure and union with the Deity through beauty and life, but for spiritual enhancement by distancing himself from worldly distraction. Peter Worsley asserts that the author of *Arjunawiwaha* presents a dichotomy between the natural world of the forests and the social world of the palace, court and human relationships. Moreover, the *Arjunawiwaha* established the popular expectations of Javanese kings. It praises one who does not use the opportunity of kingship to obtain the highest personal reward that is liberation from this world. The king should choose to remain a human and seek the welfare of others by protecting this world from various misfortunes. Rulers uphold such ideas and are even more bound to the service of humankind. This conceptualization of kingship became standards for future *kakawin*. With the focal image of Arjuna, the text allegorically associates him with the historical monarch Airlangga, who re-established the unity of Java in the early eleventh century.[7]

In the twelfth century, the *Bharatayudda kakawin* expands upon the Indic *Mahabharata* epic. It provides the thematic base for the budding East Java monarchy, that would blossom in the fourteenth-century Majapahit court and describes it in subsequent contemporary *kakawin*. In this passage, the savage wilderness of the Javanese landscape contrasts and complements the sweetness and benefits of the ordered court culture. The massage is that desire is better fulfilled by proper conduct, which brings emotional achievement, than by unrestrained passion for immediate physical or material rewards. It also depicts parallel potentials by alluding to the distinction between male and female, or more specifically between the monarch and his queen.

In the fourteenth century, *Parthayajna kakawin* highlights Arjuna's journey to Mount Indrakila, where he will be a penitent ascetic to win the favour of the Gods. Unlike the eleventh-century *Arjunawiwaha kakawin*, *Parthayajna kakawin* emphasizes on Arjuna's performance of accompanying rituals. It also enhances the role of the counseling sage, who teaches him Saivite doctrines and rituals prior to his successful spiritual quest. In other words, this text focuses on the spiritual guide as the source of ritual performance as well as knowledge, symbolic of the importance of the ritual partnership between the king and the priests.

In the late fourteenth century, *Arjunawijaya* (c. 1370) composed by poet *mpu* Tantular is a text with a hidden, magical meaning which transcends the re-telling of an old tale, a preamble to the *Ramayana* epic. It is the story of a competition between good and evil, between the virtuous king and 'World Maintainer' Arjunasahasrabahu and the 'World Destroyer' Rawana[8] (Ravana), as well as the former's submission to the spiritual guidance of a priestly 'World Renouncer'. The *Arjunawijaya kakawin* shows multilayer meanings. It indicates that a king has the potential to possess and exercise superhuman physical power; both kings Rawana and Arjunasahasrabahu are equals on the battlefield, although Arjuna is influenced by his queen. In addition, the image of queen—the feminine separates civil society from potential male barbarity and activates and channels the king's creative energies in a positive direction, often through sexual contact with him. The priest also plays an important role. He is especially capable of communicating with the divine on the king's behalf and is able to supply the king with enhanced ritual power. Peter Worsley regards it as a Buddhist epic poem about kings and queens and political order.

Sutasoma kakawin composed by same poet *mpu* Tantular, with its greater complexity in language and structure shows the 'model monarch' for Java's future. The marriage between Candrawati and Sutasoma is a combination between superior physical attributes and superior intellectual wisdom and their sexual union helps to complete Sutasoma's Liberation. While Worsley thinks that in this text, *mpu* Tantular develops the character of Sutasoma to represent the ideal of the king-priest who will overcome the shortcomings of Majapahit's monarchy, K. P. O'Brien views it as Tantular's allegorical assertion of royal legitimacy on behalf of the reigning Majapahit monarchs.[9]

The late fifteenth century witnessed a shifting of views and portrayals of new possibilities for individuals, especially relative to their spiritual welfare. This change is seen as attempts to 'put new vigour into Javanese religious life'. The representation of this new *kakawin* is *Siwaratrikalpa kakawin*, highlighting a new Saivite ritual that is potential means of achieving salvation, even for those who are among the most sinful. It focuses on the salvation of the recently dead, saving unworthy souls and those bound by curses, the role of nocturnal rituals as a means of release, and the specific association of a female intercessionary Goddess, as well as the deceased's surviving wife. It seems that this shift is a reflection of the emergence of Java's sixteenth-century Islamic courts where the *kakawin* poetic tradition of knowledge continued to flourish under Islam.[10]

Ritual inscriptions are also an important source, supplying vivid images of the ritualistic life as well as changes, developments, religious movements and religious influences on social life. Many parts of the large insular Southeast Asian region with the common language and culture linked together, enjoyed a high level of civilization, enabling their elites to adopt and adapt those elements of Indian civilization that they regarded as valuable or useful.[11] Among different religious traditions that this region absorbed from India, it seems that Brahminic Hinduism, especially Śaivism, and Mahayana Buddhism have some effect on its spiritual life. Combination of literary sources and monuments with common features diversely and deeply influences this society.

In fourth century inscriptions, different precious gifts to Brahmins, including thousands of cattle and large amount of gold are described in detail. There are also special references to the worship of the footprints of the king and of his elephants. The king's footprints were also carved into large inscribed rock. In addition, in Indonesia, there is also good evidence for the worship of footprints of ancestors in some areas. Casparis suggests that this kind of worship is a traditional Austronesian practice continuing in the guise of Sanskrit terms.

Old Javanese sources also mention two typical Hindu ceremonies in Indonesian courts called royal consecration (abhiṣeka) and funerary rites (śrāddha). The funerary rites were performed by six generations in both ascending and descending lines; the presence of a son of the deceased was essential. The participants included not only members of the royal family but also high officials, as well as simple servants with their wives, priests and monks of different denominations, dancers, musicians, storytellers. It also involves various Tantric rites carried out by both Buddhist monks and by a *purohita*. The nature of śrāddha is that "it is an essential Austronesian rite embellished by learned elements from both Sanskrit ritual literature and Buddhist thought."[12]

Besides the Brahminical influence on the performance of certain rituals, the Indian way of life for higher classes like the āśramas was also adopted. People who chose a spiritual vocation were considered to have acquired the wisdom which could attract people from elsewhere. Images of great Rishi made of yellow sandalwood were also worshiped as a God named *Haricandana*.

Another interesting feature of the spiritual life here is the worship of royal ancestors. These royal ancestors were regarded as blessed deities who 'protect the royal residence of the kings'. Inscriptions of king *Daksa*, and kings of Mataram have lists of the titles of those preceding kings who entered into the bodies of all people. This feature illustrates the idea of deification of kings as well as preferring to protect as the supreme duty of kings.[13] In addition to ancestor worship, some Austronesian cults such as Austronesian deities, supernatural powers or river spirits also matched well with Brahminic Hinduism.

The worship of Siva, as well as Gods and divine symbols associated with Siva flourished during the thirteenth to fifteenth century and were mentioned in most of the old Javanese literature and centred on the royal courts. In numerous Siva temples which have either a *linga* or a standing Siva statue in its cella (the part inclosed within the walls of an ancient temple, as distinguished from the open porticoes), most Siva images represent the God in his majestic Mahadeva form and surrounded by the Guru, Ganesa and Durga. This symbolizes the principle actors on the stage of the world: the king, his spiritual guide, his prime minister and his queen. The feature of Brahma in ancient Java is also different. Brahma always associates with fire, including the subterranean fire revealing itself through the active volcanoes.

Influences of Buddhism on maritime Southeast Asia are different from western part to eastern part. In eastern part (Java, Nusa Tenggara, and east Borneo), Buddhism was strongly patronized by Śailendra kings (c.775-860). The greatest evidence of the Buddhism flourishing in this area is Borobudur which is described as maluwa, pesāwa, stūpa-prāsāda, or Tantric mandala. In Sumatra, Buddhism also flourished under the patronage of the kings of Śrivijaya. In the thirteenth and fourteenth centuries, Buddhism flourished again not only in Sumatra but also in Java. Throughout the fourteenth century, Buddhism remained important as reflected in the art and literature of the period. The Candi Jago temple in east Java reflects its Buddhist character not only in its architecture or narrative beliefs, but also in its statues which represent a Buddhist Tantric pantheon. It particularly, has inscriptions in the Nāgarī script of the type current in northeastern India. This indicates an influx of new ideas and practices into Buddhism from India.

In Sumatra, after the decline of Śrīvijaya in the thirteenth century, Malāyu continued close relations with Java. King Ādityavarman (c. 1347-79) issued a large number of inscriptions in Sanskrit and old Malay, written in a characteristic local script, and also one in Tamil.

The relationship between the rise of maritime trade and the formation of coastal polities sometime between the last few centuries of the first millennium BCE and the beginnings of the first millennium CE has been studied through various tales and inscriptions. Pierre Yves Manguin examines some tale motifs in different places such as Buleleng (on the north coast of Bali), Sumenep in Madura, Cirebon, Barus, Kutei, island of Palawan, etc. Most of these stories appear vaguely and are often in a predominantly oral context and the characters or events undergo permutations that may obscure the contents of the tales.

Manguin points out to seven motifs in these stories. There is always a local character having powers, and an overseas ship fully laden with rich merchandise usually under the captainship of shipmaster Dampu Awang, the ship is destined to get stranded and consequently, a competition takes place—either a fight or a bet—the prize of which is the ship's cargo. After that, the local character, thanks to his śakti, wins over the riches in the ship and thus acquires considerable wealth, after which he rules over his own prosperous country.[14] From these motifs, the social contexts of these tales can be explored to study the relationship between the merchant and the king. Here in the tale, trade with overseas merchants and acquisition of wealth in the political system has a close relation. Within this relation, the symbolic value of the ruler's "treasure" is essential. Wealth is an attribute of the ruler, one of the requisite sources of his power.[15] It is not strange that in coastal polities or harbour cities, where trade was the foremost economic activity, the duty of a good ruler is to convene a sufficient number of traders into his harbour. In doing so, he would reinforce his sovereignty over potentially rival neighbouring harbour cities. Through this initiative, in proportion to the success of the trade, he would also generate income for his followers, and he would therefore accumulate prestige as the dispenser of material wealth.[16]

One special element of the tales is the term "Dang Puhawang". This term carries in itself many meanings. The term "*Dang Puhawang*" originated in old Javanese titles referring to high-ranked people, at times associated with shipmasters.[17] Dang Puhawang is also a character with an Austronesian name (or title), and has been assimilated with a well-known Chinese historical character. Therefore, Dang Puhawang is, by trade, a shipmaster who arrives from "overseas," literally from across the sea. Thus, the emphasis in these tales is on "overseas," not on a determined place of origin: the shipmaster in the tales may stand for inter-regional as well as "international" traders (including Chinese), both of which would be part of a suitable trade network.

In later Malay literature, the presence of numerous foreign merchants is conventionally seen as a desirable feature in a polity. Maritime trade is the main source of income of harbour-centred polities and, by nature, this can only be "overseas" trade, especially the economic role played by China and the Chinese market in Southeast Asian history. In the eleventh century, in a statement about Srivijaya, a Chinese chronicler writes: "Merchants from distant places congregate there. This country is therefore considered to be very prosperous."[18]

A recurrent motif of these tales is that of the competition between king and merchant. A lot has been written on their role and position—all-powerful *orangkaya*. In the sixteenth to eighteenth centuries, the *orangkaya* merchant class was the mainstay of many societies of

Insular Southeast Asia. But it has also been a constant threat to the power of the ruler. Too much wealth on their part was usually felt as a threat to the ruler's own power, challenged as it was by the rise and parallel development of commercial elites. The *orangkaya* usually lost their lives when the king became suspicious of two circumstances, "their good reputation among the people and their wealth. In a late seventh century Śrivijayan inscription, the ship-master class appears among those who threaten the "treasure" of the ruler. By the 1079 C.E. the Śrivijayan inscription at Canton describes merchants as "flying." It therefore appears that the competition motif can itself be explained when the context of the tales is examined and reference made to the dialectical relationship between ruler and merchants in harbour-centred polities[19].

Besides these tales, textiles also have been found within the area where the tales are collected. There some certain motifs of textiles—although they are not narrative motifs—the statements they make can be read as "texts" in the very same way. Especially, the motif *jong sarat* or "fully laden ship" was widely adopted in many areas. This motif encounters the tales and seems to be mentioned in relation with various rites of passage and this is essential with high-ranking or royal-blooded heroes.[20]

Ceramics are often mentioned among the goods obtained after the competition described in the tales (where they usually appear as *piring* or *piring panjang*). It is likely that the use of imported ceramic dishes in a variety of court rituals, as well as in the decoration of buildings found in harbours along the Javanese *pesisir*, has been routinely but loosely associated with past overseas trade. Gifts of ceramics were popular in foreign relations of Southeast Asian polities with overseas powers, mainly China.

In general, these trade-biased political myths underscore the fact that commerce played a prominent role in the early formative stages of coastal, harbour-centred political systems. Manguin suggests that these myths could possibly be generated when the economy of a society crosses over from simple forms of exchange restricted to kin-ordered, alliance, or tributary modes to wider-ranging networks in closer connection with market forces and ultimately, with world economies.

Although we cannot chronicle exact events, what we find in literature, myths and monuments give us some hints about the life of ancient people in maritime Southeast Asia. We can see the ideas and doctrines of courtly life, duty of kings, the relationship between kings and their queens, the connection between kings and merchants as well as the way merchants helped to enrich these maritime kingdoms. We also can see the harmonious combination between Autronesian cults and Brahminic religions and the way in which different religious traditions were absorbed in the maritime spiritual life.

NOTES

1. Kenneth R. Hall, "Traditions of Knowledge in Old Javanese Literature, c.1000 -1500", *Journal of Southeast Asian Studies*, 36 (1), p. 7.
2. *Ibid.*, p. 26.
3. *Ibid.*, p. 12.
4. *Ibid.*, p. 8.
5. *Ibid.*, pp. 2,3.
6. In Java version, Vishnu is *Wisnu.*
7. Kenneth R. Hall, *op cit.*, p. 8.
8. It is Rawana in Java Ramayana version.
9. Kenneth R. Hall, *op cit.*, pp. 22-23.
10. *Ibid.*, pp. 25-27.
11. J.G. De Casparis and I. W Mabbelt, "Religion and popular Beliefs before c.1500", *The Cambridge History of Southeast Asia*, vol. 1, p. 305, 1992.
12. *Ibid.*, pp. 306-308.
13. *Ibid.*, pp. 309-310.
14. Pierre Yves Manguin, *The Merchant and the King: Political Myths of Southeast Asian coastal polities*, *Indonesia*, vol. 52, 1991, pp. 44, 45.
15. *Ibid.*, p. 47.
16. *Ibid.*, p. 48.
17. *Ibid.*, p. 46.
18. *Ibid.*, pp. 49, 50.
19. *Ibid.*, pp. 51,52.
20. *Ibid.*, p. 46.

REFERENCES

Bentley, G.C., Indigenous States of Southeast Asia, *Annual Review of Anthropology*, Vol. 15, pp. 275-305 (October 1986).

Casparis, J.G. De and I.W. Mabbelt, "Religion and popular Beliefs before c.1500", *The Cambridge History of Southeast Asia*.

Hall, Kenneth R., "Traditions of Knowledge in Old Javanese Literature, c.1000 1500", *Journal of Southeast Asian Studies*, 36 (1), pp. 1-27.

Hoogervorst, Tom, "Travelling words and their lessons on the 'Indianisation' of Southeast Asia", *The Newsletter*, No. 66, Winter 2013.

Manguin, Pierre Yves, "The Merchant and the King: Political Myths of Southeast Asian coastal polities", *Indonesia*, Vol. 52, 1991, pp. 41-54.

Robson, S.O., "Java at the Crossroads: Aspects of Javanese Cultural History in the 14th and 15th Centuries", Bijdragen tot de Taal-, Land- en Volkenkunde, Deel 137, 2de/3de Afl. (1981), pp. 259-292.

Stanyukovich, Maria V., "A Living Shamanistic Oral Tradition: Ifugao hudhud, the Philippines", *Oral Tradition*, 18/2 (2003), pp. 249-251.

5
Understanding of Buddhism-Hinduism and Promotion of Indian Studies in India and Abroad

The Missed Opportunity in Indian Foreign Policy

Swapna Bhattacharya (Chakraborti)

I

Understanding the Scope of Indian Studies

Quite legitimately political leaders and policy makers of our country lament that India is increasingly being isolated from her immediate neighbour or neighbours within Asia at large. Obviously in a mood of comparison, the "Success Story of China" is drawing attention (H. Panth 2012). This isolation of India could have been avoided if more attention would have given to learning the history, language and civilization of the neighbouring counties. The students are often engaged in post-modern discourses. The problem is that such terms as "post-modern", "subaltern" "imagined State" etc. are not used by historians of modern Southeast Asia. Even Western scholars on Southeast Asia (N. Tarling, 1992) hardly use such terms in their works. Lack of interest to travel to Southeast Asia and learn the languages have created a strange distance between the people of India and Southeast Asia. Even, Bangladesh studies could have developed in India more successfully as has been the case. In spite of large-scale changes in connectivity between India and Bangladesh for which the governments (all previous governments included) have to be commended, teachers and students of South Asian studies have not shown enough interest to travel to Bangladesh. Interestingly with both the countries, Myanmar and Bangladesh, India has the closest historical kinship; all three have shared many historical experiences together and are now members of the BIMSTEC forum.

A teacher of Asian History, wherever he or she is engaged in teaching and research, should have a sound knowledge of the history of two major nations, India and China. Students of Asian History should read what Gandhiji precisely wanted to convey in his book *Hind Swaraj* or what the Mahatma wrote about the relationship between Hinduism and Buddhism. One should not forget the works and deeds of the great Sri Lankan monk Anagarika Dharmapala (Ven. Dharmapala 1864-1933) and Swami Vivekananda, who, in the last quarter of the 19th century brought the Hindu-Buddhist world of Asia together in a single network. Due to the tireless efforts of Ven. Dharmapala, the cities of Yangon, Sittwe (Akyab), Kolkata (Calcutta) Bodhgaya and Colombo were more closely interlinked than perhaps today. While the leading intellectuals of neighbouring countries read with great interest works of Suniti Kumar Chatterjee, Benoy Kumar Sarkar, R.C. Majumdar, D.C. Sircar, P.C. Bagchi, Himanshu Bhusan Sarkar, Nihar Ranjan Ray, Kalidas Nag, Nilakanta Shastri and such other scholars, a large section of Indian scholars preferred to ignore their contributions and even became critical about the concept of *Greater India*. While S.K. Chatterjee should be read for his excellent understanding of the Indian society within the context of the ethno-linguistic identity of a pluralist nature, Benoy Sarkar (R. Frykenberg, 2001) should be read for his wide scholarship in various disciplines, not to mention his fame across the world, from Europe, USA, to China (Benoy K Sarkar, 1916). R.C. Majumdar's *Hindu Colonies in the Far East* still remains to be referred, as are D.C. Sircar's important contributions on Sanskrit inscriptions of old kingdoms across Southeast Asia (Myanmar, Vietnam). Kalidas Nag, a close associate of Tagore, should be remembered not only for his enthusiasm for the *Greater India* (K. Nag, 1960), but also for his contributions on China, Sri Lanka and other countries. Like S.K. Chatterjee, he too was a close associate of Tagore in this mission of understanding India in the context of Asia. Nilakanta Shastri appeals to us for his brilliant understanding of importance of South India in the all-India context, as well as in the context of India-Southeast Asia relations. On the other hand, the contribution of P.C. Bagchi (Bagchi, 1981) should be read and referred for his sublime view of how the Chinese people and the Indic people (in Myanmar sources often called *Kula* people) interacted with each other through trade, pilgrimage and scholarly missions. H.B. Sarkar, whom I had the privilege to talk to on certain academic events at the Asiatic Society, intensively investigated the influence of Hindu Law, Indian Epics and various other influences on the people of Indonesia. Nihar Ranjan Ray remains the only scholar to produce three books on history of Buddhism in Myanmar. Without any prejudice he wrote on Theravada Buddhism in Myanmar, as well as on the influence of Brahmanic Gods (Nihar Ranjan Ray, 2001) and on the Mahayana tradition in Myanmar. In Myanmar as well as in many other states of Southeast Asia influenced by India, the basic idea of empire building was drawn from the concept of a total harmony with the cosmos. Call it Hindu, call it Buddhist, the state to be ruled should be taken as a part of universal duty. These ideas, so far as Myanmar is concerned, have been brilliantly explained in two important chapters of Emanuel Sarkisyanz's path-breaking book *The Buddhist background of the Burmese Revolution* (E. Sarkisyanz, 1965).

That pre-modern states in Europe and pre-modern state in Asia, South and Southeast Asia in particular, share a number of common experiences need not be reiterated. On the other hand, theories of State formation should be constructed on the solid foundation of individual country's own historical experiences. In the case of India, the social hierarchy as expressed through the caste system has to be understood in the context of forces and counter forces that ultimately determined the course. The emergence of Brahmins as bearers of knowledge and wisdom is a unique phenomenon of Indian history. At the same time, Hinduism cannot be defined only on the basis of the domination by the Brahmins. There were formidable challenges against the absolute authority of the Brahmins within Hindu society. Further, regional traditions have always been a strong force in India. Eminent Indologist H. von Stietencron saw in the Brahmans a great force for integrating the regional traditions of India (Stietencron, 1985). Students of Southeast Asian studies in India should focus their views at the regional level. Every region of India has its own charm like every individual nation of Southeast Asia. The pattern of the early Diaspora as well as colonial immigration to Southeast Asia had its bearing on recipient countries (S. Bhattacharya, 2009). Indeed, this realization convinced the Dutch and the French scholars (J.C. van Leur, C.C. Berg, F.D.K Bosch, N.J. Krom, G. Coedes) in particular; so much so that echoing their Indian counterparts, they spoke of the existence of Indianized states in ancient and early medieval periods in Vietnam, Cambodia, Indonesia, Malaysia (earlier Malay Peninsula including Singapore) Thailand and Myanmar. The founding of the *Greater India Society* in 1926 was a landmark event in this important discourse. On this platform, where the East and the West met, it is no wonder that that Gurudev Rabindranath Tagore came forward and accepted the invitation from the scholars (Suniti K. Chatterjee, Kalidas Nag and many others) to guide them. It is certainly inspiring to see that the Nalanda-Sriwijaya Centre of the Institute of Southeast Asian Studies is taking interest in this forgotten chapter of Indian Historiography (Kwa Chong-Guan 2013 and P. Duara, 2013) so that, if not at a platform in India, in Singapore, scholars from India and the rest of the world can exchange views on among many other topics, India-China-Southeast Asia linkages through trade, scholarship and culture (Tansen Sen, 2014).

No discourse on India and her place in the world can be considered complete without taking into account the vast field of knowledge covered by Indology (Ashin Dasgupta, 1988). Back in 1986 the late Professor Dasgupta (the then Director of the National Library, Kolkata) from the premises of the National Library took the initiative to bring together Indian and Western Indologists. The outcome has been published in the series *Indology and South Asia Bibliography*, which needs to be read by all concerned. This author happened to be one of the speakers in that gathering. Professor R.N. Dandekar (former Director of Bhandarkar Oriental Research Institute, Pune), one of the most well-known Indologists in the world and one of the speakers at that conference, greeted me in Sanskrit as well as in German. While conversing with him I came to know that he was also a student at Heidelberg University during the 1930s. As Dietmar Rothermund rightly pointed out in his contribution (D. Rothermund, 1988) at that conference as well as in his book *The German Intellectual Quest for India* (D. Rothermund, 1986), and later in a lecture on

"Max Mueller's Science of language and religion" delivered at the Max Mueller Bhavan, Mumbai in 2008, that the Schlegel brothers and Franz Bopp are often remembered for the initial beginnings of Indology at the institutional level. Later, Max Mueller and many other Indologists invited scholars to look at India as a destination to develop religion and language. Max Mueller (1823-1900) at the University of Oxford called upon the British administrators to learn more about the country that they were destined to rule over. Max Mueller called India a 'nation'. His multi-volumes The *Sacred Books of the East* and his theories of language on Indo-European families opened a new door—though it should be noted that long before Max Mueller, German Indologist H. Roth (1620-1668) wrote a Sanskrit Grammar, which however, could not be published. Sir William Jones' translation of *Shakuntala* (and later the founding of the Asiatic society in Kolkata in the year 1784) was a landmark event as was the establishing of the first Chair of Indology at Bonn University in 1819. A.W. von Schlegel after accepting the Chair of Sanskrit started a printing press which published *Bhagavadgita* in Devanagari script. Even German missionaries who came to the South of our country, learnt Tamil, Malayalam and preached the Gospel. In Bengal, we remember William Carey and his love and life-long mission for the promotion of Bengali language and literature.

The following subjects can be brought under the purview of Indology (H. Bechert and George V. Simson, 1979): Vedic Studies, Middle Indic (Pali and Prakrit of regional variations), modern languages, Epic Studies, Puranas, Buddhism and Jainism, Indian classical literature (mostly in Sanskrit), Poetics, Aesthetics and Metric, Philosophy (six schools of thought), Science and Medicine, Dharmashastra and Arthashastra, Epigraphy, History, Art and Archaeology, Music and Dance, Modern Indian Literature. The modern South Asian Studies have taken a large number of subjects under their jurisdiction, starting from law, political science, agriculture to modern regional tradition like the Jagannath cult in Orissa (Stache Rosen, 1990, 263). Neither the origin and development of Indology in Europe nor of the *Greater India Society* make the subject of discussion in this paper, but the discussion above has been introduced with a view that such rich traditions could be utilized as tools for a more effective foreign policy by the present and all future governments at the Centre. The respective state governments in India can play a constructive role in the implementation of the decisions through exchange of scholars, holding of joint seminars, and publishing the deliberations in the form of books, etc. As in any endeavour, in the field of foreign policy too, practical implementation of the ideas is the most important task.

The heart of Asia was simply India and in larger context, India, Pakistan and Bangladesh: the region called South Asia, and we must also add Myanmar to this group. When we think of the archaeological remains in various parts of the Rakhine State (Arakan) of Myanmar, in Bangladesh and West Bengal, without a doubt, India-Myanmar-Bangladesh was central in the civilizational realm of South-Southeast Asia. The linguistic and religious importance of Pakistan and Iran became clear through interactions with many eminent Western linguists. Even earlier, there was clarity about the Indo-Persian world from the religious and linguistic perspective when the *Rigveda* was read along with the *Zend Avesta* of Persia (old Iran). It is no wonder that in the pages of the *Journal of the Greater India Society* one could read learned essays written by such scholars as Batakrishna Ghosh on *Veda and Avesta* (*Journal of the Greater India Society*, 1934-35, 254-263). It was expected from a scholar like Dr. Pratap Chandra Chunder (former Union Minister in the Government of India and Professor of Law at Calcutta University) when we read about the world of *Vedas* and *Avesta* in his book *Glimpses of Indian Culture: Ancient and Modern* (Pratap Chandra Chunder, 2007, 18). It is interesting how sinologist P.C. Bagchi drew a vertical lineage (*Sindhu* to *Indu*) showing how the Sinitic world looked at the Indo-Persian world. Enthusiasts can go over the recently published volume, *Forty Essays on Indological Studies: A Collection from the Works of P.C. Bagchi* (Ratna Sinha and Shyamalkanti Chakravarti, 2014, 203).

II

The Hindu-Buddhist Civilization of India and Understanding of Southeast Asia in the Context of Post-Second World War India: Some Observations

Myanmar has become important as a long term partner for India in the spheres of trade and commerce and people-to-people relations at various levels. When our former Prime Minister Dr. Manmohan Singh visited Myanmar in 2012 at the invitation of President U Thein Sein, a wide range of issues covering almost all spheres of mutual cooperation were discussed (Suranjan Das, 2012). MOUs were signed which are partly yet to be fructified through quick actions. There is tremendous potential in the area of academic cooperation. A kind of cooperation that Indian scholars usually maintain with their European and American counterparts should start from within the academic communities from India and Southeast Asia. The most urgent task is to inspire the young generation not only to read Rabindranath Tagore, but also the works of scholars to whom mention has been made above. Indeed, many among them enjoyed the patronage of Gurudev Tagore. In 1937, when Tagore established the (Cheena) Bhavan, he had not only China and India in his vision, but also several other countries, the languages and literatures of which should be taught there. In this context, the books written by K.M. Panikkar, such as *Hinduism and the Modern World*, *Hinduism and the West*, *India and China: A Study of Cultural Relations,* are extremely enlightening. The importance that Panikkar gave to India and the Indian Ocean realm through his book *The Future of India and Southeast Asia* (Panikkar, 1945) is also hardly discussed now. The book was earlier published in London in 1943 under the title *The future of Southeast Asia.*

As we all know Pali was the language in which the Buddhist scriptures were written. The importance of Pali was discovered when the West and the East were engaged in discovering Buddhism, having centres in India, Myanmar and Sri Lanka. After the Pali Text Society was started by Rhys Davis in London in 1881, the trio, Haraprasad Sastri, Satish Ch. Vidya Bhusan and Sarat Ch. Ray took similar initiatives with the founding of the Pali Text Society in Calcutta in 1892 (S. Bhattacharya, 2005, 2011 and 2013). It is interesting to note that under the formal patronage of the British administrators, but with individual initiatives of great thinkers of modern India, Buddhist Studies prospered across the country. Calcutta University enjoyed a privileged position, as the Vice chancellor Sir Asutosh Mukherjee was extremely eager to explore and utilize the academic and religious (Hindu-Buddhist heritage) potentiality of Bengal. There was a keen interest on the part of the Western scholars and administrators to cooperate with their Indian and Myanmar counterparts to promote Buddhist and Pali studies at the universities of Yangon and Calcutta. Though Calcutta University (Yangon University and Judson College were under the jurisdiction of Calcutta University) formally introduced Pali in the early years of the 20th century; initially the demand for Pali to be included in the curriculum came from the Buddhist monks of Yangon in the previous century. Thus, Pali began to be taught at the School and at the F.A. (First Arts) levels in Yangon and Calcutta. Buddhist scholars E. Forchhammer, Ch. Duroiselle, Taw Sein Ko, Pe Maung Tin—were associated with the academic developments in and around the university of Calcutta (S. Bhattacharya, 2013). During the 1920s scholars like Stella Kramrisch, Suniti Kumar Chatterjee B.M. Barua and others visited Yangon University. How eager Tagore was to promote Indian Studies in Asian countries could be visualised from the fact that during the 1930s he sent Satyananda Puri to Chulalongkorn University in Thailand (S. Bhattacharya, 2007). This Indian scholar was to teach Sanskrit and Indian civilization to the Thai students. This was necessary because there was a great demand for such expertise in Thailand during the 1930s. On the other hand, through active patronage of French (Professor Sylven Levi) and German Indologists (Moritz Winternitz) he showed his keen desire to enrich the minds of his own students at Santiniketan. Today, many would perhaps not remember the name of the doyen of Pali and Buddhist Studies Pandit Vidhusekhar Shastri and his contribution. Nityanada Vinod Goswami, popularly known as "Gosaiji" in Santiniketan, was sent by Tagore to Sri Lanka and to lean Pali and Buddhism. The first generation children of post-independence India born and brought up in Santiniketan, were fortunate to be his students in early 1950s.

Tagore traveled to various countries of Asia, Europe and America with a team of distinguished scholars; he also sent Sree Santidev Ghosh, the well-known exponent of *Rabindra Sangeet* (Tagore-song) to Southeast Asia (Bali in Indonesia). And, it is not commonly known that on his way Santidev Ghosh stopped over in Yangon, to learn the techniques of choreography of Myanmar (S. Bhattacharya 2006 and 2014). To know more about Southeast Asia, Tagore went to Indonesia, the Malay region including Singapore, Thailand and Myanmar. He was keen to promote Buddhist Studies; not only during 1924, but also during the short stop-over in Yangon in 1927, private discussions were held and appointments made with the idea of future academic collaboration between Bengal and Myanmar (S. Bhattacharya, 2014). On all three occasions (1916, 1924, 1927) Tagore's vision for future relations between India and Myanmar was very clear—here Myanmar's potential to contribute to development of Buddhist studies in India played an important role.

In view of the above, it is argued here that an opportunity went a begging for the Indian people to 'globalize the world' long before the economic liberalization set in after the collapse of the Soviet Union and other major changes in world order, had we had the wisdom to maintain our Indian identity more unambiguously and without any prejudice. This is true for all religious affiliates, not only for Hindus and Buddhists of India. India is the home of all religions that in their very early stages flourished on our soil. Occasionally, splinter groups from religious communities came to India after being persecuted in their own homelands, like the Parsees or the Jews. We can draw examples from very recent history; Tibetans from China, the Bahai community of Iran or Chakmas of the Chittagong Hill Tracts or Hindus from Bangladesh. In our international relations we should not have surrendered to the forces which systematically aimed at creating divisions among Asian people and isolating India from her neighbours. After all, the term "Southeast Asia" is a modern invention; it began to be used during the end days of the Second World War, when Lord Mountbatten assumed his "Southeast Asia Command" to fight the Japanese and to re-establish the lost military supremacy of the British forces. And, it was indeed the decision of General Aung San who left the Japanese after the British promised to award Independence—that made things easier for General Mountbatten and the British administration. India's importance in post-war Southeast Asia was most acutely felt by the people and government of Myanmar, where Indian constitutional experts were in great need, as also doctors, scholars and other professionals. Prime Minister Jawaharlal Nehru played an immensely constructive and cooperative role during this difficult period of nation-building in Myanmar. However, Indian business community had to accept the hard reality that Myanmar was going through nationalization of landed and other properties. In the greater interest of the regional security Nehru had to accept the reality. However, on several occasions Nehru showed his keen interest and indeed played a very important role in promoting the spirit of Buddhist brotherhood among Asian nations. In this regard, especially in preserving Buddhist relics and relocating them from London to various corners of India, Nehru during 1948-49 worked closely with Indian leaders like Dr. Shyama Prasad Mukherjee and institutions like Mahabodhi Society of Kolkata.

Buddhism and Hinduism believe in the same philosophy of life, *karma*, rebirth or total relief from the circle, depending the degree of merit (*Punya*) one achieves, and moreover, give the people the choice to take the path considered to be the best for the individual concerned. This high adaptability of Hinduism and Buddhism make it possible for religions and faiths like Jainism, Islam, Christianity, Judaism, etc. to flourish in India. This is also why the large number of so called "Tribal people" of central and eastern India have adopted Hindu norms (Nirmal Bose, 1996) and have occasionally identified themselves as better Indians than many of us. Tribals believe that their Gods are not locked in the temples, but are omnipresent in Nature. The Nat worship in Myanmar which, though peripheral to Theravada Buddhism, still remains part of the larger religious domain.

The Hindu-Buddhist world is a vast domain, coming together among Austric, Dravidian, Sanskritic (sometime called Aryan) and Sinitic people. The Mongoloid (*Kirata*) people were found in large numbers in the eastern Himalayan region and were constantly on the move towards the plains southward, the valley of Brahmaputra in Assam. In Myanmar, it was the valley of the river Irrawaddy which gave rise to the Pagan Empire, which laid the foundation for the later rise of the Bamar (Burman) people who without any prejudice embraced Buddhism and even fought wars to preserve their identity. Just like in Myanmar various racial groups made a confluence, so was the case in India. To understand the true nature of this unique interaction one only has to think of the poem *Bharattirtha* by Gurudev Tagore. Tagore's understanding of Southeast Asia suffered no ambiguity. He located a new India beyond the geographical-political limit of India, and saw how the people of Southeast Asia created an image of their "India" in their own space and time. This view comes across very clearly in Tagore's speeches which he delivered before a distinguished gathering at the Greater India Society prior to his departure for Southeast Asia in 1927. On personal note, let me submit that when I was being taught that Shaivism influenced Cambodia (Angkor) by Professor Hermann Kulke, the overland connectivity between mainland India and mainland Southeast Asia in the ancient context was explained to me (H. Kulke, 1993) On the other hand, during the study of Srivijaya empire of Indonesia, the connectivity between the South China Sea and the Bay of Bengal in the Hindu-Buddhist realm was clearly established. Indeed, as early as in the first century CE the emergence of Funan in early Cambodia-Vietnam showed clear evidence of an Indian influence. For the Chinese travelers Indonesia was not only important for trade, but also on account of Sanskrit and Buddhist Studies. After all, it is here that Atisha Dipankar taught. Further, it is equally interesting to read what H. Kulke writes (H. Kulke 2010, 5) on how the countries of Southeast Asia at certain point of time (7th century onwards) started fearing China and thus became "tributaries" by sending missions and gifts to the Chinese emperors. Thus, slowly politically and economically, as Kulke rightly stressed, China became the "Middle Kingdom"

Coming to the modern period of our Asian history, as the developments in Indonesia, Vietnam and Myanmar during the 1940s and 1950s indicate, India's help in various forms became essential. In Indonesia, during the reoccupation by the Dutch, Indian's military help was needed, which Nehru extended wholeheartedly. A lot has been written on the Asian Relations Conference (1946) and the Conference on Indonesia (1949) which certainly attracted attention of a large number of Asian countries. Yet, Jawaharlal Nehru (V. Dutt, 1984 and G. Gopa Kumar, 2010), who was so much concerned and indeed did a lot so that the nascent nations could prosper with their individual identity, had to witness the failed peace in Vietnam, the rise of General Ne Win and end of civil rule in Myanmar and large-scale insurgencies supported by the communists to capture power. The Western powers, the United States in particular, preferred to fight the Cold War than formidable communist China and its Red Army. Though India was appointed as the Chair of the Commission for the Geneva Convention in 1957, its two partners were chosen from two mutually opposing countries, namely Poland and Canada. The first being a member of the Warsaw Pact and the second, of the NATO. No one can question Jawaharlal Nehru's keen interest to see real peace in Indo-China, Asia at large, but serious interest among countries as powerful as the United States of America was lacking. In his book *Public Policy and Global Reality* J.K. Ray (J.K. Ray 1977, 143-145) has shown the failure of the United States to pay heed to Ho Chin Minh who only wanted his country to be free of all the evil forces of imperialism and neo-colonialism. To quote Ray: "Ho Chi Minh pleaded for the recognition of Vietnamese independence by America and placing Vietnam under a system of international trusteeship. The US government did not even care to reply to his message. Ho and his associates were not subservient to Moscow. The United States was aware of this" (J.K. Ray, 1977, 144). In the same way, certainly through his sharp argument, J. K Ray has shown the failure of the American policy in the case of Indonesia, where the Dutch used the American-made bombs and bullets, thereby approving the strong arguments of the communists against the American policy in Indonesia (J.K. Ray, 1967, 152).

It is interesting to note that the people of the Southeast show their immense respect to Hinduism; in countries like Myanmar, they are indebted to the Hindu teachers who taught not only history, English, law, philosophy, etc., but even Myanmar language, to the people of Myanmar. Further, the people of Myanmar remember with great reverence many Indian names, who donated large amounts of money for the cause of education and social welfare. The eminent Myanmar historian and one of the leading thinkers of Myanmar Dr. Khin Maung Nyunt in a very recent paper delivered in Kolkata has stated that even after 1948 Myanmar had to invite Indian teachers to teach at universities and colleges of Myanmar; the names like Das, Guha, Soni, Moonie, Desai, Dutt, Subramaniam, Sundaram and Chakravarty were well known names (Dr. Khin Maung Nyunt, 2014, 190). The names of Professor W.S. Desai and Professor Nihar Ranjan Ray are familiar, but there were many Indian professors, whose students in Yangon still carry the memory and thus, the Indian tradition of *guru-shisya parampara*, to express in Myanmar language, from *saya* to *chaungtha*. Lack of knowledge in the languages of Southeast Asian countries and also the lack of knowledge in Sanskrit, Prakrit and Pali has pauperized the new generation of Indian scholars, and this led to what one often calls "sinicization of Asian Studies." At times one feels somewhat disappointed that India had to declare a formal "Look East Policy" (F. Grare and A. Mattoo, 2001; S. Devare 2006) towards countries, which actually looked "West", to India, for enrichment of their lives and legitimization of their act of ruling their own people. But the reality remains that even in a country like Myanmar which has such a longstanding relationship with India, none of the Indian languages is taught at universities or government-sponsored institutions. In a similar way, besides in the language school run by the Ministry of Defense, in no universities is Myanmar language taught, nor is there any institute existing in India which pursues the study of ancient and medieval history of Southeast Asia. It is only very recently that a group of teachers—all regular faculty members and distinguished scholars—from the Department of Ancient Indian History and Culture and Archaeology of the University of Kolkata have begun exploring the cultural linkages between India and Southeast Asia. Field trips are being undertaken and collaborative work is being done with the Department of South and Southeast Asian Studies, as also with other such centres across the world. One is hopeful that language studies as part of Area Studies, South and Southeast Asia will be given the due importance. One remembers when the derivation of the word *Saya* from the Sanskrit word *Acharya* was explained by U. Tin Htway (former Lecturer in Myanmar language and Literature at the Suedasien Institute/South Asia institute, Heidelberg University), or the derivation of the word *Takatai* ('University' in Myanmar language) from the word Takshashila, the Buddhist centre of learning, once a part of the great realm of learning under the Indic world, but now in Pakistan.

III

The Study of Indology: Urgent need to look Beyond "Look East"

Instead of arguing the way Mahatma Gandhi did, viewing Buddhism as a reformist religion out of Hinduism, a large number of scholars and policy makers considered Hinduism and Buddhism as two very different religions, almost as if they were contrary to each other! Even for many orthodox Buddhists, when it comes to Hinduism, they have no hesitation to admit that Hinduism has shown the maximum accommodativeness among all religions. Mahatma Gandhi rightly stated that Buddhism is to Hinduism what Protestantism is to Catholicism. In one of the *Dhammapada* verses it is said a true Brahmin is one who does not necessarily wear the *Upavit* (sacred thread), but who possesses the real virtue of a Brahmin. The Brahmins were so much respected for their scholarship in various fields of knowledge and also rituals that they were called to perform in the courts during coronation, they were invited to preach, read their texts, addressing subjects like Astrology, Logic, Philosophy, *Dharmashastras* and other Shastras. Generations of Myanmar kings looked West, to India, in search of knowledge in the form of texts and teachers. Royal protection and respect made the Indian Diaspora (S. Bhattacharya, 2009) in countries like Myanmar, Cambodia and Thailand a well integrated segment of the society. Hinduism like Buddhism is a way of life, a path to achieve the supreme through the practice of *Dharma*. This is why, as A.L. Basham says "India was a thorough 'melting pot' long before the term was invented for America. In spite of attacks, Hellenic, Muslim, and European among others, Hindu culture has maintained its tradition unbroken to the present day" (A.L. Basham, 1975, 62). Basham, a true lover of India and a great Indologist, submits "The history of Hinduism is chequered by tragic failures and wonderful victories, by opportunities missed and taken".

Those who are familiar with the history of mainland Southeast Asia, would know that in many of the ancient centres (*Pura*), the kings who ruled were of Indian descent. Herein comes the Kshatriya theory within the discourse of Indianization. They married indigenous princesses and thus acquired the real legitimacy to rule over the land. If one follows the pattern of early Indian trade in Southeast Asia (John Guy, 2011, 243-262), one could see that the Indian maritime trade was so powerful that it brought about urbanization in the coastal regions, while in the heartland, the intrusion of the Sinic people, known by the name *Kiratas*, continued, with scattered settlements. Every country located between China and India, whether surrounded by sea (like Indonesia) or by land (Myanmar) had to learn to adjust the Indic (Austric and later Sanskritic) with the Sinic. While India in the minds of the ancient Southeast Asians was represented by scholarship and wisdom, China or the Sinitic people, were represented by the vigour of trade and commerce. That Indian values of eternal wisdom and merit won over the wealth accumulated by trade, could be read, for example, in the naming of a temple, Nandamanna in the Pagan archaeological site. The Myanmar word, *Nadamanna* is derived from the Sanskrit word, *anantapunna*, the eternal merit. It is in search of this eternal merit that the people of Southeast adopted various styles of Indian art, like Amaravati, Gupta and Pala-Sena.

Today, India and Southeast Asia have developed a very mature friendship and a relationship of mutual trust. India today is not only a Full Dialogue Partner of the ASEAN, it has successfully hosted the meetings of the ongoing Delhi Dialogue (S.T. Devare and V. Shekhar, 2012). In this achievement the Indian diplomats deserve more applause than the scholars of modern India. It is even more inspiring to see that scholars and ordinary people of Southeast Asia continue to look at India with a deep feeling of cultural kinship and co-sharer of common knowledge. On the basis of one's own experiences it can be said that the Nalanda Sriwijaya Centre of Southeast Asian Studies, Singapore and the Institute of Asian Studies in Leiden are fulfilling an important mission; yet, more attention could be given to bring the Indian Classical Studies within the domain of Southeast Asian Studies. We should not forget that there were hundreds of Nalanda and Takshashila-like centres of learning in the real Majjhimdesha, i.e., India. Near home we had the great centre of Navya Nyaya tradition, Navadvipa, which was well connected through Manipur, with Mandalay, the centre of learning in the heart of upper Myanmar. Everyone, especially from Buddhist countries of Southeast Asia wanted to come here, to India, for spiritual fulfillment, wisdom and scholarship. Next to India was and still is, Myanmar, the *Brahmadesh*, as the region of Upper Myanmar was known in the literature of the time (S. Bhattacharya, 2014). That the word Prome, the site of the Pyus of Myanmar, who being Sinic (Sino-Tibetan), embraced the highly liberal Hindu-Buddhist faith, comes from the word "Brahma", has been very brilliantly established by none other than the eminent archaeologist from colonial Myanmar, Taw Sein Ko, in his book *Burmese Sketches*. It is amazing to see how little attention this great archaeologist from colonial Myanmar draws. It is deeply disappointing, as his understanding of the Sino-Indic world and importance of Myanmar in that realm are too precious to be ignored.

Now-a-days, a lot of debates are ensuing to predict the future of Myanmar. Real democracy will flourish only when the people of Myanmar will realize that their ancestors were the real bearers of civilization, a major component of which was the Theravada Buddhism with a strong tradition of Pali scholarship. Sometime in the history of Asia, the *Bhogavada* (consumerism) replaced the ethos of *Tyaga* (renunciation). The ruthless sense of business and diplomacy, with Buddhist relics, maximum profit and similar convictions and actions, were never considered to be part of the Indian tradition. It came with the emergence of later developments when religion and scholarship turned into tools of profit making. Certainly, Mahayana Buddhism with all its philosophical ramifications (Sahajayana, Kalchakrayana, Mantrayana, etc.), also contributed to constant progress of rituals, which generated a spirit of entrepreneurship among the people affiliated with northern (Mahayana) Buddhism. This included Vietnam among other countries, where Mahayana Gods found their places along with Confucian and Taoist thoughts. Yet, the core remained the emancipation from the cycle of birth and rebirth, and thus, the only way to be followed was the way of renunciation, best epitomized in the verse of the *Ishoponishad* which says in short that the whole world is represented by a single God. Therefore, learn to enjoy sacrifice and don't be greedy about others' wealth (*ma gridha kasyaschit dhanam*). No wonder that Tagore in his writings repeatedly quoted this verse and thereby perhaps warned the people of India, not to be envious of others' wealth, but to give up, to get more in form of wisdom and knowledge.

Now-a-days we read a lot in the print media about the escalating conflict over energy resources in the South China Sea; conflict between Vietnam (also the Philippines) and China is coming to the fore. Let the two countries or for that matter, Japan and China settle their problems with or without the help of a Third Party; for scholars, the fact that Vietnam is rediscovering her Buddhist past is significant, and, thus, the urgency to come closer to India has never been felt so urgently before. No other country has fought independently with her own strength as Vietnam did. China occupied Vietnam for almost thousand years. Thus, the country is ethnically perhaps more "sinacized" than many other countries, yet, Vietnam has not shifted from her Buddhist roots and has not lost her strong identity as a nation.

Thus, the history of the old city kingdom of Champa has to be studied by emerging Indian scholars keeping in mind that such names as Champa and Vesali (in the Rakhine State of Myanmar) carry the age-old linkages between the Buddhist centres of modern Bihar in India and Southeast Asia. It is also our moral duty to remember those Vietnamese Buddhist monks who sacrificed their lives to save the country, to save *Dhamma* during the early years of the 1970s when the 'imperialists' were involved in a shameless battle over occupation (reoccupation) of this wonderful country. The leadership of the ASEAN countries during the 1990s should be praised for the inclusion of Vietnam as one of the member-states in 1995. One is sure that like Myanmar, Vietnam will also be a balancing factor within the ASEAN.

IV

Ground Realities of Southeast Asia during the 1940s and 1950s

While going through the Frank Trager Collection, kept in Heidelberg University, at the Suedasien Institute (South Asia Institute), one came across a specific piece (article or small monograph), written by Frank Trager, the founder of the Cornell School of Southeast Asian Studies and the father of Myanmar studies. Trager believed in India and Myanmar (Burma) having the real potentiality to bring peace and prosperity in post-Second World War Asia. Consequently, he wanted these two countries forming an alliance, to establish a solid democratic foundation of an emerging Asia. During the early 1950s there were positive signs of future collaboration between the two countries at all levels; Jawaharlal Nehru enjoyed complete trust from the leadership of U Nu and other leaders belonging to the socialist fold. Nevertheless, after the signing of the Panchsheel in 1954 many developments in the relationship between Myanmar and India culminated in the advent of a precarious time from the 1960s onwards. While Communist China was successful in utilizing the political space for herself in Indo-China by backing Ho Chi Minh against the French in 1946 (Hall, 1987, 885), Indian leaders were not thoughtful enough about the post-World War reality in this part of Asia. Certainly, the twists and turns during the War forced India to take a position where she had to declare her formal submission to the Allied Powers and the Commonwealth, and thus become one of the founding members of the United Nations.

One can legitimately ask the question, why with such a grand position in the international platform during the 1940s and 1950s, could the Indian government not protect the interests of Indians worldwide: whether in Pakistan or in Myanmar. While a large number of Hindus had to leave Myanmar (then called Burma), the majority of Muslims decided to stay back in Myanmar, as their India was divided into two countries: Pakistan and India. In contrast to the Indian policy of taking back its nationals, the Chinese policy was well planned in bargaining: the Franco-Chinese Agreement was signed on 28 February 1946, only when in return concessions were made on the Yunnan-Hanoi Railway and recognition of the special position of their nationals in Indo-China was given (D.G. Hall, 1987, 886). Hall even provides statistical data, showing the number and the ratio between the Chinese and the native people. Quoting King Vajiravudh of Siam, who called the Chinese "the Jews of the East", Hall justified his apprehension about the future of Southeast Asia, so far as the Chinese community is concerned (D.G. E. Hall, 1987, 909). Hall emphasized two aspects very distinctively: first, the economic importance, and second, the cultural distinctiveness of the overseas Chinese (D.G. Hall, 1987, 909). Hall further argued that the Communist victory of 1949 considerably contributed to these two factors. To quote D.G.E. Hall: "...Hence, with the communist victory in China every country of South-East Asia became uneasily aware of the presence of a potential Chinese 'fifth column' in its midst." (D.G. Hall, 1987, 909). Hall further described how the Geneva Conference succeeded in bringing about a ceasefire in Vietnam, and yet, there was such an apprehension of further conflict that the South East Asia Collective Defence Treaty was signed in Manila. Its signatories were the United States, Britain, France, Australia, New Zealand, Pakistan, Thailand and the Philippines. They joined hands with each other in forming the SEATO—the Southeast Asia Treaty Organisation. As we know, Nehru was much against this Treaty as he saw in such measures neo-colonial aspirations of the West. China's policy was to weaken the pro-Western influence in Asia in order to prepare communist victory everywhere, yet, at the same time she was engaged in gaining support in the United Nations.

While most of the Indian scholars ignore religion (especially the Buddhist identity of the Asian people) it is J.K. Ray, who in his monumental work *India's Foreign Relations 1947-2007* clearly highlighted the significant mistakes that were committed during the 1950s (J.K. Ray, 2011, 253). Naturally, the subject of Tibet was part of his discussion, besides the usual themes like unresolved boundary issues between India and China, etc. It may be important to note that Myanmar was allowed to resolve the boundary problem with China in 1960, when in January 1960 Chou En-Lai and Ne Win signed a boundary Agreement (R.H. Fifield, 1963, 365) Several Western authors though, not exactly criticising Nehru wrote in plain and simple terms that it was due to Nehru's special interest that China was invited to participate in the Bandung Conference (Ralph Pettman, 1973, 19). Nehru was a socialist, he believed in the cultural unity of India and was particularly careful so that the idea of Hindu tradition is not over-emphasized at the state level. For this, occasionally he had to face difficult situations even from the highest office (Romit Bagchi, 2014).

It is interesting to note that U Nu's Burma initially thought that such a meeting as Bandung would be futile. Yet, when Nehru took interest in China, U Nu agreed to participate. And, interestingly Chou En-Lai, otherwise an unknown figure, became known to other participants through U Nu (Ralph Pettman, 1973, 19). The necessary groundwork was certainly done by Chou En-Lai in 1954, on his way back from Geneva, when he visited Yangon (Rangoon) and later, New Delhi. As we know, later in 1956-7 Chou En-Lai embarked on his grand Asian tour, which included Myanmar (Burma). He took the opportunity to get his Five Principles of Non-interference, Panchsheel, endorsed by Burma (Ralph Pettman, 1973, 20) A question could legitimately be raised: Was the basic principle of Panchsheel regarded, when Tibet was occupied by China?

Little research has been done so far by Indian scholars on the degree of disappointment brought on with the decolonization in Southeast Asia. We should not forget that decolonization in Southeast Asia led to yet another intra-Asian colonialism, for which, as has been explained above, D.G. Hall had already expressed his apprehensions in 1955. And, the largest democratic and most powerful country of the post Second World War, the United States of America either remained a silent spectator, or fought a proxy war, or got itself involved in the "war", of all the countries, against Vietnam! It is indeed Vietnam where the Communist uprising was most natural and anti-colonial (anti-French) in its spirit. Elsewhere (Myanmar, the Philippines, Malay, Indonesia) across Southeast Asia, the Communist parties followed a hard anti-nationalist line. Indeed, the Calcutta Youth Conference (February 1948), directed by the Cominform and patronized by Moscow, made no secret of the fact that the Communists did not endorse the kind of freedom that was achieved. The Indian Communists used the slogan *ye azadi jhut hai*. Yet, in India, as in Myanmar, the Communists backed the British during the War, on plea that the war had to be fought to fight the fascists.

Therefore, a call was given to offer armed resistance against the "fake" independence (Brian Crozier, 1968). In the Calcutta Conference of 1948, the Communists of Myanmar were represented by the White Flag Communist, Than Tun. That the United States of America was closely scrutinizing the developments in this part of the world (J.K Ray, 1967, 152), is evident from Ruth McVey's work, *The Calcutta Conference and the Southeast Asian Uprisings*, published by the Cornell University Press in 1958 (Ruth McVey, 1958). It is interesting to see that the US looked at the Communist uprising in Myanmar as a minor challenge. Instead of granting something like a "Marshall Plan" for the Southeast, the US acted passively. It preferred to "wait and watch". The Soviet Union was busy at the European (East European) Front, leaving the matter of mobilizing the Communist forces to the respective country's Communist Party. Moscow had no time to get itself engaged in the internal feuds of the communist parties in Asia. This rather "passive role" from Moscow created a comfortable space for China to enter the arena. This was exactly the global reality about which D.G.E. Hall and other scholars spoke very clearly.

India, however remained a trusted partner, for, it was India which was her closest cultural kin. Nevertheless, India-China relations and the war between China and India in 1962 was a formidable challenge before Myanmar. While monks of the Theravada order, disappointed by the rising dependence of Myanmar on China, turned to India for spiritual refuge, diplomacy with Buddhist missions continued between China and Myanmar (S. Bhattacharya, 2010). U Win, Burma's Minister of Religious Affairs, visited China, and a Chinese Buddhist mission went to Rangoon. Yet, we must not forget that during the 1950s there were two very powerful movements in India: one was the Buddhist Resurgence Movement led by Dr. B.R Ambedkar and the other was a very strong Socialist Movement led by Jaya Prakash Narayan. There are other names too, like Ram Manohar Lohia, Ashoke Mehta. They were in best of friendship with the Myanmar socialists like U Ba Swe and Kyaw Nyein. Indeed, the city of Yangon (then called Rangoon) was hosting the First Asian Socialist Conference in the year 1953. The Conference was the result of the longstanding efforts by three sponsoring parties/countries: Burma, India and Indonesia. Besides socialists from nine countries of Asia, international participation from European countries, Africa the Socialist International and other socialist groups was visible.

The importance of such socialist movements in the context of the Buddhist Resurgence Movement, the waves of which were also sweeping over India was highlighted by Jaya Prakash Narayan: "...But I believe socialism will soon develop national peace and also work for international peace. The Indians are not formal Buddhists but, I believe, there is no Indian whose life has not been vitally shaped and moulded by the teachings of Lord Buddha and only a few years ago there lived amongst us a Mahatma Gandhi" (Report on First Asian Socialist Conference, 1954, 11). According to Gandhiji, Gautam Buddha should be worshipped by every Hindu since Gautam Buddha made a great sacrifice to reform and purify Hinduism. Buddha did that since he himself was a Hindu (R. Iyer, *The Moral and Political Writings of Mahatma Gandhi,* Oxford 1986, vol. I, 492-43).

At yet another front India and Myanmar could have worked together to make a different Asia than we have today: i.e., the Buddhist Resurgence Movement (S. Bhattacharya, 2011) Here, we must remember Dr. B.R. Ambedkar and his close contact with Myanmar, his friendship with Dr. R.L. Soni of Mandalay and the story of his formal initiation in Buddhism. Dr. Ambedkar's social misery of being born in a family of Dalits certainly was the cause of his rejection of Hinduism. Yet, little is known of how much inspiration he drew from Myanmar and how was his vision of a future India. It is no wonder that he totally rejected Communism, irrational partition of his motherland, protested the annexation of Tibet by Communist China and foresaw a brighter future of India within the axis of a Buddhist

Asia. In 1956, after his return from Yangon, where he was sent by Nehru to take part in the Sixth Buddhist Council, he embraced Buddhism as his new religion. Nagpur, his *Dikhshabhumi* has remained witness to one of the most landmark events in the history of Buddhism in India and Asia as a whole. However, one would also like to suggest to the young Indian scholars that they visit Kushinagar, the place where Dr. Ambedkar met U. Chandramani, the Rakhine-Myanmar monk (S. Bhattacharya, 2010) whose life-long mission was to promote *Buddha Shasana* in India through basic education, social welfare and development along the lines of *Dhamma.* Dr. Ambedkar was born in India, suffered in India, but fortunately not forgotten in India. Yet, his vision of India's future international relations failed to impress those who were at the forefront of policy making during the 1950s. Perhaps, the challenges of decolonization and nation-building in that complex world with formidable forces all around, especially Communist China, were too much to cope with.

Conclusion

Compared to many countries which got their independence around the same time as India got hers, India was far better placed, not only due to the political leadership of Jawaharlal Nehru, but also due to the presence of a large number of scholars who were active researchers, internationally reputed through their writings and activities. There were universities and institutions all over India which were widely known across Asia: universities of Calcutta, Bombay, Madras, Benares Hindu University (BGU), Visva Bharati, just to name a few. During the Second World War India even became a place of refuge for some intellectuals. For example, the great Myanmar writer and Tagore expert, Paragu spent the war years at Benares Hindu University learning Sanskrit and Hindi. Even, during the early 1950s academic exchanges took place between Buddhist countries of Southeast Asia and India. Thailand and Myanmar were at the forefront, so also Sri Lanka from the South Asian region. While war-torn Germany went on with her great tradition of promoting Indology at various universities, India somehow missed the opportunity to promote Indian Studies in various countries of Asia and Europe. At the university and college level Indian students should be equipped with proper texts and reference books, many of which we read, but our students do not. The students of today will be the policy makers of tomorrow. Thus, a thorough review of the state of affairs in the education sector is the need of the day.

The four Indian states with which Myanmar shares 1600 kilometre border, Manipur, Arunachal Pradesh, Mizoram and Nagaland, were the most important trade and cultural routes which connected the Indian heartland with the cultural centres of Upper Myanmar. The Tibetan monk Lama Taranatha described this region as Kokiland (*Kokibhumi*) which included Pugan (Pagan of Myanmar) and Rakhan (Rakhine state of Myanmar). It was indeed the Indo-Myanmar civilizational heartland. The astrologers, pilgrims, Brahmin Pundits with manuscripts in their hands, the Vaishnavas, and traders came and went using the roots. To properly understand the very cultural and knowledge-based continuum along this vast route, one has to take up serious studies with field researches, and should stop looking at these states as "exclusive" "exotic Northeast" or the "Frontier". Many lost Indian assets have been brought back by the people of this region: Theravada Buddhism among the Khamti people of Arunachal Pradesh should be mentioned in this regard. The contributions of scholars affiliated with the Greater India Society Movement should be read with an open mind. Early Southeast Asia was Indianized from the top, as the Indian idea of empire as a manifestation of the cosmos became extremely popular among the royalty. In this discourse it was not important whether a particular king hailed from India, or not.

At the bottom, the Austric, Dravidian, Sinitic people assimilated with each other through peaceful means, and in their quest for eternal wisdom and merit looked at the civilizational norms brought by the Sanskritic people from India. Had it not been the case, we would not have found Sanskrit inscriptions across Southeast Asia and also the numerous archaeological monuments built after Indian art styles, Gandhara, Gupta, Amaravati and Pala-Sena. India and Southeast Asia experienced the same processes of state and nation-building, from the top as well as from the bottom.

Acknowledgements: I am deeply indebted to the Director of Maulana Abul Kalam Azad Institute of Asian Studies (MAKAIAS), Dr. Sreeradha Datta for inviting me to the seminar so that I could share my views with the distinguished scholars from Vietnam and various parts of India. To Dr. Arpita Basu Roy, Fellow, MAKAIAS and Coordinator of the Seminar, my special thanks, as she showed immense patience and extended necessary cooperation so that I could bring this paper to a satisfactory end. I deeply appreciate her kind gesture. To all other colleagues from MAKAIAS I remain grateful for their constant inspiration to write on many things that I studied many years ago. To Professor Jayanta Kumar Ray, Maulana Azad Fellow (former Chairman, MAKAIAS) at MAKAIAS and Founder Director of our Centre (Centre for South and Southeast Asian Studies, University of Calcutta) I remain indebted for his constant inspiration and support. To my former teacher and eminent South Asia specialist Professor Dietmar Rothermund (Former Director of South Asia Institute and former Head of the Department of South Asian History) I am particularly grateful for sending me a paper on Max Mueller which he presented at Max Mueller Bhavan, Mumbai in 2008. Last, but not the least, I must acknowledge my indebtedness to Professor Hermann Kulke, my first Ph.D Supervisor (former Professor of South and Southeast Asian History, South Asia Institute, Heidelberg University and later Kiel University). He taught me the history of Ancient Southeast Asia with great care, perhaps a special care, given my argumentative posture when it came to the discourse on Indianization. To all my teachers in Santiniketan, who taught me from the early 1950s to the mid-1970s I remain indebted, for, they were my first inspiration to search for an "India outside India". Most of them are no more in this mortal world, but their memory keeps my quest alive and active.

BIBLIOGRAPHY

Bagchi, P.C. *India and China. A Thousand Years of Cultural Relations*, Calcutta: Saraswat Press, 1981.

Bagchi, Romit. 'Jawaharlal Nehru and Hindutva' *The Statesman*, Kolkata, 13 June, 2014.

Basham, A.L. *A Cultural History of India*, New Delhi: Oxford University Press, 2014 (first published 1975).

Bechert, Heinz and Von Simson, George, *Einfuehrung in die Indologie: Stand Methoden Aufgaben*, Darmstadt,: wissenschaftliche Buchgesellschaft, 1979.

Bhattacharya, Swapna. History of Buddhism in Myanmar: Interpretation from an Indian Perspective', *Journal of the Asiatic Society*, Vol. 47, No. 4, Kolkata, 2005, pp. 65-81.

Bhattacharya, Swapna. 'From Mahabodhi Movement of the late 19th century (1891) to Neo-Buddhist Revival (1956) in Post-Colonial India', in *Myanmar Historical Commission Conference Proceedings* Part II. (12-14 January 2005), Golden Jubilee Publication Committee, Myanmar Historical Commission, Ministry of Education, Union of Myanmar, Yangon, 2005, pp. 339-359.

Bhattacharya, Swapna. 'Rabindranath Tagore in Myanmar (Burma) and Tagore's Perception of Southeast Asia-India Relations', in S.K. Panda and M. Brandtner (eds.) *Interrogating History: Essays for Hermann Kulke*, Delhi: Manohar, 2006, pp. 212-229.

Bhattacharya, Swapna. *India-Myanmar Relations 1886-1948*, Kolkata: K.P. Bagchi & Co., 2007.

Bhattacharya, Swapna. 'Political Implication of Resurgent Buddhism in India with Special Reference to the Eastern Region' in J.K. Ray and Arpita Basu Ray (eds.), *Political Roles of Religious Communities in India*, Stockholm: Institute for Security & Development Policy, 2008.

Bhattacharya, Swapna. 'Indians in Myanmar', in Jayanta Kumar Ray and Binoda Kumar Mishra (eds.), *Interpreting the Indian Diaspora: Lessons from History and Contemporary Politics*, vol. X. pt. 8, Project of History of Indian Science, Philosophy and Culture (PHISPC), General Editor D.P. Chattopadhyaya, Centre for Studies in Civilizations, Delhi pp. 165-188.

Bhattacharya, Swapna. *India and Myanmar: People, Pilgrimage, Histories and the Present,* Occasional Paper, Centre for South & Southeast Asian Studies, University of Calcutta, 2010.

Bhattacharya, Swapna. 'Contributions of Kripasharan Mahasthavir in the world of Buddhist Reform and Buddhist Scholarship of the 19th century India and Beyond', *Jagajjyoti*, 2555 Buddha Jayanti Volume, 2011, pp. 88-93.

Bhattacharya, Swapna. 'Situating Pilgrimage: Evaluating the role of Myanmar Monasteries in South Asia' in Suchandana Chatterjee, Anita Sengupta and Susmita Bhattacharya (eds.), *Buddhism in Asia*, New Delhi: Shipra Publications and MAKAIAS, 2012.

Bhattacharya, Swapna. 'The University of Calcutta and Myanmar: Urgent Need for Revisiting the Golden Era', paper presented at the Annual Congress, Myanmar Academy of Arts and Sciences (MAAS), 24-27 October, 2012 Yangon University (In Press).

Bhattacharya, Swapna. 'Experiencing the Continuity in Art, Culture and Life in Bengal and Myanmar', *Journal of Bengal Art*, vol. 8, 2013, The International Centre for Study of Bengal Art, Dhaka, pp. 305-316,

Bhattacharya, Swapna. 'Gurudev Rabinbdranath Tagore in the minds of the Myanmar people', in Mamata Desai, Manis Kumar Raha and Chitra Ghosh (eds.), *Rabindranath Tagore: A Many-Splendoured Personality*, Kolkata: K.P. Bagchi & Co., 2014, pp. 118-141.

Bose, Nirmal Kumar. *The Structure of Hindu Society* (Translated from Bengali with an Introduction and Notes by Andre Beteille), Hyderabad: Orient Longman (First published 1975).

Chunder, Pratap Chandra. *Glimpses of Indian Culture: Ancient and Modern*, Kolkata: Indian Museum, 2007.

Chatterjee, Suniti Kumar. *Bharat Samskriti.* Calcutta: Mitra & Ghosh, BE 1364

Chatterjee, Suniti Kumar. *Rabindrasangame Dvipamaya Bharat O Shyamdesh* (First published 1940), Calcutta: Prakash Bhavan, 1980.

Chong-Guan, Kwa (ed). *Early Southeast Asia Viewed from India: An Anthology of Articles from the Journal of the Greater India Society.* N. Delhi: Manohar, 2013 (First published by ISEAS, Singapore in the Nalanda-Sriwijaya Series. General editors Tansen Sen and Geoff Wade).

Coedes, George. The *Indianized States of South-East Asia,* Honolulu: University of Hawaii Press, 1968.

Cohen, Stephen P. *Emerging Power India*, Washington DC: Brookings Institution Press, 2001.

'Compete with China on skill, scale and speed: PM', *The Indian Express*, 9 June, 2014.

Crozier, Brian. *Southeast Asia in Turmoil*, Baltimore: Penguin, 1965.

Das, Suranjan *The Hindu,* 31. May, 2012, http://www.thehindu.com/todays-paper/tp-national/tp-otherstates/article (reporting of view of Vice Chancellor Professor Das on India-Myanmar relation).

Dasgupta, Ashin (ed). *Indological Studies and South Asia Bibliography*, Kolkata: National Library, 1988.

Dahm, Bernhard, 'Religious Revival, Ethnicity and Nationalism in Southeast Asia', in G. Berkemer, T. Frasch, H. Kulke and J. Luett (eds.), *Explorations in the History of South Asia: Essays in Honour of Dietmar Rothermund*, New Delhi: Manohar, 2001, pp. 301-310.

Devare, Sudhir. *India and Southeast Asia: Towards Security Convergence*, Singapore: ISEAS, 2006.

Dharmapala, Anagarika Hewavitarne. *Buddhism in its Relationship with Hinduism,* (First published in 1918). Kolkata: Mahabodhi Book Agency, 1997.

Duara, Prosenjit. *Asia Redux: Conceptualising a Region for Our Time*, New Delhi: Manohar, 2013.

Dutt, V.P. *India's Foreign Policy,* New Delhi: Vikas Publishing House, 1984.

Fifield, R.H. *Southeast Asia in United States Policy*, Frederick A. Praeger 1963

Frykenberg, Robert E., 'Benoy Kumar Sarkar, 1887-1949: Political Rishi of Twentieth Century Bengal', in G. Berkemer, T. Frasch, H. Kulke and J. Luett (eds.), *Explorations in the History of South Asia: Essays in Honour of Dietmar Rothermund*, Manohar, New Delhi, 2001, pp. 197-217.

Ganguly, Sumit, *India's Foreign Policy: Retrospect and Prospect,* New Delhi: Oxford University Press, 2010.

Gopa Kumar, G. *Nehru and Modern India: An Anatomy of Nation Building*, New Delhi: New Century Publications, 2010.

Grare, Frederic and Mattoo, Amitabh (eds.), *The Politics of India's Look East Policy,* New Delhi: Manohar, Centre de Sciences Humaines, Institute of Southeast Asian Studies, Centre for the Study of National Security Policy, 2001.

Guy, John. 'Tamil Merchants and the Hindu-Buddhist Diaspora in Early Southeast Asia', in Manguin, Pierre-Yves Mani, A. and Wade, Geoff (eds.), *Early Interactions between South and Southeast Asia: Reflections on Cross-Cultural Exchange*, Manohar: New Delhi, 2011. pp. 243-262. (First published in ISEAS, Singapore).

Hall, D.G.E., *A History of South-East Asia*, London: Macmillan, 1987.

Hundred Years of the University of Calcutta 1857-1956, edited by Board of editors with Professor Pramathanath Banerjee as chairman, published by Dr. D. Chakravarti, Registrar, Calcutta University, Calcutta, 1957

Iyer, R. The *Moral and Political Writings of Mahatma Gandhi,* volume. I, N. Delhi: Oxford University Press, 1986.

Journal of the Greater India Society, 18 volumes (1934-59). ed. by Ghosal, U.N., Nag, K. & Dutt, N. with a Preface and Index by Lokesh Chandra, N. Delhi: Aditya Prakashan, 1987.

Kulke, Hermann, *Kings and Cults, State Formation and Legitimation in India and Southeast Asia*, New Delhi: Manohar, 1993.

Kulke, Hermann, 'The Naval Expeditions of the Cholas in the Context of Asian History' in Kulke, Hermann & Kesavapany, K. Sakhuja, V. (eds.), *Negapattinam to Suvarnadwipa: Reflections on the Chola Naval Expeditions to Southeast Asia* Manohar, New Delhi, 2010, pp. 1-19. (First published in Singapore by ISEAS 2009)

Majumdar, R.C. *Hindu Colonies in the Far East*, Calcutta: Firma KLM 1991.

McVey, Ruth. *Calcutta Conference and Southeast Asia Uprising*, New York: Cornell University Press, 1968.

Menon, K.P.S., *Many Worlds Revisited: An Autobiography* (4th ed), Bombay: Bharatiya Vidya Bhavan, 1981.

Nag, Kalidas (ed). *Tagore and China*, published by Sj. Pranabesh Chandra Sinha, Hony General Secretary, Federation of Indian Music and Dancing and Calcutta Art Society, Calcutta, 1945.

Nyunt, Khin Maung. 'Indo-Myanmar Cultural Relations: Past Present and Future' in Arindam Mukherjee (ed.), *Indo-Myanmar Relations: New Horizons,* Proceedings of an International Seminar organized by the Institute of Social and Cultural Studies, India held at National Library, Kolkata, 8-9 February, 2014, pp. 9-15.

Pant, Harsh V. *The Rise of China: Implications for India*, New Delhi: Cambridge University Press, 2012.

Panikkar, K.M. *Hinduism and Modern World* Kitabistan, Allahabad, 1938.

Panikkar, K.M. *India and China: A Study of Cultural Relations*, Bombay: Asia Publishing House, 1957.

Panikkar, K.M. The *Future of India and Southeast Asia*, London: George Allen and Unwin Ltd, 1945.

Pettman, Ralph. *China in Burma's Foreign Policy,* Canberra: Australian National University Press, 1973.

Pochhammer, Wilhelm von. *India's Road to Nationhood: A Political History of the Subcontinent,* New Delhi: Allied Publishers, 1981.

Ray, Jayanta Kumar. *Transfer of Power in Indonesia*, Bombay: Manaktala & sons, 1967.

Ray, Jayanta Kumar, *Public Policy and Global Reality: Some Aspects of American Alliance Policy,* N. Delhi: Radiant Publishers, 1977.

Ray, Jayanta Kumar, *India's Foreign Relations 1947-2007*, New Delhi: Routledge, 2011.

Ray, Nihar Ranjan, *Brahmanical Gods in Burma* Bangkok: Orchid Press, 2001 (First published by Calcutta University Press, 1932.

Report of the First Asian Socialist Conference, Asian Socialist Publications, Rangoon, 1953.

Rothermund, Dietmar. *The German Intellectual Quest for India*, Manohar: New Delhi, 1986.

Rothermund, Dietmar. 'Max Mueller's Science of Language and Religion', Lecture delivered at Max Mueller Bhavan, Mumbai, 8 December, 2008

Sarkar, Himanshu Bhusan. *Cultural relation between India and Southeast Asia.* N. Delhi: ICCR & Motilal Banarashidas, 1985.

Sarkar, Benoy Kumar, *The Futurism of Young Asia*, Julim Springer, Berlin, 1922.

Sarkar, Benoy Kumar. *Chinese Religion through Hindu Eyes: A Study in the Tendencies of Asiatic Mentality (with an Introduction by Wu Ting-Fang)*, Shanghai: Commercial Press, 1916.

Sarkisyanz, Emanuel. *The Buddhist Background of the Burmese Revolution*, The Hague: Martinus Nijoff, 1965.

Sen, Tansen. *Buddhism Across Asia: Networks of Material, Intellectual and Cultural Exchange* Volume I, N. Delhi: Manohar and Singapor: Institute of Southeast Asian Studies, 2014.

Sengupta, Sukumar. 'A Short History of Pali Studies in the University of Calcutta (1880-1983)', in Haldar, Manikuntala (ed.), *Centenary Volume of the Department of Pali*, University of Calcutta, 2010, Kolkata, pp. 41-86.

Sharma, Anjana (ed),. *Civilizational Dialogue: Asian Inter-Connection and Cross-Cultural Exchange,* New Delhi: Manohar, 2013.

Sinha, Ratna and Chakravarti. Shyamakanti (eds). *Forty Essays on Indological Studies: A Collection from the Works of P.C. Bagchi* volumes I and II, Kolkata: Pritonia Publishers & Distributors, 2014.

Stache-Rosen, Valentina. *German Indologists: Biographies of Scholars in Indian Studies* (second revised edition by Agnes Stace—Weiske), N. Delhi: Max Mueller Bhavan, 1990.

Stietencron, H. Von. 'Brahmanen als Integratoren und Interpreten von Regionaltraditionen', in H. Kulke und D. Rothermund (eds.), *Regionale Tradition in Suedasien*, Wiesbaden: Steiner Verlag, 1985, pp. 23-56.

Tarling, Nicholas, *The Cambridge History of Southeast Asia*. Volume II, Cambridge: Cambridge University Press, 1992.

Taw Sein Ko, *Burmese Sketches* Volume II, Rangoon: British Burma Press, 1920.

Tinker, Hugh, *The Union of Burma*, London: Oxford University Press, 1967.

6
Some Features of Tantrism in Vietnam

Nguyen Ngoc Quynh

Vietnamese Tantrism in the Historical Context

When one talks about Vietnamese Buddhism, one often talks about the integration of three sects—Zen sect (or Ch'an); the Pure Land (Sukhavati) sect; and Tantrism. At every juncture of Vietnamese history, the role, influence and effect of each sect is different. Scholars have not been able to identify the time when Tantrism came to Vietnam. Other Tantric sects were also in existence here. There have been indications that the presence of Tantrism within Vietnamese Buddhism was established quite early in its development there. One scholar even assumes that Vietnamese Tantrism came into existence there much earlier than in China. It is said that the period from the 10th to the 13th centuries A.D. was the most prosperous period for Tantrism in Vietnam.

Researchers claim that the Tantric element was rooted in Vietnam since the presence of Master Vinitaruci, not from the independent period (1st to 10th century) in the 10th century. Vinitaruci (?-594), a Brahmin from a southern kingdom in India, was eager to become a monk and seek Buddhist compassion all over India at his very early age. He moved south-eastwards. In 574, the monk came and met Seng Ts'an—the Third Patriarch of the Chinese Zen Sect—in Zhang An, China. He had said: "You should go to the South for teaching and converting, do not stay here for long". Vinitaruci went to Guang Zhao for studies. In 580, he came to Vietnam and stayed at Phap Van Monastery (present day Dau pagoda, Dien Ung Tu, Thuan Thanh,

Bac Ninh province) and translated *Dharani sutra* (*Dai Thua Phuong Quang Tong Tri* in Vietnamese)—a Tantric sutra. *Dharani* in Pali means holding, maintaining or preventing. *Dharani* has connections with meditation. *Dharani sutra* of Tantrism was used since the start of the Vinitaruci Zen sect. Some researchers say that Vinitaruci followed the Zen sect but the tantric characteristic presented itself very clearly in his studies. Nguyen Duy Hinh supposes that this was a kind of primary Tantrism without any institutions.

Vinitaruci left India around the first half of the 6th century and became a Tantric. He remained in Vietnam for 14 years (580-594). We can see traces of Tantrism in his sect. It is possible that he brought with him at least the Tantric sutra in Pali such as *Dharani* which he translated.

There were many outstanding scholars and researchers in his sect like Dinh Khong (?-808), La Quy An, Phap Thuan (925-990), Sung Pham (1004-1087), Van Hanh (?-1025), Dao Hanh (?-1117), Tri Bat (1049-1117), and Minh Khong (1066-1141). The tradition of combining study, numbers, magic and warfare techniques in Vinitanuci's Zen sect and among monks is common in Vietnamese Buddhism. Thus, it is not surprising that all of the monks were intellectuals among whom the nation's great intellectuals contributed to building of a new civilization of Dai Viet (old name of Vietnam).

In the tenth century, crown prince Dinh Lien (?-979) had an Usnisavijaya Dharani, which was a popular Dharani in Tantrism, inscribed in stone pillars to prevent evil dharma and pray for Bodhisatva's blessings for individuals, the crown prince and the court. Since then, Tantrism was popularized among the elites and played a vital role in the state's rituals. Many Buddhist monks had significant roles in building and constituting the administrative apparatus such as Van Hanh, Minh Khong, Giac Hai and so on. Buddhist festivals which were rich in Tantric characteristics were celebrated, like the Quang Chieu lantern festival, *'Nhan vuong ho quoc'* sutra chanting festival, etc. The above activities show that Buddhism through Tantrism has made a vital and practical contribution to the protection of the state since the formation of the country.

Tantrism was developed and popularized on a large scale because it accepted the presence of the Gods worshipped by the people. This kind of spiritual approach was quite suitable to Vietnamese beliefs and customs that constituted the system of *Tu phap* (Four Dharmas: Cloud, Rain, Thunder and Lightning) in Vietnam. As a result, Tantrism integrated and became an important element of Buddhist and religious activities at that time. The manner in which Tantrism was studied and practiced, also gave Buddhism the ability to embrace the native religion. Some of the Zen sects originating from India and China like the Vinitaruci Zen sect (?-594), the Wu-Yun-T'ung Zen sect (無言通派) (Vo Ngon Thong) (759?-826) vm Tsao-T'ang Zen sect (草堂派) (Thao Duong in Vietnamese), were partly Tantric, especially its studying forms and meditation of Dharanisamadhi, focusing on keeping secrets on the body and chanting mantras for miracles.

Besides the Vinitaruci Zen sect, Tantrism also penetrated into Vietnam through many other ways, i.e. through Vietnamese monks travelling to India for studies, influence of Champa Buddhism and visits of Chinese Tantric monks. Among Vietnamese monks who studied in India, Sung Pham (1004-1087) belonged to eleventh generation of the Vinitaruci sect. He studied in India for nine years and established a Dharma hall at the Phap Van monastery when he came back. Monk Dao Hanh was one of numerous disciples there and became famous on Tantrism. Dao Hanh also tried to go to India, but he could only reach present-day Van Nam province. After that, he was recognized by Sung Pham. Sung Pham had another disciple named Tri Bat (1049-1117) who belonged to the twelfth generation of this sect.

One of Champa's monks was Mahayana (around tenth century), belonging to the tenth generation of the Vinitaruci sect. He was famous for magic and studied with Phap Thuan. The name Mahayana shows us the origin of Saivism. In 875, Indrapura established a Buddhist monastery in Champa where all the relics proved the presence of the Buddhist Mahayana, in the ninth century. The monastery in question was the *Lakshmindralokesvara (Dong Duong)* monastery. In the ninth and tenth centuries, Mahayana Buddhism was practiced together with Saivism in Champa. The book *Thien Uyen tap anh* says that Mahamaya had ancestors in Chiem Thanh. His grandfather used *Duong* as family name and his father—*Boi Da*—was good in Pali books and became a *'boi'* mandarin in the Tien Le Dyansty (Boi mandarin was a mandarin in charge of Buddhist music). He mastered both Pali and Chinese. He headed Quan Ai Pagoda in place of his father. His tantric dharma was enriched when he studied with Phap Thuan (925-990) who belonged to the tenth generation of Vinitaruci sect. He was professional in practicing Ksamayati and chanting the Great Compassion Mantra (*Chu Dai Bi*). Thereafter, he returned to Truong Yen for further studies and gained *Dharani Samadhi* (*Tong tri tam muoi*) and other magic powers.

From the Dinh Dynasty (968-980) to the Ly Dynasty (1010-1225) the movement of practicing Tantrism flourished. The *Quang Chieu lantern* festival, together with the *Nhan Vuong sutra* chanting festival, which were written in orthodox history, were typical evidences showing that Tantrism was practiced popularly in activities of Dai Viet's Buddhism. Speaking in a different way, Tantrism served the practical need at that time—of blessing and saving, Buddha's and Bodhisattvas' recognization of ksamayati towards human beings, either king or civilians—Buddhism did meet that need.

From the Dinh-Tien Le Dynasty to the Ly Dynasty (tenth to eleventh century), pagodas and Buddhist stupas were built in large numbers. Currently, Buddhist remnants in general and Tantric traces in particular still remain in some localities. Tantric thought developed at its highest level around the 11th-12th century in the Kien So and Dau sects. Considering the influence of Tantrism on other traditions, Nguyen Lang assumed that "Tantrism flourished in Vietnam from 7th-8th century, though [the] Wu-Yun-T'ung Zen sect tried to [be] free from its penetration, influence of this dharma still existed. This event demonstrates the importance of Tantrism in Vietnam since the day Vinitaruci came to Vietnam".

Up to the Tran Dynasty (13th-14th century), occasionally there appeared some Indian Tantric monks who came and propagated dharma in official history. *Dai Viet su ky toan thu* (*the full book of Dai Viet*) recorded that a Tantric monk named Du Chi Ba Lam came to Vietnam during the reign of King Tran Nhan Tong (1278-1293) as follows: "He—the black skinned man at his three hundred as he claimed—is able to sit floating on the water, to withdraw all his zang to his chest, to make his abdomen as empty as nothingness with only skin and spine". He ate only some herbs, honey and vegetables. He stayed in Vietnam for several years and then returned to India. In 1311, he was back with his daughter—Da La Thanh. When the king got his daughter to the royal harem, he stayed and died in the capital city. During the reign of King Tran Minh Tong (1311-1329), there was another Indian Tantric monk named Bo De That Ly (Vietnamese name) who came and had similar powers.

In later dynasties like the Hau Le, Mac, Le Trung Hung and Nguyen (15th -19th centuries), there were a few direct records on Tantrism in bibliographies, but we can sieve some details relating to Tantrism such as the worship of Bodhisattvas, local names, praying festivals, books of prophecies or we can consider some rituals in worshiping, the way of disposing statues, mantras, rituals in worshiping Mother Lieu Hanh, ancient languages and so on.

Activities of Tantrism in Vietnam Today

Historically, in Vietnam's Buddhism till date, three elements—Zen, Pure Land (Sukhavati), and Tantrism have been omnipresent without displacement. Even a monk can express his Zen ideas in poems while following Tantric rituals in ceremonies and practicing Sukhavati methods.

Nowadays, many rituals are influenced by both Tantrism and the Pure Land sect, and meditation plays a major role in Zen monastery. In Buddhist rituals such as praying for blessing, salvation and eliminating evil fates, chanting dharani of Tantrism and evoking the names of Buddha of the Pure Land sect are used. Even in daily studies, the combination of these elements is quite clear, these are: chanting the Great Compassion Mantra and other mantras (of Tantrism), reading the Amitabha Sutra and evoking the names of Buddha's (of the Pure Land sect), and reading the Prajnaparamita Sutra (of Zen sect). Generally, combination of Zen, the Pure Land, and Tantrism has become a unique characteristic in studying the traditions of Vietnamese Buddhism in recent times.

Today, Tantrism is attracting many Buddhist and non-Buddhist followers because it can meet people's spiritual needs in current social conditions in Vietnam, and help people to solve problems in their life. However, Tantrism does not develop strongly and officially within the Tantric pagodas, but exists in the form of activities within the traditional pagodas and among the people who follow Tantrism through its different sects (from Tibet, Bhutan, India, China, Taiwan...).

There are various sects with different methods of teaching and studying Tantrism. The teachers can be monks who master Tantrism, or those who practice it at home. The most acceptable official form of teaching is in the Huong pagoda (Fragrant pagoda). The late Venerable Thich Vien Thanh founded the Drupka sect with the method of "*Tinh Mat song tu*" (practicing the Pure Land and Tantrism together) in Vietnam after he finished studying in Bhutan. Nowadays, after awareness and study, the late Venerable Thich Vien Thanh's disciples continue to propagate Tantrism in many areas of the country. According to available statistics, in Hanoi city itself, thousands of people study and use Tantric powers to address daily issues.

Major uses/functions of studying Tantrism include:

- To obtain tranquility of mind, and eliminate bad karma.
- To pray for good family life, prosperous country, mild climate and good fortune.
- To address some practical issues in life such as feng shui, house, health, treatment for diseases.

Now various sects of Tantrism are assimilated due to lack of official transmission. Tantrism does not develop systematically but appears only in some pagodas where monks are knowledgeable about it. Thus, it is difficult to provide a detailed assessment on the development trends of Tantrism in Vietnam in the future. Nevertheless, as of now, Tantrism has an increasing influence in society because it satisfies the spiritual needs of the people who follow and practice it to help solve problems and issues like peace of mind, generation of fortune and cure for diseases.

REFERENCES

Đức, Monk Thích Viên (1996), *Tantrism*, Ho Chi Minh City Publishing House.

Gyatso, Tenzin (2009), *Tibetan Tantrism*, Oriental Publishing House.

Harris, Elizabeth J. (1998), *What is Buddhists Believe*, Oneworld, Oxford,

Hinh, Nguyễn Duy, (1999), *Ideology of Vietnamese Buddhism*, Social Science Publishing House, Hanoi.

Ikeda, Daisaku, (1996), *Buddhism the First Millennium*, Middleway ISBN 9780977924530, Nguyễn Phương Đông dịch, Trần Quang Tuệ hiệu đính, Chính trị Quốc Gia, Hà Nội.

Kiểm, Monk Thích Thanh (1989), *Brief History of Indian Buddhism*. Ho Chi Minh City Buddhism Sangha.

Kiểm, Monk Thích Thanh (2001), *History of Chinese Buddhism*, Publishing House, Hanoi.

Lang, Nguyen (2000), *Discussion of Vietnamese Buddhism*, Literature Publishing House.

Ninh, Vu Thoa-Nguyen (2011) *1000 Issues about Tantrism*, Time Publishing House.

That, Le Manh (1999), *The History of Vietnamese Buddhism*, Episode 1 Thuan Hoa Publising House.

That, Le Manh (chủ biên), (2005), *Buddhism in New Age, Challenges and Oppotunities*, Ho Chi Minh Publishing House.

Thu, Nguyen Tai (1988), *History of Vietnamese Buddhism*, Social Science Publishing house.

Tuan, Nguyen Quoc (2006), *Characteristics and Roles of Vietnamese Buddhism*, Vietnam Academy of Social Science Institute of Philosophy, *Some Issues of Vietnamese Ideology History* (1986). Hanoi.

India and Vietnam

7
India and Vietnam

The Historical Strategic Friendship in Asian Domain

Tridib Chakraborti

Kautilya, in his *Arthashastra* mentioned that there are no permanent friends or foes, only permanent interests. In the history of statecraft and foreign policy formulations between countries in the academic discipline of international relations, there are contextual imperatives that prompt building of strategic relationships or their nemesis. While the phrase 'strategic', used to exemplify relations between and among nations has been worn to some extent broadly, and to some extent flaccidly, it has some defining connotations, according to prevalent situations. Although it has often been assumed that India has no strategic culture and thinking in its foreign policy decision-making, throughout its annals of external policies, it has proved that the vision and long-term philosophy of its past years are quite pragmatic and mostly rational in nature. India, in the present century, has been emerging as a major strategic power to be reckoned with, in the Asian region and stands fully integrated, politically and economically with South, Southeast and East Asia and other parts of the world. Likewise, Vietnam, after its long heroic struggle and multifarious economic challenges, has also emerged as a major economic and strategic player in the Asian region. Its geo-political existence has become vitally important for the external powers. It is a "gateway" from the Asian landmass to the Pacific Ocean or a "bridge-head" on the shores for the trading routes, both maritime and airborne, across the South China Sea. Thus, in the context of emerging global power relations, both India and Vietnam are promising as true strategic partners, in order to achieve their mutual national security interests. Over the years, both have consistently continued their solidarity, friendly mindsets and policy approaches, time and again, and have proved trustworthy to each other, initiating a newfangled partnership in the 21st century. Except a minor hiccup, their relations continued even in the post-Cold War years and gathered momentum on account of India's officially declared "Look East" policy on the one hand, and Vietnam's adherence to a liberal, market-oriented economy, on the other. The cordiality, which has evolved since the late 1990s, reached its zenith due to the convergence of strategic interests in the backdrop of China's growing penetration in the South and Southeast Asian regions. The present strategic understanding was so deep-rooted, that even the recent Chinese threat to both India and Vietnam to stop oil drilling in the South China Sea has been simply ignored by them and this displayed that the 21st century is a century for all; not like the 20th century, during which, New Delhi and Hanoi experienced common threats from the former. In this backdrop, the purpose of this paper is to highlight the evolving eco-political and strategic understanding between India and Vietnam, based on certain parameters in the context of the present global order.

India and Vietnam: Pages from the Dawn of History

In the narration of world history, Vietnam symbolizes the morality of strength. Although many scholars still imagine Vietnam through the lens of war, it is in reality a country that captivates through its show of strength. Over the decades, after its heroic war against the US, it was officially united, and has done a commendable job of healing its wounds and war-shattered economy that it had inherited from the colonial and imperial powers. The real history of this war was that it was fought without connotation. Struggle, death, destruction, sorrow and imposition of someone's dream made her constantly suffer for years. It was the resistance history, which motivated the Vietnamese to be more vivacious and increased the sense of endurance against all odds, making them more realistic and effervescent in the face of vicissitudes throughout its history—from the very inception to the present day, and toughened its moral strength to build the country to keep its head high in emerging global politics.

India, except for a brief period of inactivity has maintained long traditional, close and dependable relations and multi-faceted bilateral cooperation with Vietnam. India's ties with Vietnam date back to over 2000 years as evidenced by the existence of ancient Hindu temples in this Southeast Asian neighbouring country. History is replete with chronicles of Indian merchants' voyages in those ancient times, which have opened up a glorious chapter of mutual exchanges, leading to the blossoming of civilization and culture that has endured the passage of centuries. Today, Indian influences are seen in Vietnamese folklore, religion, philosophy, art and architecture. India had trade relations with Vietnam, and many Indians, especially from the south India, have permanently settled in Ho Chi Minh City. The existence of four big south Indian temples, particularly the Champa Temple in former Saigon, bears a clear testimony to the long-standing Indo-Vietnamese bonhomie. So, Indian influences have spread in the region in a peaceful way.[1]

However, the spread of Chinese influence in Vietnam was an offshoot of political tumult and consequential sinicization of that country. This state of history lost its entity with the arrival of the Western colonial powers in Asia, resulting in the unexpected end of cultural exchanges between India and Vietnam. Yet, it is significant that all through her struggle for independence against the colonial powers, India remained deeply conscious and empathetic towards the interests of her neighbour. Moreover, the experience of national liberation movements of the two countries, based on the ethics of anti-colonialism and solidarity, brought India and Vietnam closer to each other.[2] Thus, over the years, India and Vietnam have been enjoying a traditional friendship and multifaceted cooperation. The two countries have been doing their best to broaden and deepen bilateral cooperation via several agreements that cover a broad range of areas including strategic cooperation, economics, trade, investment, science and technology, culture, education, training etc. that have made each other more dependable and trustworthy.

India-Vietnam: Mapping Out Bonds in the Cold War Period

The end of the Second World War, followed by the Cold War placed the Indian foreign policy makers in a grave quandary. India, in the context of the changed global environment, developed an alternative path of engaging with the newly independent countries of the Asia and Africa. Its goal for quest of peace was to be obtained not through the association with any military alliance, but by joining and judging an issue on its merits. In a world where alliances and counter-alliances were the order of the day, India indicated clearly that it did not wish to join any military alliance. This initiative by India later came to be known as non-alignment. New Delhi's response to the then emerging bipolar world politics stood different from the experiences of the Southeast Asian countries, with most of the latter getting embroiled in Cold War military alliances. As a corollary, India's foreign policy strategy towards Vietnam during the Cold War period was generally determined in terms of the then global power politics and political turbulence that existed within that region. In spite of such trends, India's relations with Vietnam remained extremely cordial, except for minor bitterness in the early years of the Cold War era.[3] If one evaluates the overall trajectory of India-Vietnam relations during the Cold War, it is amply clear that both the countries enjoyed convergence of strategic interests, which largely provided the path for building and reinforcing mutual cooperation. India, in the past, has stood by Vietnam in opposing US military intervention at the cost of embittering Indo-US relations. New Delhi's deep strategic and political understanding with the former Soviet Union, prompted by circumstantial rationale and Hanoi's development of proximal and warm relations with Moscow, at the cost of its policy of friendship with the Peoples' Republic of China (PRC), had further narrowed the gap between India and Vietnam. Thus, in the post-Vietnam War period (since 1975) New Delhi's ties with Hanoi improved very rapidly. India, during these years, vehemently opposed the American and Chinese role on the Cambodian issue at the UN. Besides antagonizing Washington, Beijing and the ASEAN nations by staunchly attesting to its recognition of the pro-Vietnamese Heng Samrin government in Cambodia, it isolated itself from the ASEAN's economic and political sphere. This decision by India, under the leadership of Indira Gandhi, in 1980, was preferred on the ground that the Heng Samrin government was far better than the Pol Pot regime from a moral and humanitarian point of view[4] and it was thought to be strategically rewarding to adopt an identical stand with that of the then Soviet Union. This outlook of the then Indian government was judged as being internationally significant, mainly from the viewpoint of the Indo-Soviet alliance, since New Delhi's major objective was to consolidate and promote this alliance and she judged other issues in the light of this intention.[5] This decision of India acted as a bridge between New Delhi and Hanoi, followed by a steady and sustained progress in economic, commercial, scientific and technological cooperation between them, on the one hand and naturally tarnished New Delhi's non-aligned image in the international arena, on the other. Therefore, this pro-Soviet and pro-Vietnamese political image of India incalculably hindered her chances of improving political and economic relations with the ASEAN countries.

Besides this, geographically and geopolitically, India's connection with the Southeast Asian region had been governed by two important links—land and sea. Southeast Asia comprising Myanmar, Laos, Cambodia, Thailand, Malaysia and Vietnam geographically forms a contiguous region with India, connected by land routes. Thus, India's relations with Vietnam have always been governed by their common enemy i.e., China, on account of a familiar war and other bitter experiences faced by both India and Vietnam over the years. This bitterness prompted New Delhi and Hanoi to amalgamate their strategic interests against China and provided them the foundation for building and reinforcing strategic cooperation against the latter. Given such a common outlook, New Delhi's strategic and military relations with Hanoi even in the Cold War years developed slowly but steadily. Moreover, in the Cold War period, India with its limited capacity, contributed substantial credit and other resource support to Vietnam to restructure its war-shattered economy. India had signed a series of agreements with Vietnam, such as the Cultural Cooperation Agreement (1976); the Trade Agreement and the Agreement of Scientific-Technological Cooperation (1978); the Agreement on Encouraging and Protecting Investment; Agreement on Avoiding Double Taxation; and Agreement on Cooperation in the fields of Mining, Health Care and Environment. Besides this, the Government of India, under the patronage of the Indian Technical and Economic Cooperation (ITEC) Programme, had not only set up the O'Mon Water Rice Research Centre and the Song Be Milk Buffalo

Forage Research Centre, but had shared its experience in cross-breeding of a number of animals (milk buffalo, milk goat, fish and shrimp) and supplied Vietnam with an amount of highly productive breeds and seeds (maize, cotton etc) as well.[6]

Furthermore, Vietnam also remained one of India's largest aid beneficiaries for restructuring its decrepit economy and received Indian credit assistance of Rs. 141.15 crores on soft terms, with repayment being spread over 15 years, at a modest 5 per cent rate of interest, to import railway, telecommunication and sugar production equipment.[7] Till 1985, Vietnam received 5 lakh tons of wheat and rice as a commodity loan from India during her severe food crisis that had inflicted her in the late 1970s. Not only that, while treating Vietnam as a 'Most Favoured Nation' (MFN), in 1982, New Delhi signed an agreement with the latter for setting up a 'Joint Economic, Scientific and Technical Commission', which it had not done with any other country of the Southeast Asian region during the period under review. In fact, besides COMECON countries, India's economic assistance to Vietnam featured prominently in the latter's national reconstruction process. These promising economic relations between New Delhi and Hanoi during the Cold War years (i.e. between 1977 and 1990) were not shaped by their Soviet linkages, but developed primarily as a self-styled, coordinated bilateral approach on the basis of shared resilience and deep understanding. Although Indian economic assistance to Vietnam figured scantily in contrast to core members of the COMECON (before it was dissolved in early 1990s), New Delhi's stature displayed its priority in Vietnam's overall national reconstruction process.

Besides this, one of the most striking incidents, which took place between India and Vietnam during the Cold War period, was New Delhi's initiative to assist Hanoi in developing its alternative energy sources through peaceful use of nuclear energy. Although Vietnam's venture to acquire energy is a recent phenomenon, its mindset about the utility of this resource was visible in the early 1980s, when it wanted to upgrade its Da Lat Nuclear Reactor with the help of the erstwhile Soviet Union, which was disbanded by US before it left Vietnam in 1975. India agreed to help Vietnam in this scientific endeavour. The process of Indian assistance started in August 1988, when a delegation of the Indian Atomic Energy Commission led by its Chairman, M.R. Srinivasan, paid an official visit to Vietnam and on August 15 (1988), signed an accord on peaceful use of atomic energy. Under the Protocol and Work Plans signed under this agreement, a number of Vietnamese scientists and experts have received training in India. This nuclear accord, described as a "memo of cooperation in the use of atomic energy for peaceful purposes",[8] remained another significant chapter in Indo-Vietnamese contemporary history. Interestingly enough, the Indian Prime Minister, Morarji Desai, during Vietnamese Prime Minister Pham Van Dong's visit to India in February 1978, offered to assist Vietnam with her programme of developing peaceful uses of nuclear energy. The kind of nuclear technical aid that New Delhi agreed to provide Hanoi was not initially made public. However, following the 1988 agreement between India and Vietnam, New Delhi began assisting the Vietnamese government in re-activating the Da Lat nuclear research reactor for future nuclear power generation programmes to analyze mineral or biological samples, and produce necessary isotopes for medical and agricultural research institutions, with technical assistance from the Indian scientists.

During the Cold War period, India's political and economic aid to Vietnam displayed an archetypal image of a developing country helping another developing economy and thereby created close interdependence, which has been often referred to as "an ideal model for South-South economic cooperation for the developing world".[9] This Indian role may be described as the first individualistic pragmatic solidarity policy towards any country of Southeast Asia, against the backdrop of the then closer politico-security and political relations with the former Soviet Union and Vietnam. This explicit pro-Vietnam policy, as followed by India mainly during the last two decades of the Cold War years, amply reflects New Delhi's overall foreign policy priority towards this country, rather than the ASEAN members. Thus, in the last two decades of the Cold War, India's political and economic ties had compromised her regional image in two ways: On the one hand, it had de-linked itself from the ASEAN orbit to a great extent. On the other, its image had graduated on a compact footing in the psyche of the Indo-China States (mainly Vietnam).

The Demise of the Soviet Union: The Shifting Paradigm of Indian Foreign Policy

The disintegration of the Soviet Union, accompanied by the emergence of the new global order, positioned India's foreign policy-makers in a quandary, and stimulated the initiation of her economic liberalization policy in 1991. This uneven situation also significantly changed the gamut of India's overall foreign policy approach towards the Southeast Asian region. In the context of the changing global environment, India radically modified its earlier mindset of domestic, economic and foreign policies, based on economic and strategic imperatives rather than political expression. In the initial phase of the post-Cold War years, India, under its New Economic Policy, identified ASEAN as a major focus of interest in her foreign, economic and defence policies, which is otherwise known as the 'Look East' Policy. Interestingly enough, this new 'Look East' economic outlook of New Delhi, which coincided with ASEAN's Look West and rationalization thrust, practically inaugurated a new segment of re-discovery and revival in India-ASEAN relations, and largely spawned confidence among India's leaders who believed that this integration might prove useful to New Delhi in politics, economics and strategy. Thus, in the initial post-Cold War years, New Delhi was mostly engaged in establishing institutional linkages with ASEAN and the economically developed countries of Southeast Asia and attempted to generate a more secure and reliable image of itself to them. As a result, India, within a short span of time, through its officially declared 'Look East' Policy uplifted its status from 'Sectoral Dialogue' (1992) to 'Full Dialogue' (1995) Partner, from 'Full Dialogue' to 'Summit Partner' (2002) of ASEAN and from 'Summit Partner' to 'East Asia Summit Partner' in 2005. Furthermore, in July 1996, India's inclusion in the ASEAN Regional Forum (ARF) was not only hailed as a major diplomatic achievement, but a salutation of its "Look East" doctrine as well. However, during the initial years, New Delhi had ephemerally lost rhythm of continuing its fraternal ties with Vietnam. The cadence, however, was re-issued with the inclusion of Vietnam (in 1995), Myanmar and Laos (in 1997) within the ASEAN orbit, followed by the formation of BIMSTEC in June 1997 and the Mekong-Ganga Cooperation (MGC) Initiative on November 10, 2000. All these events were naturally aimed at broadening and spiraling joint efforts at economic cooperation between India and ASEAN in the Mekong Basin, apart from establishing a Delhi-Hanoi road and railway link in the near future, and the development of transportation networks, including the East-West Corridor project and the Trans-Asian highway. With these landmarks, India's economic interests, national security and strategic imperatives towards Vietnam convalesced the momentum and restored positive bilateral relations, thereby gradually converting each other as promising "strategic partners" in emerging global politics. Presently, India's 'Look East' policy has crossed more than twenty years and during these two decades, Vietnam has emerged as a prime strategic partner of India. The rationale behind this emerging strategic partnership between India and Vietnam can be estimated on the basis of certain factors.

Major Rationale behind the Emerging Strategic Understanding between India and Vietnam

India's outlook towards Southeast Asia through the 'Look East' policy clearly painted the principles and scripted the potential roadmap of ASEAN-India cooperation with its consequent spillover on the overall visage of Indo-Vietnam linkages. The major rationale behind the growing understanding between New Delhi and Hanoi can be identified as follows:

First, the changing global milieu due to the process of globalization, resulted in New Delhi's announcement of New Economic policy in 1991, followed by its 'Look East' policy, which coincided with Vietnam's transformation from a centralized planned economy to an open, liberalized market-oriented economic system in 1986, through Doi Moi (renewal), thereby brought the two countries economically and geo-politically closer to each other. Geo-strategically, India and Vietnam occupy important positions in their respective regions and in so far as the safety of Sea Lanes of Communication (SLOC) is concerned, India has a vital interest in ensuring that the Straits of Malacca remain in friendly hands. Its 'Look East' policy has led to an increasing engagement with Southeast Asia and the sea lanes to the further East are growing in significance for its energy security, as New Delhi is looking for oil and gas supplies from Myanmar, Vietnam, Indonesia and other countries from that region. India's 'Look East' naval diplomacy in tandem with the two versions of the Naval Doctrine (2004 and 2009) ranks high in the new global agenda of the country's foreign policy. New Delhi's joint naval exercises, conducted regularly with most of the countries of Southeast Asia, are a manifestation of a more organized and tactical 'Look East' policy. Moreover, India's realistic maritime profile, the absence of maritime dispute with any ASEAN country and its benign image has helped to develop strong naval ties between South and Southeast Asian regions. Besides this, Indian naval operations during the Tsunami disaster (of 2004) and its recent assistance to the Malaysian government to trace the location of the missing Malaysian airline have clearly manifested a direct challenge to some countries of East Asia and promises a redefinition of the naval balance of power in the region.[10]

Second, India's membership in the East Asia Summit (EAS) has narrowed the gap between India and East Asia. If the EAS could establish a realistic structure for Asian community-building, then Asia might appear as a new and independent centre of growth and influence, which may change the strategic equations within Asia as well as the entire world. If the 21st century is to be a truly "Asian" one, it cannot be so without India playing a central role in this endeavour.[11] So, in this effort, India's importance as a core player cannot be ignored and this consideration led Vietnam to reach a strategic understanding with the former.

Third, the historical solidarity and no-war experience as well as the economic assistance provided by India for national reconstruction to re-build Vietnam's economy in the 1970s and 1980s, brought both New Delhi and Hanoi closer to each other in the post-Cold War years.

Fourth, India's burgeoning strategic, political and economic importance not only among the Southeast Asian countries, but also beyond the region, has made the Vietnamese leadership develop a pragmatic outlook towards India and thereby brought the two countries closer to each other.

Fifth, strategically placed on the western fringe of Southeast Asia, Vietnam figures prominently in the US and Chinese strategic calculus in order to wield influence in East Asian security, where India considers Vietnam as the main barrier for China's southward expansion. So, convergence of geo-strategic interests, on account of China's emerging economic and naval strength with reference to the pivotal location across the sea-lanes of East Asia, with particular reference to the South China Sea, and thereby an occasional display of strength by Beijing, brought India and Vietnam closer to each other. Both are also cautious about the Chinese entry into the Indian Ocean and the South China Sea. China has prolifically created strategic pressure over India by bringing Myanmar and Pakistan within its sphere of influence. It was never vocal and sensitive regarding Pakistan's initiative to build nuclear weapons and nuclear-capable missile arsenal. Then why should India be concerned of what China thinks with reference to Vietnam? Thus, India can play a crucial role in the capacity building of Vietnam's military deterrence and a strategic partnership with Vietnam can afford India space to pressurize China. With this mindset, India built her capacity with the Vietnamese Armed Forces, since the latter's pivotal location makes New Delhi extremely strategic for the role envisaged by her in the given situation and which probably has been endorsed by Vietnam in principle. So, convergence of strategic interests compelled both India and Vietnam to establish a strong bond to contain the growing Chinese influence in the existing power structure in Asia. Thus, the 'China factor' plays a key role in the emerging strategic calculus of both India and Vietnam.[12]

Sixth, the rising multi-directional defence diplomacy in Asia, on account of the shift away from economic issues in the first phase to a broader agenda in the second that involved security cooperation through India's 'Look East' policy, brought India closer to Vietnam. The military diplomacy, which India started with the ASEAN countries at a rudimentary level in the early 1990s, has expanded into full-fledged defence cooperation with them (including Vietnam), and thereby gave New Delhi enough space as an eminent naval power offering a balancing role, against the growing Chinese military in the region.[13] Moreover, India's participation in the first ASEAN Defence Ministers' Meeting Plus (ADMM+) in October 2010 at Hanoi is another milestone of its 'Look East' policy. New Delhi's participation has made it a strong claimant for APEC (Asia-Pacific Economic Cooperation) membership, which has been deadlocked since 1997.

Finally, owing to its geo-strategic setting in China's neighbourhood, Vietnam is one of the key players for any future strategy of containing the former's hegemonic rise in the Asian region. The ongoing strategic partnership evolved both by the US and Japan with Vietnam as well as with India, brought both New Delhi and Hanoi closer to each other in the emerging global profile. Since 1995, the US opted for a policy of rapprochement with Vietnam after a long period of isolation. In recent years, the two countries have expanded their political and security exchanges through initiation of dialogues on economic and regional security issues. Though both US and Vietnam emphasize the budding bilateral strategic relations are not aimed at China, nevertheless, Hanoi, being a major offshore oil producer in the South China Sea, has had an incentive to involve as many foreign powers as possible to reinforce its claim in the region. However, the Obama administration's recent emphasis towards Vietnam through aid, military assistance and most significantly, the signing of the transfer of nuclear technology deal, on October 10, 2013 in Brunei, brought both the countries nearer to each other. Like India, the US-Vietnam Civil Nuclear Cooperation Agreement, known as the '123 Agreement', will allow US industries to tap Vietnam's nuclear power market as part of the US push to strengthen both economic and security ties with Vietnam in the face of China's growing influence in the region. For Vietnam, its ports, membership in ASEAN, as well as its growing market for American goods could make it an important regional partner. As a result, presently Vietnam considers the United States as a more significant ally than China from the perspective of its strategic interest, in spite of common philosophical beliefs harboured by China and Vietnam. Besides this, the growing strategic understanding followed by the Civil-Nuclear Energy Agreement in 2008 brought New Delhi and Washington close to each other and also generated a better diplomatic understanding between New Delhi and Hanoi. The changing regional profile in the Asia-Pacific region as well as the signing of the 'Strategic Partnership' Agreement between India and Vietnam in July 2007 at New Delhi, was described by the Vietnamese Prime Minister, Nguyen Tan Dung, as a "new strategic partnership between the two countries, their potential, efforts and determination, we can believe that in the future, Vietnam-India relations will see strong, intensive and effective development steps."[14] Therefore, in recent years, both India and Vietnam pragmatically realized the importance of evolving a strategic partnership, based on national security interests, on account of China's growing military, economic and strategic footing in the South, Southeast and East Asian regions. The strategic cooperative and solidarity mindset, which evolved during the Cold War period between India and Vietnam, enhanced its space and tightened their embrace.

Outfit of Closer Strategic Understanding between India and Vietnam

The 21st century is celebrated as the Asian Century, in which India and China are the two emerging powerhouses. This enhanced status is chiefly due to New Delhi's spectacular achievements, premised on the New Economic Policy. While honouring this belief, India bestows the appellation "strategic partnership" in its diplomacy to every set of relationship in pursuit of developing better equations with those countries which are strategically important and amenable in its foreign policy domain. From that perspective, New Delhi intended to develop a long-range and substantial relationship and strategic partnership with Vietnam. Although belated, India has initiated this process and it is reflected in multifarious spheres with Vietnam. Among these, defence, naval and nuclear cooperation remain the most important sectors.

Defence and Naval Cooperation

Historically and geopolitically, India's links with the Southeast Asian region have been governed by two important links—land and sea. Peninsular Southeast Asia is a geographically contiguous region with India connected by land routes. In this backdrop, their common adversary, i.e., China, has governed India's relations with Vietnam. Given such a common outlook, New Delhi's military ties with Hanoi developed slowly but steadily since the Cold War era. However, that situation gathered impetus in the post-Cold War period, following a number of defence agreements signed by New Delhi and Hanoi over the years. In September 1994 the then Indian Prime Minister P.V. Narasimha Rao paid an official visit to Vietnam and signed a defence agreement with the latter. Its main focus was to promote cooperation between the defence establishments of the two countries, centred on safeguarding and preservation of military equipments mostly supplied to Vietnam by the erstwhile Soviet Union. However, the agreement was not intended against any third country.[15]

Following this meeting, in the Eighth India-Vietnam Joint Commission meeting held at Hanoi in August 1997, India offered to supply spare parts to Vietnam, apart from providing its service of Soviet-origin defence equipment on a commercial basis. The documents, which were finalized after the meeting, clearly stated that, "Cooperation in defence is an important aspect of bilateral relations between India and Vietnam."[16] It was also decided that New Delhi and Hanoi would take essential steps to execute the provisions of the 'Protocol on Defence Cooperation' signed during the visit to Vietnam by the Indian Prime Minister P.V. Narasimha Rao in 1994 and agreed that periodic exchange of visits of defence personnel, exchange of information, transfer of relevant technologies and repair, maintenance and up-gradation of defence equipments were all "important elements" of Indo-Vietnamese defence cooperation. The growing understanding further strengthened, when India's then Defence Minister, George Fernandes paid an official visit to Hanoi, marking the first ever visit by an Indian Defence Minister to Vietnam, in late March 2000. The most notable facet of this visit was that a 15-point agreement was signed between the two countries which had among its highlights, the two Navies, the Indian Coast Guards and the Vietnamese sea-police agreeing to cooperate with each other in combating piracy, repairing Vietnamese Air force fighter planes and the training of Vietnamese Air Force pilots by the Indian Air Force.[17] It was also agreed by India to revamp the Vietnamese Air Force, providing MiG-21's with fresh avionics and radars to maintain Russia's latest missiles, including the R-77 AMRAAMSKI and the R-27 dogfight, and also to assist Vietnam to build up its domestic arms industry, to make small and medium weapons and definite kinds of ordnance. At the end of this agreement, the Indian Defence Minister hailed Vietnam as India's "most trusted friend and ally", and clearly mentioned that Hanoi "stood by us after the nuclear tests because they understand that if [India] went nuclear there were good security reasons for it", thereby implying the China threat as unmistakable.

Finally, the Indian Defence Minister described this cooperation as the beginning of a "periodical security dialogue", and decided to support Vietnam in the course of setting up its defence industry and opened its doors to the research done by the Defence Research and Development Organization (DRDO). The agreement reflected India's strategic aim to assist in building Vietnam's armed forces as militarily strong and self-reliant, and thereby institutionalized regular meetings between the Defence Ministers of the two sides to discuss matters relating to shared threat perceptions, apart from paving the way for visits of Indian ships to Vietnamese ports and more collaboration in naval exercises.[18] In fact, this defence accord has institutionalized the framework for regular meetings between the Defence Ministers as well as for visits by Indian naval ships to Vietnamese ports and extensive collaboration through bilateral naval exercises. Moreover in May 2003, India signed a "Joint Declaration on Framework of Comprehensive Cooperation" with Vietnam, within which, Vietnam agreed to train the Indian armed forces in guerrilla warfare in order to tackle the terrorist problems faced in various parts of India.[19]

Historically, Vietnam mostly experienced adverse relations with China, having fought its last war with the latter in 1979. Although Vietnam has been able to resolve its land border dispute with China skillfully, the mutual confidence between the two countries has not yet been fully refurbished. Presently, India and the US are primarily considering Vietnam's importance vis-à-vis their anti-China stance, as a result of Hanoi's past bitter relations with Beijing and its geo-strategic location in the Asia-Pacific region, in terms of its proximity to the SLOC area, prompting both New Delhi and Washington to come closer to Hanoi. Thus, axiomatically, the imperative of India's strategic endeavour to support building Vietnam's armed forces to be militarily powerful and autonomous has been justified. The growing strategic importance of Vietnam in Indian foreign policy gathered impetus following Vietnam Prime Minister, Nguyen Tan Dung's visit to India, on July 6, 2007. During this visit, both countries signed a Joint Declaration on establishing a bilateral 'Strategic Partnership' in six areas and agreed to promote regional security, by pledging to strengthen cooperation in defence supplies, joint projects, training cooperation and intelligence exchanges. It was also decided by New Delhi and Hanoi that they would work closely on defence and security establishments, enhance cooperation in capacity building, technical assistance and information-sharing between their respective germane agencies for ensuring security of sea-lanes, including combating piracy, preventing pollution and conducting search and rescue operations.[20] Besides this, it was agreed by both the countries that they would hold annual Strategic Dialogue at deputy minister level, to enhance contacts and exchange visits between their defence and security establishments, to strengthen bilateral cooperation to combat terrorism and to promote cooperation in cyber security, to address non-traditional security issues including drug trafficking, natural disasters, climate change, energy security, HIV/AIDS, avian influenza and other epidemics. Thus, the core stipulation of this strategic partnership is neither pertinent in the corporate sense nor in terms of a defence pact, but impinges more upon the convergence of views on strategic issues, on account of a new strategic realignment in Asia.

Following this historic event, India and Vietnam approved a plethora of measures to further expand their relations in defence and 'take it to new heights', when the then Indian Defence Minister, A.K. Antony paid a three-day official visit to Vietnam in December 2007. During his meeting with his Vietnamese counterpart, Gen. Phung Quang Thanh in Hanoi, Antony agreed to transfer 5,000 items of naval spares belonging to Petya class of ships to Vietnam to infuse life into many of the ageing vessels. The Indian leader also suggested an increase in the frequency of goodwill visits by naval ships, application of information technology in defence, e-technology and technical support to the Vietnamese Navy. Additionally, India agreed to dispatch a four-member army team to Vietnam during the first half of 2008 to conduct training on UN peacekeeping operations. Finally, the two sides agreed to set up a Joint Working Group to facilitate the signing of a Memorandum of Understanding on defence cooperation (including national defence, navy, air defence and personnel training). The Indian delegation also visited defence industries in Ho Chi Minh City. The Vietnamese Defence Minister sought Indian support in training of defence personnel, enhancing the exchanges of delegations, expanding training cooperation, an increase in the frequency of goodwill visits by naval ships, application of information technology and e-technology, and technical support for the Vietnamese navy. So far, 49 officers have attended various army and navy courses in India and 64 officers have attended English language courses. Furthermore, at the 3rd India-Vietnam Security Dialogue meeting held in New Delhi in November 2007, both the countries converged on a number of important decisions, like the exchange of visits for better appreciation of requirements and problems, greater cooperation in the field of training of Service personnel—particularly involving junior level officers, security dialogue at least once a year, sharing of expertise on issues of common concern such as maritime security, border management and counter-insurgency, conduct of training for Vietnamese officers in the field of UN Peacekeeping operations, invitation to Vietnamese officers to Indian military exercises as observers etc., which were aimed at providing greater impetus to their budding relationship.[21]

In the succeeding years, a number of visits and counter-visits took place between India and Vietnam, related to the ongoing defence collaboration between them. Among these visits, the Indian Army Chief, General V.K. Singh's July 2010 visit remained quite significant in nature. Like the Cold War period, this was the first time in the post-Cold War years that an Indian Army Chief visited Vietnam to implement the roadmap of the 2009 Memorandum of Understanding between the two Ministries of Defence. Nevertheless, the most remarkable event, which took place in 2010, was the First ASEAN +8 Defence Ministers' Meeting (ADMM+8) held in Hanoi in October. This ADMM+8 is a newly-formed gathering of ASEAN Defence Ministers and their counterparts beyond the region including Australia, China, India, Japan, New Zealand, South Korea, Russia and the US and thereby, provides an inclusive and focused configuration, bringing together the key regional players to collectively handle security issues such as terrorism, piracy, disaster relief and transnational crime. In this meeting, the Indian Defence Minister, A.K. Antony held discussions with the Vietnamese leadership and agreed to provide support to the latter to enhance and upgrade the capabilities of defence services in general, and Navy in particular.[22] He also assured that India would help Vietnam in its capacity building for repair and maintenance of its platforms. The Armies of the two countries would also cooperate in areas like IT, English training of Vietnamese Army personnel and that both the armies would conduct joint training in mountain and jungle warfare in India the very next year. While expressing deep satisfaction regarding this Indian gesture to modernize Vietnam's defence and other strategic areas, the Vietnamese Prime Minister, Dung said, "The Vietnam-India strategic partnership is a good model. Our traditional and friendly co-operation has always been consolidated by generations of the two sides' leadership."

However, the growing defence understanding between India and Vietnam reached a slightly low ebb, when Hanoi expressed its dissatisfaction about India's lack of occasional commitment to supply some of the missile systems as agreed to by the BJP government to modernize Vietnam's military. It was committed by New Delhi during the BJP government's tenure that it would gift Vietnam the Prithvi and BrahMos missile systems, in order to counter Chinese naval dominance in the South China Sea, so as to greatly aid Vietnam in its strategy of sea denial and coastal defence. The word 'BrahMos' is an acronym of the two rivers, *Brahmaputra* of India and *Moskva* of Russia. These stealth missiles, capable of being launched from submarines, aircraft or land, are the fastest supersonic missiles in the world. Unfortunately, India failed to maintain its commitment due to two important reasons and they were: First, the Congress government had increasingly focused on economic rather than military cooperation with Vietnam, and thereby, had tried not to antagonize its immediate neighbour, China, with which New Delhi was evolving better ties. Second, some analysts felt that the BrahMos must first be fully inducted into the Indian Armed Forces before a surplus can be generated for friendly states such as Vietnam. As against such arguments, Vietnam had procured 100 SMG-PK 9 mm submachine guns and 50 sniper rifles from the state-run Pakistan Ordnance Factories (POF) in Rawalpindi in 2007, in a veiled but nevertheless significant expression of its displeasure to New Delhi.[23] Auspiciously, this state of misunderstanding finally withered away from the Vietnam mindset, when India in September 2011, entered into negotiations with Vietnam to sell its first BrahMos cruise missile to an outside country, crossing into neighbouring hands. The process of delivery of this missile to Vietnam has not yet commenced and negotiations are still on. To procure this cruise missile, the Vietnamese Communist Party General Secretary, Nguyen Phu Trong, during his visit to New Delhi on 3 December 2013, once again requested India to supply the BrahMos cruise missiles and initiate training for Vietnamese pilots to fly Sukhoi-30 aircrafts to meet its immediate requirement. It was stated by the BrahMos Aerospace chief, Sivathanu Pillai on 2 August, 2013, that this Russian-Indian joint venture BrahMos Aerospace would transfer the first Su-30MKI jet fighter to the Indian Air Force in September 2015.[24] Already more than fourteen countries have expressed interest in buying different modifications of a BrahMos supersonic cruise missile. Interestingly enough, this decision comes after an Indian ship was halted by the Chinese after leaving port, and following China's recent admonition that India best stay away from exploring the South China Sea. The BrahMos missiles are the result of a joint venture between Russia and India, and will be of immense value in boosting Vietnam's defence preparedness. This move by New Delhi further underscores the importance of ongoing strategic ties between India and Vietnam in the face of China's assertiveness in the South China Sea region.[25] Besides this, the secretary-level Eighth Annual Security Dialogue was held in Ho Chi Minh City on November 8, 2013. In this meeting, both the countries have discussed in detail the ongoing capacity—building of the Vietnamese Armed Forces, particularly the Navy and the areas like training, repairs and maintenance support, exchanges between think tanks, study tours and ship visits. Following this meeting, in December 2013, India decided to give a $100 million credit line to Vietnam to buy military equipment, including four offshore naval patrol vessels. This decision remains an extension of the first military credit that India agreed to provide to any country.[26] So, these multifarious defence projects are the pillars of strategic partnership between the two countries, through which India endeavours strengthening its relationship with Vietnam. There is a clear strategic mindset that gradually Hanoi would become the linchpin of this eastward move by New Delhi and if China wants to expand its presence in South Asia and the Indian Ocean region, India can follow suit to act as a counterweight in the same manner that Pakistan is for China and also in East Asia.

Besides this, another area where India and Vietnam's growing strategic partnership is expanding quite rapidly is the ongoing naval understanding. The brisk defence understanding had a spillover effect in the development of naval cooperation between them in recent times. Both India and Vietnam have embarked upon a mission to strengthen their naval ties and establish a sustainable maritime presence, as Indian naval warships have been granted permission to drop anchor at the Na Trang port in southern Vietnam. The Vietnamese move to allow the Indian Navy to drop anchor at the South Vietnamese port assumes significance because the Indian Navy is the only foreign navy in the world to have been granted such a privilege at a port other than Halong Bay near Hanoi, and will facilitate the presence of Indian Navy in the South China Sea, enabling a greater strategic role for India in Southeast Asia. India and Vietnam are wary of the growing Chinese military capacity as well as their increasing incidence in the region. The decision to develop this naval strategic tie was actually processed following the visit of Vietnamese Naval Chief Nguyen Van Hien to India in late June 2011. During this visit, Nguyen Van Hien visited the public sector defence shipbuilder, Mazagon Dock Limited in Mumbai and Hindustan Shipyard Limited in Vishakhapatnam and realized the potential of Indian naval ship-building capacities and functioning of the defence shipyard.[27] Finally, he agreed to secure Indian help for augmenting the size and capabilities of the Vietnamese navy. In other words, this achievement of the Indian Navy in Na Trang port, not only added military heft to India's 'Look East' policy, but is also emblematic of a larger Indian effort to counter China's activities in South Asia, and allow New Delhi to monitor the South China Sea side of the Straits of Malacca as well, effectively securing India's energy and commercial shipping originating in the Far East, while putting a greater drape of China's SLOCs within the Indian Navy's accomplishment. Besides this, in September 2011, both India and Vietnam jointly decided that the former would train the Vietnamese in submarine operations, mainly to help Vietnam with "intensive" submarine and underwater warfare training as part of its expanding military ties with the East Asian region, both of which are concerned with China's "increasingly assertive behaviour" in the region.[28] The proposed training programme for Vietnamese sailors would take place at Indian Navy's submarine school INS Satavahana in Vishakapatanam, which is equipped with advanced training aids and other facilities. Furthermore, it was agreed by India to continue to train Vietnamese naval personnel and help maintain any equipment that Vietnam sourced from Russia, in addition to providing aid to Vietnam to increase its naval strength by building ships and other necessary training facilities.

While defending India's stand on docking rights for its warships and facilities to post naval instructors long-term in Cam Ranh Bay on Vietnam's south-central coast, and at Na Trang 60 km north of the bay, which are on a busy commercial route cutting through South China Sea, Vishnu Prakash, the spokesperson of the Ministry of External Affairs, Government of India, in an interview said: "What I know is that security and defence co-operation are again important facets of co-operation with Vietnam. We have a memorandum of defence co-operation that was concluded in 2009. We have regular high-level exchanges, visits—both military to military, as well as at the political and official levels. Our ships regularly pay port calls in Vietnam and vice versa. We have joint training. We have exchange of information."[29] Moreover, the Indo-Vietnam bilateral joint naval exercise in the South China Sea on June 8, 2013, was not favourably looked upon by China and it was treated as an attempt to undermine its sovereignty over uninhabited islands in the South China Sea.[30] Over the years, regular bilateral joint naval goodwill visits between India and Vietnam have taken place, as demonstrated in Table 7.1.

Therefore, the growing defence and naval linkages between India and Vietnam have been premised on a number of important determinants, which are as follows: First, the longstanding territorial disputes with China, in which India and Vietnam are the common sufferers; Second, China's disputable mindset and recent muscle flexing with reference to the South China Sea. It was felt by the Indian policy makers that Vietnam's location is ideal to avert China's increasing naval growth and thereby, to deny Beijing total supremacy in the South China Sea. Both feel that growing Chinese influence is a threat for the existing power structure in Asia and to counterbalance Beijing's fledgling military prowess in the region, it is imperative to work together as well as lend a helping hand to major powers involved in the region's security dynamics; Third, it has been also pragmatically realized by the Indian policy-makers that its 'Look East' policy should not be confined only to trade, but also be extended to the new military-security power projection mainly in the Southeast and East Asian region, particularly through naval deployments and maritime diplomacy; Fourth, the growing defence and naval cooperation between India and Vietnam as well as the former's display of strength, existence, mobility, coincided with Vietnam's anti-China ties and its

Table 7.1: Goodwill Ship Visits between India and Vietnam

Serial Numbers	*Date of the Journey*	*Name of the Ships*	*Place of the Visits*
1.	October 1-4, 1998	INS Rajput, INS 21 Delhi, INS Khanjar	Vietnam
2.	September 28-October 1, 2000	INS-Rajput	Ho Chi Minh City
3.	June 7-9, 2001	Coast Guard vessel Sangram	Ho Chi Minh City
4.	October 29-31, 2001	INS Mumbai and INS Jyoti	Ho Chi Minh City
5.	November 2004	INS Ranvijay, INS Sukanya and INS Kirch	Ho Chi Minh City
6.	June 9-13, 2005	INS Magar	Ho Chi Minh City
7.	June 8-11, 2006	INS Rajput; INS Kulish; INS Kirpan	Tien Sea Port, Da Nang City, Vietnam
8.	May 7-11, 2007	INS Mysore, INS Ranjit	Ho Chi Minh City
9.	May 12-14, 2007	Coast Guard ship ICGS Sagar	Ho Chi Minh City
10.	April 17-21, 2008	INS Kora; INS Kirpan	Hai Phong Port
11.	April 7-11, 2009	INS Mumbai; INS Ranvir	Northern Port of Hai Phong City, Hanoi
12.	May 30–June 2, 2010	INS Ranjit; INS Kulish	Kulish Northern Port of Hai Phong City, Hanoi
13.	May 10-13, 2011	INS Delhi, INS Kirch	Saigon Port
14.	July 19-28, 2011	INS Airavat	Nha Trang in South-Central Vietnam and the Northern Port of Haiphong

Serial Numbers	*Date of the Journey*	*Name of the Ships*	*Place of the Visits*
15.	May 19-23, 2012	INS Shivalik, INS Karmuk	Chua Ve Port, Northern Port City of Hai Phong
16.	December 31, 2012 - January 3, 2013	INS Sudarshini,	Da Nang Port
17.	June 6-10, 2013	INS Satpura (F48), INS Shakti (A57), INS Ranvijay (D55) and INS Kirch (P62).	Tien Sa Port in Da Nang City

Source: Compiled by the author based on various Annual Reports (1998-1999 to-2011-2012), Ministry of External Affairs, Government of India, New Delhi and Newspapers and Internet sources.

geo-strategic location, in terms of its proximity to the SLOCs, on account of the growing Chinese naval manoeuvre in the Asia-Pacific region, brought the two countries closer to each other; Finally, a number of non-traditional security threats, which evolved in the Straits of Malacca and the Indian Ocean Region, provided India an opportunity to upgrade its naval strength through its Naval Doctrine announced in 2004 (modified in 2009). Presently, like Vietnam, India has also started dialogue with Japan, South Korea and the US in order to safeguard the SLOC as well as China's so-called 'String of Pearls' encirclement. Thus, India's regular deployment of warships, which visit the Asia-Pacific region regularly, clearly sounded a frequent alarm to China's increasing forays into the Indian Ocean region, since this region is poised to become the new cockpit for the 21st century version of the Great Game in the coming years.[31] With these naval activities, India has clearly signaled that the Asia-Pacific region can no longer be compartmentalized and New Delhi is more assertive in Asian affairs and is gradually trying to evolve as a maritime balancer in the Asia-Pacific in the coming years. However, in the eyes of both India and Vietnam, the necessity of this strategic partnership is neither in the corporate sense, nor in terms of defence pact, but impinges more on convergence of views on strategic issues evolved in the Asia-

Pacific region. For India, deepening defence ties with Vietnam would create a resolute partnership in Southeast Asia and beyond and accentuate the larger and long-term role it envisions, viewed through its 'Look East' prism.

Cooperation on Peaceful Use of Atomic Energy

In the emerging global order of the 21st century, acquisition of energy remains one of the most decisive mechanisms for any country in the world. In the Asia-Pacific region, the procurement and preservation of energy is the key factor of a country's national interest. Based on such a necessity, like India and China, Vietnam also joined this race and it was mainly confined to the South China Sea, since it is preparing for nuclear power electricity generation, to reduce its dependence on hydro and fossil fuel resources. Till date, Vietnam has no nuclear power plant. Although the State-owned EVN (Electricity Vietnam) has done a feasibility study on nuclear energy, concluding that the country has the capability for nuclear power, concerns remain about experience, safety, technology and management of such a plant. In this context, the government has called for international support and cooperation, as a result of which, since the 1980s, Vietnam has paid attention to building the strategy and policy for national energy development, and the peaceful use of nuclear energy has remained an important objective. Vietnam is a signatory to both the International Atomic Energy Agency (IAEA) Regional Cooperation Agreement (RCA) and South Asian Frameworks for Environmental Data-Sharing. Although Vietnam's motivation to procure energy is a recent phenomenon, its mind about the utility of this resource was made up in the 1980s itself, when it wanted to upgrade its Da Lat Nuclear Reactor with the help of the erstwhile Soviet Union. The Reactor was disbanded by the US before it left Vietnam in 1975. Therefore, since the mid-1980s, besides the former Soviet Union, Vietnam procured assistance from many other countries (including India) in order to develop its nuclear power plants for scientific research. India, owing to its cordial historical ties, substantially helped Vietnam in this scientific endeavour. In fact, the process to develop nuclear power plants for scientific research with Indian assistance took off in August 1986 when a delegation of the Indian Atomic Energy Commission, led by its then Chairman, M.R. Srinivasan, paid an official visit to Vietnam and on August 15 signed an agreement on peaceful use of atomic energy (ratified in 1987).[32] This Cold War understanding between India and Vietnam was revived in the post-Cold War years and presently, Vietnam has drawn up plans to harness nuclear energy for electricity generation to diversify its energy needs and also lessen its reliance on hydrocarbon-based energy resources. Vietnam plans to build eight nuclear power plants in five provinces by 2030 with a total capacity of 15 Gigawatts, or 10 per cent of all electricity produced in the country. Vietnam's first nuclear power plant is expected to be built between 2015 and 2020 in Ninh Thuan province and for that it is looking towards a plethora of nuclear technology-capable countries such as Canada, China, Russia, France, Japan, South Korea, India and the US for cooperation and assistance. So far, Vietnam has signed two agreements in 2010 with the US and Russia for acquiring nuclear reactors. The Russian agreement visualizes building two power units with an ability of 1.2 Gigawatts each and also provide for a loan for the construction of the nuclear power plant. However, Vietnam has not acquired trained human resources to handle the nuclear infrastructure, has not drafted national legislation and has not conceptualized nuclear safety and security arrangements. Furthermore, in the wake of the Fukushima nuclear disaster in Japan, the Vietnamese government is paying greater attention to the safety of the nuclear power plants and has established a special committee for training the scientists.[33]

As a part of the earlier understanding, on April 23, 1999, the Indian Atomic Energy Commission (a part of the IDAE) and the Vietnam Atomic Energy Commission (VAEC) signed another agreement for cooperation in the field of nuclear power, exchange of scientists and assistance in setting up a training centre in Vietnam. Under this agreement, about 30 Vietnamese nuclear scientists have received training at the Bhabha Atomic Research Centre (BARC) in Mumbai and Indian scientists have visited Da Lat in order to complete Vietnam's nuclear energy programme by 2015. Furthermore, in January 2001, the then Indian Prime Minister, Atal Behari Vajpayee paid an official visit to Vietnam. During his stay in Hanoi, the two countries signed a MoU between the Department of Atomic Energy and the Ministry of Science, Technology and Environment of Vietnam.

The basis of this MoU has been the agreement between the two governments for cooperation for Utilization of Atomic Energy for Peaceful Purposes signed in 1988, which was valid till May 2002. It also accorded continued cooperation in the fields of human resource development and exchange of expertise.[34] This agreement was an extension of the earlier MoU signed by New Delhi and Hanoi on April 23, 1999. Moreover, in 2005, India supplied, under international nuclear regulatory norms, cobalt, a critical source for a nuclear unit at Ho Chi Minh City built by the Hungarians in the 1980s. India with a rich experience in nuclear energy operations can offer Vietnam its capacities in training skilled nuclear human resources to pave the way for bilateral cooperation in nuclear trade and fuel reprocessing. Unfortunately, Indo-Vietnamese cooperation in the field of nuclear energy has not worked successfully so far, in view of the pressure exerted on both India and Vietnam by the US, as also the availability of more options to Vietnam. However, of late, cooperation in this field has been revived and may hopefully produce some positive results by 2015 or 2020.[35] This situation changed direction following the agreement signed between United States and Vietnam on October 10, 2013 in Brunei, within the framework of which, the US would transfer nuclear technology to the latter. This US-Vietnam Civil Nuclear Co-operation Agreement, otherwise known as the '123 Agreement', would allow US industries to tap Vietnam's nuclear power market as part of the US push to strengthen both economic and security ties with Vietnam in the face of China's growing influence and further support India's position with Vietnam. The issue of civil nuclear cooperation has been a major plank in the bilateral ties between New Delhi and Hanoi and a clear manifestation of a major thrust in India's 'Look East' Vietnam policy in the post-Cold War era.

India's Energy Diplomacy with Vietnam in the South China Sea: China's Display of Red Eyes

Another major event, which took place in global politics in recent years, is the procurement and preservation of energy sources, since the demand for energy sources has been deeply connected with the degree of economic development. Like China and India, Vietnam, as a leading producer of oil and gas, is a vital cog in India's quest to diversify its energy supply sources. India has been investigating overseas exploration rights and Vietnam has been a success story in this regard.[36] The ONGC Videsh Ltd. (OVL) was selected as the successful bidder in the global competitive bid for nine offshore exploration blocks in Vietnam in 2004, and it signed a petroleum sharing contract with Petro-Vietnam for three blocks—06, 12E and 19 in the Nam Con Son basin, about 370 km offshore. Moreover, it also signed an MoU with Petro-Vietnam Investment and Development Company (PIDC) on January 9, 2001 for collaboration between OVL and PIDC in the exploration and production of hydrocarbons in Vietnam.[37]

Although China had not objected to Vietnam regarding the India-Vietnam joint exploration actions dating back to 1988 when Vietnam agreed to offer block 06.1 in Nam Con Son Basin of South China Sea to India, it came into limelight since 2011, when China opposed to India's involvement in the exploration of oil and gas in the South China Sea region. In recent years, there have been diplomatic rows between the two countries on the issue of gas exploration by Petro-Vietnam and British Petroleum (BP) in the planned US$2-billion gas field and pipeline venture, southeast of Vung Tau on the southern coast, close to the Lan lay-Lan Do project in which ONGC is a partner. China has not been entirely content with ONGC in the South China Sea and has been trying to entice Vietnamese oil companies into joint exploration so that Indian companies may face stiff competition in coming years.[38] Moreover, in recent times BP, which is raising capital to cover the cleanup costs of its oil spill in the Gulf of Mexico, has put many of its global assets up for sale, including an investment in the Nam Con Son basin off the southern coast of Vietnam. The Vietnamese government has approved a consortium of state-owned Indian energy firms and Petro Vietnam to buy out BP's stake. Significantly, this large-scale natural gas project is located in an area of the Nam Con Son basin where BP announced in March 2009 that it would cease exploration in response to pressure from China.[39] Against such a backdrop, in October 2010, the Indian Petroleum Minister, Murli Deora agreed to buy BP's 35 per cent stake in the US $1.3 billion Nam Con Son gas project in Vietnam, and thereby integrate India's presence in the oil exploration venture with Vietnam in the South China Sea region, which was not at all favourably looked upon by China. In these joint oil and gas exploration activities in the South China Sea between India and Vietnam, India's state-owned oil company, OVL has so far invested approximately US$ 360 million in the three acquired blocks namely 06.1, 127 and 128. India had invested US$ 342.78 million in block 06.1 till March 2012; US$ 68 million in block 127 till March 2010; and US$ 49.14 million in block 128 till March 2012.[40] [Indian operations in extracting natural gas in Block 6.1 since 2003 in the region which is not under dispute continue from where it got two billion cubic metres (bcm) of gas in 2011-12 for its 45 per cent participating interest.[41]]

Meanwhile, at the invitation of the Foreign Minister of the Socialist Republic of Vietnam, Pham Binh Minh, India's Minister of External Affairs, S.M. Krishna, paid an official visit to Vietnam from September 15-17, 2011, in connection with the 14th India-Vietnam Joint Commission Meeting (JCM) on Trade, Economic, Scientific and Technological Cooperation. During this meeting, both the countries expressed their satisfaction with reference to the evolving Strategic Partnership initiatives and agreed to add greater content to bilateral relations in the fields of defence and security, trade and investment, education, culture and other areas. Before this meeting took place, on September 15, 2011, China officially objected once again to the agreement signed between India's state-owned OVL and Vietnam's Petro Vietnam for conducting oil and gas exploration in the South China Sea, on the ground that India's venture with Vietnam would naturally weaken its long-term claim that the entire South China Sea is its "indisputable sovereignty". In other words, on this account, China had sent a demarche to India and warned against launching exploratory projects in that region. This event naturally stimulated international attention when China began to resist India's oil exploration in blocks 127 and 128 in the Phu Kanh Basin. These blocks were allotted to India in 2006 with 100 per cent stakes. Ironically, logistic restraints coupled with non-availability of enough oil in the block 127 led India to withdraw from the block, which was, unfortunately, seen as a feeble strategic move.[42]

However, the Chinese objection was flatly rejected by India on the basis that the "energy ties with Vietnam are as per international regulations". Before S.M. Krishna had embarked on a three-day visit to Hanoi, Vishnu Prakash, the spokesman of the Ministry of External Affairs, in an interview, firmly reiterated New Delhi's stand on this issue and said, "Our cooperation with Vietnam or any other country is always as per international laws, norms and conventions. Trade is an important aspect of India's relations with Vietnam and the field of energy, hydrocarbons and renewable energy is one such important area. We want to see this relationship grow and expand, and China's objection to OVL's explorations in South China Sea has no legal basis as the blocks belonged to Vietnam".[43] He also categorically pointed out that India has an investment of $400 million in Vietnamese hydrocarbon sectors, with OVL investing $225 million in oil exploration projects in South China Sea, some of which have been objected to by China. He further added: "India supports freedom of navigation in the South China Sea and hopes that all parties to the dispute will abide by the 2002 Declaration of Conduct in the South China Sea". Besides this, India's official position has been that engagement with Vietnam for oil and gas exploration activities in the South China Sea serves commercial purposes and has little to do with China. It reiterates its support for freedom of navigation in the waters of South China Sea and other international waters. However, the Indian response has not been auspiciously looked upon by the Chinese government and as a rejoinder to this Indian stand, a Chinese daily, on September 18, 2011, wrote, "India and Vietnam's insistence on jointly tapping oil resources in the disputed waters of the South China Sea, may risk setting off a new round of tension in the troubled waters. India and Vietnam should understand that China will not back off when it comes to issues concerning its territorial integrity. Beijing is determined to defend its indisputable sovereignty in the South China Sea. Both countries should understand the sensitive and complicated nature of the South China Sea issue, must refrain from making reckless moves that could escalate tensions in the disputed waters. Their planned oil exploration in the waters is not simply an economic issue but one of security and political importance. Any misstep or misjudgment by them could hurt their relations with China. So, jumping on the bandwagon to provoke China on the maritime disputes is not a sensible move on New Delhi's part", the daily further cautioned.[44] Consequently, S.M. Krishna told his Vietnamese counterpart Pham Binh Minh, during his meeting on September 16, 2011, that OVL will go ahead with oil and gas exploration in the disputed region of the two offshore blocks which Vietnam claims as its own, and which were fully endorsed officially. In fact, New Delhi had brushed off China's objections to ONGC's oil exploration projects in two Vietnamese blocks in South China Sea[45], and thereby dismissed Beijing's reprimand. The tension re-surfaced following the Vietnamese Communist Party General Secretary, Nguyen Phu Trong's India visit in November 2013, in the course of which, Vietnam offered to India seven oil blocks in the South China Sea—including three on an exclusive basis—and joint prospecting in some Central Asian countries on a nomination basis to OVL. These were exempted from competitive bidding according to the MoU signed for joint development of the new blocks, between them at the end of this visit. The joint statement issued at the conclusion of this official sojourn clearly mentioned: "The leaders reiterated their desire and determination to work together to maintain peace, stability, growth and prosperity in Asia. They agreed that freedom of navigation in the East Sea/South China Sea should not be impeded and called the parties concerned to exercise restraint, avoid threat or use of force and resolve disputes through peaceful means in accordance with universally recognised principles of international law, including the UNCLOS".[46] It is a fact that China has always accorded a rigid rejoinder to India-Vietnam joint exploration; however, this time, China has remained silent on the issue of joint exploration. While not directly voicing its opposition to the newly-signed MoU on joint exploration, China conveyed its optimism that countries would "do more things that are conducive" to stability.[47] As far as Hanoi is concerned, it sees New Delhi's existence as a positive move and has been encouraging it to take a stake in the disputed sea through the acquisition by OVL.[48] Thus, the prime objective of this offer is not merely to enhance economic and energy cooperation but also to elevate the bilateral relationship in order to strengthen the strategic partnership announced in 2007.

Envisioning India-Vietnam Growing Understanding: Reflecting Through Chinese Mirror

Historically, India-China relations have developed on the basis of both pro-active and re-active flavours and as a result, neither has developed a workable strategy towards the other. However, the emerging global order, followed by India and China's changing economic and strategic parameters in the South, Southeast and East Asian regions, as well as the improving strategic understanding between India and Vietnam, has led to regional and geo-strategic rivalry and bilateral competition between India and China. For both India and Vietnam, China has always dominated the crucial determinants in processing their foreign policy decision-making. For India, China remains a major natural geo-strategic rival, which claims a large chunk of its northeastern frontier. During its long history, India-China relations have been skeptical in nature. In fact, the border war of 1962 between India and China left a trail of deep-rooted mistrust whose traces are still present in their bilateral relations. Like India, China, in the eyes of the Vietnamese leadership, except some years during the national liberation phase, remained a suspect power. Vietnam's historical border problem and its border clash in February 1979 with China, clearly demonstrated Beijing's hegemonic posture towards the Southeast Asian region. This outlook was further entrenched when territorial disputes to take control over the Paracel and Spratly Islands in the South China Sea between Vietnam and China raised their ugly head. The Paracel (1974) and Spratly (1988) clashes between Beijing and Hanoi have clearly exhibited the hegemonic ambition of China in the Southeast Asian region. Similarly, China's close understanding with Cambodia further damaged Vietnam-China relations. The remark of India's former Defence Minister, George Fernandes in 1998, where he described the Chinese threat as an impulse for New Delhi's nuclear weaponisation, was amply demonstrative of India's mindset towards China.[49] Likewise, Vietnam is also suspicious and apprehensive of China's intentions, which was explicitly manifest in an official remark by a Vietnamese Foreign Ministry official in 2000, when he said: "We don't trust China".[50] Therefore, both India and Vietnam enjoy a seam of strategic interests, creating the basis for building and reinforcing cooperation between them, where China figures prominently in the respective strategic domains.

Besides this, in the post-Cold War years, China's emergence as a major strategic and economic power in the Asia-Pacific region, due to the absence of former Soviet Union and the United States (in the region), has deeply influenced both India and Vietnam. The growing unease across this region over China's rise led Vietnam to approach other countries receptive to friendlier ties. Like the Philippines, which sought to maximize its long-time relationship with the United States and recently with Japan, Vietnam has cast a wider net for friends and over the last two decades, it has made fast friends with a number of external powers, including India, Japan, Russia, Australia, Germany, Italy, Sweden and the United States.[51] Like Vietnam, India has become wary of China, since the latter strategically regarded the Asia-Pacific region as vital to its security and any Indian attempt to intrude into it was viewed with suspicion. However, New Delhi has made it clear that it perceives its strategic interests to be stretching from the Gulf of Aden to the South China Sea. Besides this, the growing importance of the Straits of Malacca, from where more than 50 per cent of India's trade and more than 80 per cent of China's oil passes, makes this route one of the world's most vital strategic waterways at present. The joint patrolling between India and US in the sea lanes along the Straits of Malacca, in conjunction with other countries of Southeast and East Asia in recent times are representations not only of greater cooperation between the two countries, but also signal India's emergence as a key player in the region. Moreover, India's 'Look East' policy has led to an increasing engagement with Southeast Asia and the sea lanes to the further east are growing in significance for its energy security, as New Delhi looks for oil and gas supplies from Myanmar, Vietnam and Indonesia. Furthermore, the idea of upgrading the security structure of the Andaman and Nicobar Islands and the surrounding areas due to China's growing presence in Myanmar's Coco islands has also emerged as an important security concern for India. Thus, India's 'Look East' naval diplomacy, along with the new naval doctrine, ranks high on the agenda of Indian foreign policy in the present global order. Like India, the Vietnamese leadership, through its past experience, looks at India as "a friend and neighbour," which does not force her views or prescribe solutions, but is ready to work together and address common problems.

Moreover, since the fall of former Soviet Union, the Chinese leadership has shown inclination to support ASEAN's central position in the region and has developed an extensive bilateral relationship with its member-states. It is friendly towards Southeast Asia and has tried to develop an image of a constructive actor and "soft power" by persuasion, rather than coercion, in regional politics. It has initiated various measures—including cultural, diplomatic, participation in multinational organizations, business actions abroad, the gravitational pull of its economic strength, and the employment of several strategies—to boost its win-win stance in this region. Like China, India's integration with Southeast Asia has been primarily market and private sector-driven; the government's commercial diplomacy has also played a positive role. It has been felt by India's policy makers that Vietnam is gradually becoming the linchpin of this eastward move by New Delhi. Besides this, there has been domestic political and public consensus on India's 'Look East' Policy. Presently, New Delhi's desire to deepen its friendship with all members of ASEAN, including Vietnam, has been in making its presence felt in the Southeast Asian region to compete with and ignore China's presence in the region. Moreover, India's strategic and national security interests demand that Vietnam emerges as a strong state and where, India is better placed to contribute towards this aim in all fields compared to China—defence cooperation, political cooperation, economic and technical assistance and technology transfers. This display of a firm politico-strategic mindset helped India to strengthen its relationship with Vietnam. If China wants to expand its presence in South Asia and the Indian Ocean regions, New Delhi also felt that it can do the same in Southeast Asia. Therefore, for India, Vietnam is already seen as a counterweight in the same way that Pakistan is for China. However, China knows that India is the only country that could possibly challenge its ascendancy and potential hegemony in Asia, and therefore it makes sense for China to try to keep India under pressure. India and Vietnam enjoy a convergence of strategic interests, which could provide the basis for building and reinforcing strategic cooperation between them, which China never endorsed as reflected in confrontational situation quite often on a number of issues. Therefore, the major subject of discussion in the triangular relations between India, Vietnam and China will be the manner in which China is either contained or diplomatically engaged in future.

Conclusion

Having analyzed the emerging trends of strategic partnership between India and Vietnam in the post-Cold War years, it is evident that New

Delhi has taken a pragmatic, constructive gesture towards Vietnam in the backdrop of the changing global order, and modified its past solidarity-cum-friendly policy. As a part of this policy, India presently concedes Vietnam's strategic position in the realm of Southeast, East and Asia-Pacific politics. This growing attention towards Vietnam is stimulated not only by burgeoning trade but also by the speed at which China's navy is modernizing and expanding its wings in the South China Sea region. To counter this growing Chinese expansion, India diplomatically tries to play a more pro-active role in Southeast Asia, where strategic shipping lines are located. With such a policy, India has tried to balance the far-reaching plans of China to increase its sphere of influence. New Delhi's experience with the China policy in the South Asian region is not without its pros and cons. Beijing's interference in the Indian Ocean, including port construction in Myanmar and in southern Sri Lanka and through Pakistan etc. has placed New Delhi in a continuously disadvantaged strategic position in the South Asian region. To contain such a Chinese strategic posture, India is helping Vietnam strengthen its Defence, Air Force and Naval power, and thereby acting as a catalytic pressure point against Beijing. So, New Delhi's defying of Chinese objection and threat and agreeing to continue the ONGC oil and natural gas exploration projects in multiple Vietnamese blocks in South China Sea, adequately exhibits a new dynamics of its 'Look East' policy, which is strategically correct and diplomatically pragmatic. Furthermore, this gesture of India also mirrors its greater assertiveness in the politics of Asia and clearly signals that Asian politics can no longer be monopolized by any single power. Thus, India's strategic thrust towards Vietnam, has added new content in the implementation of its 'Look East' policy. Unlike China, Vietnam as a regional power would not be hostile to India or Indian national security interests in the region. So a strategic partnership with Vietnam provides India with an opportunity to pressurize China and restrict Chinese ambitions. Moreover, a strong and robust India-Vietnam partnership is important for realization of India's strategic interests in the maritime domain and Vietnam's pursuit for engaging reliable international stakeholders in the region. In essence, Vietnam views India as its most trusted strategic partner and their relations are certainly going to take a more productive shape in the future. Needless to say, this strategic initiative and India's re-activated 'Look

East' policy needs to be sustained as essential without losing track of its core objectives, in the context of the changing regional order in the Asia-Pacific.

NOTES

1. Tridib Chakraborti, "India-Vietnam Relations: A Time Tested 'Look East' Friendship", *Jadavpur Journal of International Relations,* Vol. 6, 2001-2002, Jadavpur University, Kolkata, pp. 239-240.
2. *Vietnam Courier* (Hanoi), No. 1, January, 1986, p. 4.
3. Tridib Chakraborti, No. 1, pp. 240-242.
4. Tridib Chakraborti, *India and Kampuchea: A Phase in Their Relations–1978-81,* Minerva Associates, Calcutta, 1985, p. 89.
5. *Ibid.*, p. 127.
6. Tridib Chakraborti, "India's Economic Support to Socialist Vietnam: An Aspect of India's Foreign Policy", in A. Lakshmana Chetty (ed.), *The States of Indochina: Stability, Development and Foreign Relations*, Centre for Studies on Indochina, Sri Venkateswara University, Tirupati, 1997, p. 45.
7. Tridib Chakraborti, "India's Southeast Asia Policy in the 1980s and 1990s: Contrasting Shades in Foreign Policy Priorities", *Jadavpur Journal of International Relations*, Vol. 1, 1995, Jadavpur University, Kolkata, p. 155.
8. *The Indian Express*, August 17, 1988.
9. Tridib Chakraborti, "India and Vietnam: A New Dimension in South-South Economic Cooperation", *Asian Studies* (Calcutta), Vol. 8, April-June, 1990, pp. 55-56.
10. Tridib Chakraborti, "Strategic Convergence between India and Vietnam in the Twenty-first Century: "Look East" as a Parameter", *Indian Foreign Affairs Journal,* New Delhi, Vol.3, No. 4, October-December 2008, p. 43.
11. Rajiv Sikri, "India's Foreign Policy Priorities in the coming Decade", ISAS Working Paper No. 25, September 25, 2007, p. 47.
12. Tridib Chakraborti, "India and Vietnam: Sprouting Strategic Partnership", *World Focus*, Annual Number, Vol. 32, No. 11-12, November-December 2011, pp. 896-897.
13. *Ibid.*, p. 896.
14. For details see 202.151.160.183/qdndsite/en-US/75/72/182/155/.../Default.aspx (accessed on September 25, 2011).
15. *The Hindu*, September 8, 1994; see also *The Pioneer* (New Delhi), September 8, 1994.

16. *The Times of India*, August 3, 1997; see also *The Statesman* (Kolkata), August 3, 1997.
17. For details see Subhash Kapila, "India-Vietnam Strategic Partnership: The Convergence of Interests", Paper No. 177, South Asia Analysis Group, at http://www.saag.org/papers2/paper177.htm (accessed on March 28, 2014).
18. Tridib Chakraborti, no. 10, p. 45.
19. Ian Storey and Carlyle A. Thayer, "Cam Ranh Bay: Past Imperfect, Future Conditional", *Contemporary Southeast Asia*, Vol. 23, No. 3, December 2001, p. 468.
20. *Nhan Dan*, July 7, 2007.
21. http://www.india-defence.com/reports-3652 (accessed on September 22, 2011).
22. For details see http://indiadefenceonline.com/2256/india-to-boost-ties-with-vietnam/ (accessed on September 25, 2011).
23. For details see http://www.defencetalk.com/forums/military-strategy-tactics/india-vietnam-strategic-partnership-9559(accessed on September 25, 2011).
24. "Indian Air Force to get first BrahMos-armed Su-30MKI fighter in 2015", August 2, 2013, at http://in.rbth.com/economics/2013/08/02/indian_air_force_to_get_first_brahmos-armed_su-30mki_fighter_in_ 201_27927.html (accessed on 16 April, 2014).
25. Robert Johnson, "India Is Preparing To Sell BrahMos Supersonic Cruise Missiles to Vietnam", September 20, 2011 at http://www.businessinsider.com/india-to-sell-brahmos-missiles-to-vietnam-china-2011-9.
26. Vivek Raghuvanshi, "India to Train Vietnamese Sailors, Expand Ties", December 12, 2013 at http://www.defensenews.com/article/20131212/DEFREG03/312120020/India-Train-Vietnamese-Sailors-Expand-Ties (accessed on 16 April, 2014).
27. http://www.defencenow.com/news/223/vietnamese_naval_chief_visits_india_to_foster_defence_ties.html (accessed on September 25, 2011).
28. Rajat Pandit, "India to help train Vietnam in Submarine Operations", *The Times of India*, September 15, 2011.
29. Sujan Dutta, "China in Mind, Salute & Port Plea to Vietnam", *The Telegraph*, September 17, 2011.
30. For details see http://www.wantchinatimes.com/news-subclass cnt.aspx?id=20130610000067&cid=1101 (accessed on 16 April, 2014).
31. Tridib Chakraborti, "A Time-tested Friendship in the New Global Order", in Vijay Sakhuja (ed.), *India-Vietnam Strategic Partnership: Exploring Vistas for Expanded Cooperation*, Pentagon Press, New Delhi, 2011, p. 180.
32. Tridib Chakraborti, "Strategic Convergence between India and Vietnam in the Twenty First Century: 'Look East' as a Parameter', *Indian Foreign Affairs Journal* (New Delhi), Vol. 3, No. 4, October-December 2008, p. 47.

33. Vijay Sakhuja, "India, Vietnam: Time to Expand the Strategic Partnership", September 10, 2011, at http://sspconline.org/opnion/India_Vietnam_Timeto Expand_StrategicPartnership_10092011 (accessed on September 25, 2011).
34. For details, see http://www.pib.nic.in/archive/pm_visit_iv/indoiv.html (accessed on October 2, 2011).
35. Tridib Chakraborti, no. 10, p. 47.
36. For details see http://www.ongcvidesh.com/op_vietnam.asp (accessed on October 2, 2011).
37. Tridib Chakraborti, no.10, p. 51.
38. For details see Pankaj K. Jha, "India–Vietnam Relations: Need for Enhanced Cooperation", *Strategic Analysis,* Volume 32, Issue 6 , November 2008, pp. 1085-1099.
39. For details see http://thehanoist.wordpress.com/2010/07/29/vietnam-hedges-its-china-risk/(accessed on April 13, 2014).
40. ONGC Videsh Limited, "Assets", http://www.ongcvidesh.com/Assets.aspx?AspxAuto DetectCookieSupport=1 (accessed on April 13, 2014).
41. P. K. Ghosh, "Binding Vietnam and India: Joint Energy Exploitation in South China Sea", RSIS Commentaries, December 17, 2013, at http://www.rsis.edu.sg/publications/Perspective/RSIS2282013.pdf (accessed on April 13, 2014).
42. For details see, Harsh V. Pant, "Why India must not withdraw from the South China Sea", Rediff, June 1, 2012, at http://www.rediff.com/news/column/why-india-must-not-withdraw-from-the-south-china-sea/20120601.htm (accessed on April 14, 2014).
43. www.daijiworld.com/news/news_disp.asp?n_id=115968 (accessed on October 4, 2011).
44. http://ftpapp.app.com.pk/en_/index.php?option=com_content&task=view&id=154075&Itemid=2(accessed on October 4, 2011).
45. *The Times of India*, September 17, 2011.
46. For Joint Statement see http://www.mea.gov.in/bilateral-documents.htm?dtl/22510/Joint+Statement+on+the+occasion+of+the+State+Visit+of+the+General+Secretary+of+the+Communist+Party+of+Vietnam+to+India (accessed on April 16, 2014).
47. Ananth Krishnan, "Measured Chinese Response to India-Vietnam Deals, *The Hindu,* November 22, 2013.
48. Cited in David Brewster, "India's Defence Strategy and the India-ASEAN Relations", in Ajaya Kumar Das (ed.), *India-ASEAN Defence Relations*, RSIS, Singapore, 2013, pp. 124-145.
49. J.N. Dixit, *Across Borders: Fifty years of India's Foreign Policy*, Picus Books, New Delhi, 1998, p. 408.

50. S.Prasamrajan, "Ahoy Hanoi: With India and Vietnam reviving old bonds, the chances of a strategic tie-up become stronger", *India Today*, New Delhi, November 20, 2000, p. 50.
51. See Julian Kerr and James Hardy, "Australia, Vietnam signal closer Defence Ties", *Jane's Defence Weekly*, March 21, 2013.

REFERENCES

Asian Studies (Calcutta), Vol. 8, April-June, 1990.

Chakraborti, Tridib, *India and Kampuchea: A Phase in Their Relations—1978-81,* Minerva Associates, Calcutta, 1985.

Chetty, A. Lakshmana (ed.), *The States of Indochina: Stability, Development and Foreign Relations*, Centre for Studies on Indochina, Sri Venkateswara University, Tirupati, 1997.

Contemporary Southeast Asia, Vol. 23, No. 3, December 2001.

Das, Ajaya Kumar (ed.), *India-ASEAN Defence Relations*, RSIS, Singapore, 2013.

Indian Foreign Affairs Journal, New Delhi, Vol.3 , No. 4, October-December 2008.

Jadavpur Journal of International Relations, Vol. 6, 2001-2002, Jadavpur University.

Jadavpur Journal of International Relations, Vol. 1, 1995, Jadavpur University.

Jane's Defence Weekly, March, 2013.

Sakhuja, Vijay (ed.), *India-Vietnam Strategic Partnership: Exploring Vistas for Expanded Cooperation*, Pentagon Press, New Delhi, 2011.

Strategic Analysis, Volume 32, Issue 6, November 2008.

World Focus, Annual Number, Vol. 32, No. 11-12, November-December 2011.

8
Vietnam-India Economic Relations from a Geo-political Perspective

Ngo Xuan Binh and *Ngo Minh Duc*

Introduction

Vietnam and India are the two countries located in important strategic positions in Southeast Asia and South Asia. Over the past 40 years, the traditional friendship between Vietnam and India has continuously developed, especially in the fields of economy and trade. The paper discusses factors promoting Vietnam-India relations, as well as characteristics and prospects of Vietnam-India economic relations in the new international context.

Reasons for Promotion of Vietnam-India Relations in the New International Context

Vietnam-India traditional relationship has grown since President Ho Chi Minh and Prime Minister Jawaharlal Nehru laid the foundation of the relations in the 1940s. Since then, generations of leaders and people of the two countries have continued the tradition and raised the two countries' ties to a new level—that of a "Strategic Partnership".

In the new international context with many changes, starting from the end of the Cold War in the early 1990s, together with the disintegration of the Soviet Union and economic globalization, Vietnam-India relations have also been witness to many significant achievements. Which were the reasons for such changes?

Internal Reasons

It could be affirmed that subjective reasons promoting Vietnam-India relations in the present context are the close and friendly ties of the two countries with many similarities, the strategic location of the two countries, and India's "Look East" policy.

Firstly, the traditional friendship has been longly cultivated by leaders of both countries. Both sides actively supported and assisted each other in the struggle for independence and nation-building. This was an important basis for both countries to establish strategic partnership in the twenty-first century.

Secondly, there are many similarities, including the social-cultural links and commercial interests of India with the eastern coastal states dating from ancient times. India had a wide trade linkage with many countries like China, Vietnam, Cambodia, which created a foundation for the similarities and close cultural resemblance (religion, architecture), in history (victims of colonialism, the struggles for independence, country's reform), and the same level of development. Besides, both India and Vietnam are grappling with border disputes with China. This creates a convergence of interests in foreign policies of both countries towards China and is the basis for Vietnam and India to strengthen trade as well as many other areas.

Thirdly, both countries have strategic and geopolitic locations. Vietnam serves as a bridge connecting the Indian Ocean with the Asia-Pacific which gives it political advantages over other countries in Southeast Asia. In addition, with a full length eastern coast, Vietnam has an open space accessible to the route connecting to the wider Asia-Pacific which also accounts for nearly 50 per cent of India's commercial activities with the Asia-Pacific and across the Pacific Ocean to North and South America.

India has a geopolitical land position amd a sea space linking the East and the West and is surrounded by the Indian Ocean. This means that India has great advantages in areas like economic cooperation and maritime security; concomitantly, India can enhance its position and important role in maintaining peace and security in the region.

Fourthly India conducted its Look East Policy with large spatial scope, stretching from New Zealand to Southeast Asia and up to

Northeast Asia since 1991. In particular, India paid special attention to ASEAN countries including Vietnam. India regarded Vietnam as a "springboard" to expand relations with ASEAN countries and then reach out off the region and far beyond. Furthermore, in order to adapt to Chinese policies in the East Sea, India needs to manifest its role and position in the region for its significant interests here.

External Reasons

Entering the twenty-first century, the strong growth of science and technology, the rise of trade and investment, and continuous changes in the region and the world, create great challenges for each country in this region. Policies of major countries in developing relations with ASEAN countries in general and with Vietnam in particular have an impact on the development of Vietnam-India relations.

After the Cold War, Russia's withdrawal from Vietnam and the US' withdrawal from the Philippines created a "power gap" in Southeast Asia—a region having the potential of strategic importance in politics, economy, and military. In addition, high-speed dynamic development of many economies in the region have attracted many countries to boost ties with ASEAN in general and Vietnam in particular. Many bilateral and multilateral trade agreements were signed. China and Japan are two of the countries enhancing relations with Southeast Asia, and China's foreign policy in recent times has focused on ASEAN and Vietnam in particular.

Vietnam-China relations since its normalization (in 1991) have flourished in all fields, especially in political and economic fields. This created favourable conditions for a comprehensive strategic partnership between Vietnam and China, which is seen as one of the fastest growing bilateral relationships in Vietnam today. With its foreign policy, China has far exceeded India in developing relations with ASEAN in general and Vietnam in particular. The rapid development of Vietnam-China relations is an important factor in promoting India's ties with ASEAN, alongside Vietnam, in order to demonstrate its influence and interests in this region.

Vietnam-India Economic Relations

Trade

Vietnam-India comprehensive strategic partnership has been growing strongly and has gained significant momentum. Along with good political relations, bilateral trade and economic cooperation are also enhanced. In recent years, trade relations of the two countries are on a growth path, as shown in the following table:

Table 8.1: Export-Import Turnover and Growth of Import and Export of Vietnam and India in 2006-2012

Year	*Turnover (US$ mil.)*			*Trade Balance*	*Increase/decrease as compared with the previous year (per cent)*		
	Export	*Import*	*Total*	*(US$ mil.)*	*Export*	*Import*	*Total*
2006	138	880	1018	–742	0	0	0
2007	180	1357	1537	–1177	30	54	51
2008	389	2094	2483	–1705	116	54	62
2009	420	1635	2055	–1215	8	–22	–17
2010	993	1762	2755	–769	136	8	34
2011	1554	2346	3900	–792	56	33	42
2012	1782	2161	3943	–379	15	–8	1

Source: General Department of Vietnam Customs.

From the Table 8.1, it is seen that the value of Vietnam's exports to the Indian market keep rising higher than the value of imports. The total value of exports in 2006 was only $138 million, but by 2012 it increased to $1,782 million, an increase of 13 times. In particular, the speed of growth reached 116 per cent and 136 per cent in 2008 and 2010 respectively, as compared with the previous year.

Also, during this period, Vietnam has always been a net importer from India; however, this trend has decreased markedly. In 2012, the trade deficit fell to $379 million, down to 50 per cent as compared to $792 million in 2011. The growth of imports and exports between Vietnam and India and the trade balance are shown in the figure 8.1:

As shown in the above figure, the total value of annual import and export had increased steadily. However, in terms of the relative

Fig. 8.1: Turnover of imports and exports and trade balance between Vietnam and India in the period of 2006-2012

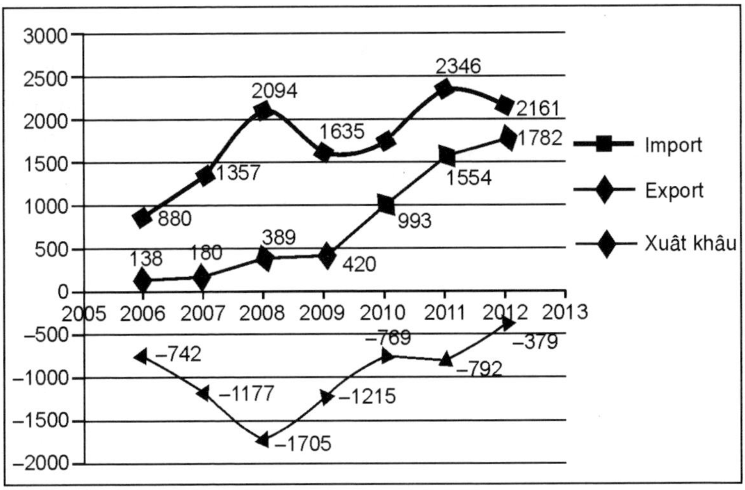

Source: General Department of Vietnam Customs

index, the index showed a significant downward trend if it is compared to the growth rate of the previous year. Total imports in 2012 fell by nearly 8 per cent as compared to 2011.

The ASEAN-India Trade in Goods Agreement (AITIG) under the Framework Agreement on Comprehensive Economic Cooperation, was signed on 16 August 2009 and is valid from 1st June 2010. This agreement has spurred growth of exports in Vietnam, including a number of goods which have very high growth rates, such as rubber (641%), telephones and components (448.6%), and so on.

The density of five groups of Vietnam's major exports (mentioning these five would be useful) to India increased rapidly over the years and accounted for a large proportion of the total 24 exported items. In 2012, mobile phones and components accounted for 41.3 per cent. The density of the five commodity groups increased from 38.9 per cent in 2009 to 63.8 per cent in 2012.

Rubber goods are one of Vietnam's significant exports to the Indian market. In 2012, the total export value of rubber goods reached

Table 8.2: Export Turnover of Vietnam's Five Major Commodity Groups to India in the period of 2009-2012

No.	*Goods*	*Export turnover (US$ mil.)*				*Increase/Decrease as compared to the previous year (per cent)*		
		2009	*2010*	*2011*	*2012*	*10/09*	*11/10*	*12/11*
1	Phones and components	46,63	255,8	371,3	469,1	448,6	45,2	26,3
2	Equipments and Spare parts	39,6	61,1	245,2	238,59	54,3	301,3	–2,7
3	Rubber	10,2	75,6	109,2	211,57	641,2	44,4	93,7
4	Computer, electronic products and components	44,22	67,1	95,9	159,54	51,7	42,9	66,4
5	Coffee	22,51	24	45,7	57,75	6,6	90,4	26,4
	Total of 5 commodity groups	163,16	483,6	867,3	1136,55			
	Density compared to total value of exports	38,9	48,7	55,8	63,8			

Source: General Department of Vietnam Customs.

Table 8.3: Turnover of Vietnam's Five major import groups from India—2009-2012

No.	*Goods*	*Import turnover (US$ mil.)*				*Increase/Decrease as compared to the previous year (per cent)*		
		2009	*2010*	*2011*	*2012*	*10/09*	*11/10*	*12/11*
1.	Corn	60,74	121,3	166,2	329,78	99,70	37,02	98,42
2.	Raw materials and foodstuff for cattle	470,04	412	529	284,65	–12,35	28,40	–46,19
3.	Raw materials and medicine	148,64	167,7	218,7	235,76	12,82	30,41	7,80
4.	Machines, equipments and spare parts		118,8	199	120,7		67,51	–39,35
5.	Raw plastic materials	56,84	55,4	112,3	110,99	–2,53	102,71	–1,17
	Total	736,26	875,2	1225,2	1081,88			
	Density compared to the total value of imports	45,03	49,67	52,23	50,06			

Source: General Department of Vietnam Customs.

US $211.57 million, increasing by 93.74 per cent compared to US $109.2 million in 2011.

For imports, Vietnam focused on raw and production materials such as corn, foodstuff for cattle, pharmaceuticals, machinery, equipment and accessories, plastic, etc.

It is to be noted that the import turnover of these commodities in 2012 witnessed a decrease—or only minor increase—except for corn (an increase of 100 per cent).

The density of the five major imports in a total 39 import groups, accounted for a relatively high proportion, from 45-52 per cent. Total exports and imports of the two countries have increased sharply in recent years, Vietnam and India hope and strive to increase the total bilateral trade volume up to US$ 7 billion in 2015.

Direct Investment

According to data from the Department of Public Policy and Industry Promotion belonging to the Indian Ministry of Commerce and Industry, in the period from 1991 to 2005, Vietnam had an investment of about $ 100,000 in India. According to the Foreign Investment Agency, Vietnam now has three investment projects in India with a total investment of US$ 23.6 million, ranking 45th of 57 countries having capital investment in India up to January 2013.

A typical such project is Rohto Pharma (India) Private Ltd, licensed on June 23,2011 with a total investment of US$ 22.8 million. The scope and mandate of its production business is importing and selling pharmaceutical products, and foodstuffs in India and a major investment share of the Rohto-Mentholatum Co., Ltd. (Vietnam).

Meanwhile, until January 2013, Indian investment in Vietnam was quite large with 68 valid projects with a registered capital of US$ 251.35 million, ranking 30th among 98 countries having invested in Vietnam[1]. Specifically:

Regarding the industry structure: Indian projects are mostly focused on processing and manufacturing with 33 projects and a total investment of US $134.9 million (accounting for 49 per cent of the total projects and 53.7 of the total investment). The next in line is the mining sector with three projects and a total investment of US $86 million (accounting for 4 per cent of the total projects and 34.2 per cent of the total investment).

Regarding investment areas: Excluding three projects of oil and gas exploration, India has investments in 19 localities but invested capital is mainly used in the Tuyen Quang province with Alliance's mining projects and a total invested capital of US $15 million, as well as in the Ninh Thuan province with Vietnam Dhampur's sugar production project. The total investment is US$22 million.

Regarding investment forms: Most of India's invested capital is in the form of 100 per cent foreign capital with 49 projects (accounting for 72 per cent of the total projects and 56.5 per cent of the total investment). The remaining capital is in the form of business cooperation contracts and joint ventures.

Two typical Indian projects in Vietnam are the production-sharing contracts to explore Oil Block 127 and 128, licensed on June 16, 2006, with a total investment of US$ 40 and 20 million respectively. The investor is India's ONGC Videsh Ltd.

Tourism

Vietnam and India are the two countries sharing a long history with many similarities. The richness, diversity of lifestyle, cultural heritage and festivals are advantageous for both Vietnam and India to become important tourist destinations. However, due to lack of information about each other, the difficulty of travel etc., tourism has still not been developed appropriately to its potential. According to Vietnam's National Administration of Tourism, about 14.5 million Indians are estimated to travel abroad, of which about 2.5 million travel to the ASEAN countries. However, the number of Indian tourists to Vietnam is not significant.

A workshop on Vietnam-India Investment and Trade Cooperation under the framework of the Vietnam-India Economic Forum suggested measures to improve tourism between the two countries. Specifically, five issues that need to be resolved soon are a direct air route from Vietnam's urban centres to the capital and cities of India and vice-versa, enhancing cooperation in tourism at various levels such as state-to-state, locality-to-locality and especially business-to-business;

and boosting market research with specific products suitable to visitors. Tourism products like destination (especially the demand for destinations associated with culture and spirituality), and food services have attracted attention from both the countries. Besides, the two countries have been proceeding to simplify visa procedures and promote cooperation to popularize bilateral tourism potential.

Prospects for Vietnam-India Economic Relations

Looking back at Vietnam-India relations in all fields of economics, politics, culture, education, science and technology and national security, there is a good prospect for the two countries' ties in the future. The change in the relationship, from the mutual trust and understanding relationship to the comprehensive cooperation relationship, and then to the strategic partnership, reflects a positive change as well as a strong determination of the leadership of the two countries.

The economic cooperation, particularly in trade between the two countries, has been positive, bringing practical results for both sides. The visit of Vietnamese General Secretary Nguyen Phu Trong to India was an important one towards promotion of cooperation more practically, and more effectively, especially in economic ties.

The Vietnamese General Secretary and Indian leaders agreed on the critical guildlines and issued a Joint Declaration. Some key highlights of boosting economic ties between Vietnam and India as per the Declaration are:

- On strategic engagement, both sides agreed to further enhance high-level visits and meetings between the two countries. There still remains considerable potential for cooperation and there was agreement on enhancing the comprehensive strategic partnership between the two countries based on the key pillars of political, defence, security, economic, cultural and human resource development cooperation. The leaders agreed to further deepen the strategic partnership, by adding more concrete programmes and projects and broadening it to new areas for cooperation, taking into account the changing political and economic situation both at the regional and international levels. Both sides agreed to continue strengthening cooperation in the areas of politics, economy, trade and investment, finance, science and technology, human resource development, culture, agriculture, fisheries, aquaculture, etc., while striving to expand cooperation in areas such as high-tech science and technology, justice, public health, information and communication, tourism, sports, press, and other areas of mutual interest.

- The two sides welcomed the further strengthening of cooperation in the fields of defence and security. They expressed satisfaction at the outcome of the 6th India-Vietnam Security Dialogue at the Deputy Defence Minister level and the establishment of a mechanism of a biennial dialogue on security issues between the Ministry of Home Affairs of India and Ministry of Public Security of Vietnam and agreed to work towards the early completion of the Indira Gandhi Hi-tech Forensic Laboratory in Ho Chi Minh City. The Vietnamese side welcomed the offer for training and capacity building of Vietnamese police forces.
- The two sides stressed the importance of maintaining peace, stability and of ensuring the safety, security and freedom of navigation in the high seas. The two sides agreed that disputes in the East China Sea should be settled through peaceful negotiations, without resorting to the threat or use of force by the parties concerned, in accordance with universally recognised principles of international law, including the 1982 United Nations Convention on the Law of the Sea and the 2002 ASEAN-China Declaration on the Conduct of Parties in the East China Sea.
- The leaders agreed to further strengthen cooperation at regional and international fora, especially the ASEAN-India and Mekong-Ganga forum as well as in the East Asia Summit (EAS), ASEM, ARF, WTO, UN and the Non-aligned Movement. The Vietnamese side reaffirmed its strong support for India's Look East Policy and the strengthening of the ASEAN-India relationship. The Indian side congratulated Vietnam for its success in fulfilling its role as ASEAN Chair in 2010 and thanked Vietnam for its support to India's

candidature for permanent membership in an expanded United Nations Security Council and the G4 short draft resolution on reform of the UNSC.

- Both sides also agreed to closely cooperate to promote dialogue and cooperation within the EAS with the aim of promoting peace, stability, development and prosperity in East Asia.
- The two sides strongly condemned terrorism in all its forms and manifestations and resolved to increase cooperation in the common efforts of the international community in preventing this scourge in a comprehensive manner. Both sides agreed to closely cooperate for an early finalisation of a Comprehensive Convention on International Terrorism, for which India had presented a draft at the United Nations in 1996.
- Especially, on the economic cooperation front, the two leaders unanimously agreed to lift the economic partnership for it to become one of the main contents of the strategic partnership between the two countries. The two sides unanimously agreed to create favourable conditions to increase the bilateral trade to US$ 15 billion by 2020 and boost the investment between the two countries, especially in fields such as education, infrastructure, oil and gas, energy, new energy and renewable energy, agriculture, textile, information technology and pharmacy. The two leaders also unanimously agreed to cooperate to soon deploy the ASEAN-India Free Trade Agreement in the tourism and investment fields in order to develop further based on the motive force from the ASEAN-India Free Trade Agreement in the fields of goods. The two sides also unanimously agreed to cooperate to soon implement the Regional Comprehensive Economic Partnership (RCEP) in order to support India to join the ASEAN Economic Community.
- The Vietnamese side welcomed the new investments of the Indian companies in the upstream and downstream oil and gas projects in Vietnam. The two leaders expressed their satisfaction that PetroVietnam has given priority to introducing India to the new area for exploration and exploitation of oil and gas. The two leaders particularly welcomed and supported the introduction of the Tata Group to join as the bidder of the

Project of the Long Phú 2 Thermal Power Electric Plant with a capacity of 1,200 MW. This is India's largest investment project in Vietnam and will be the pioneer project to encourage larger investment flow from India.

- Besides, the two sides encouraged cooperation between the private sectors of the two countries and affirmed the private sector support towards the Vietnam-India Enterprises Forum and the activities of the chambers of commerce and industry of the two countries. The Vietnamese side also unanimously agreed to give active support to the "Vietnam-India Enterprises Council". The two leaders decided to enhance the connection between Vietnam and India in land, marine and air transportation. The two sides welcomed the signing of the Agreement on Air Transportation with the aim of boosting cooperation in the civil aviation sector and welcomed the signing of the Agreement on Marine Transportation. They also proposed to start official negotiations on the agreement on the sub-region transportation network between India and Cambodia, Laos, Myanmar and Vietnam. The two leaders highly valued the importance of expanding the road connections between Vietnam and India and welcomed India's proposal to start discussions on the requirements for the soft infrastructure so as to create conditions for the transportation of the goods and services through the economic corridor and start negotiations for the ASEAN-India Transit Transportation Agreement (AITTA), expected to be completed in late 2015.
- Both sides noted with satisfaction that the two-way trade had increased steadily in recent years and the trade deficit on the Vietnamese side had declined. President Truong Tan Sang affirmed that Vietnam would create favourable conditions for Indian enterprises to invest in the country. Both sides agreed to step up trade and investment linkages, inter-alia by encouraging cooperation between the private sectors. Both sides set a target of US $7 billion in bilateral trade by 2015 and welcomed the entry into force of the India-ASEAN FTA in Goods and agreed to work for the early finalization of the India-ASEAN FTA in Services and Investments.

During the visit, the two sides signed eight cooperation agreements in the fields of trade, finance, energy, transportation, education-training, and people-to-people exchange. This is one of the important bases to determine that a bright future exists for Vietnam-India economic relations.

With geopolitical, geo-economic advantages, resources and potential, the need for reform, integration and development in each country, along with the increasingly strengthened bilateral relations, the trend of strengthening economic cooperation in the region has been creating and will create favourable conditions for the further development of the bilateral economic relations of the two countries in the future.

NOTES

1. Department of Foreign Investment, Ministry of Plan and Investment, Vietnam http://fia.mpi.gov.vn/news.aspx?ctl=news&mID=464

REFERENCES

Do Duc Dinh, *50 years of Indian Economy*, The World Publishing House, Hanoi, 1999.

Nguyen Van Lich, "Promoting Vietnam-India Relations", in Promoting Vietnam-India Relations in the New Context, International Conference Proceedings, Hanoi, 2012.

Tran Thi Ly (ed.), *The Modification of Republic: Indian Policies from 1991 to 2000*, The Social Sciences Publishers, Hanoi, 2002.

Truong Sy Hung, *Religions in Cultural Life of Southeast Asia*, Culture Publishing House, Hanoi, 2010.

Pranav Kumar, "Multilateral Trading System: Is it India's Best Option?" *Policy Analyst*, CUTS Centre for International Trade, Economics & Environment (CUTS CITEE), April 2008.

Southeast Asia—South Asia—Pacific Department, Ministry of Foreign Affairs, *India and Vietnam—India Relations*, The World Publishing House, Hanoi, 2011.

Ngo Xuan Binh, Le Thi Hang Nga, "Promoting Vietnam-India Strategic Partnership in the New context", in *Promoting Vietnam-India Relations in the New Context*, Internatiomal Conference Proceedings, Hanoi, 2012

9
Urban Environmental Pollution in India and Vietnam

A Comparative Study

Nguyen Thi Ngoc

Introduction

The process of urbanization takes place in most countries around the world. This is also one of outstanding features in developing countries. Urbanisation is usually the focus of a large population, administrative centres, commercial and cultural centres, etc. The process of industrialization and modernization in Vietnam and India has gone together with the urbanization process. In addition, urbanization is the positive characteristic in developing countries, but it is difficult to manage its negative effects not only in India but also in Vietnam. In this paper, some general comparisons are provided on the current situation of urban environmental pollution in India and Vietnam, and common challenges that the two countries need to address in the future are enumerated.

As two developing countries in Asia, India and Vietnam have made efforts in promoting economic development while protecting the natural environment. However, both countries are now grappling with many serious environmental concerns such as air, water and soil pollution, domestic and industrial waste, loss of biodiversity, etc. These are much more urgent problems for people, especially those living in urban areas and large cities.

Water Pollution

In India, the problem of water pollution in urban areas is becoming increasingly serious. According to a survey of the United Nations, the number of deaths due to diseases relating to water pollution is greater than the number of people killed by terrorists in this country. Approximately 90 per cent of water sources suffer from contamination or "sick water", discharged directly into the river and the ground from plants and industrial parks, without treatment. In addition, 80 per cent of the water and waste in urban areas of India, dumped directly into rivers flowing through urban areas, makes the level of water pollution more serious. The survey results also indicate that a major source of water for daily living does not meet the quality standards[1]. For example, along banks of the Ganga river, where 82 per cent of the Hindus are living, people are struggling with serious illness and they face death due to water pollution. Along the Ganges near Varanasi, the amount of coliform and harmful bacteria found in water samples is 3,000 times higher than the quality standards of drinking water for daily use[2].

Some Indians have a habit of using a lot of plastic and glass bottles to store beverages, after use. This waste is discharged directly into the environment; it is noteworthy that it is dumped into rivers flowing through the area. Previously, India had some landfills, but they have been overloaded. So, currently, waste is almost pouring into river after collection. Specifically, 57 per cent of garbage in Delhi city is dumped daily into River Yamuna. Only 55 per cent of the 15 million people living in Delhi have sewage systems connected with the common sewage system of the city; others use water from rivers and also discharge directly into them. According to calculations of the Centre for Science and Environment, untreated wastewater system accounts for 75-80 per cent of the pollutant recourses to rivers. Besides that, industrial waste water and waste water leak from the landfills lead to rivers gradually "dying". According to estimates by Indian scientists, it will cost $ 500 million to be able to clean up such dead rivers[3].

Exploitation and overuse of groundwater is also warned by scientists as a source of causing water pollution in India. In April 2010, over 18 per cent of new-born children in Bihar's Bhojpur suffered from temporary blindness within three months; the causes were attributed to the use of arsenic-contaminated groundwater. According to estimates by the World Health Organization, each year there are about 4 billion people in the world suffering from diarrhea due to unsafe drinking water that fails to meet hygiene standards. Nearly 2 million people die from diarrhea, most of whom are children and poor people living in developing countries. Ground water in Indian cities is polluted due to discharge of waste water from living activities and industrial parks.

In Vietnam, the results of water quality observation in major rivers flowing through urban centres such as Hanoi, Ho Chi Minh City, Hai Phong, Da Nang, Viet Tri, Thai Nguyen, Dong Nai, etc. show that the pollution has increased significantly over time, especially in the dry season, when water flow falls. The content of BOD_5, NH_4^+, TSS, metals, and pesticide in rivers exceeds the permissible Vietnamese quality standards in each different region.

Fig. 9.1: Water Pollution at West Lake, Hanoi

Source: http://www.tienphong.vn

In urban areas, water in rivers and lakes, ponds, canals and small rivers that receive industrial or domestic wastewater, is eutrophication and the concentration of substances is 5 to 10 times higher than the permissible standards (compared to the Vietnamese Quality Standards for surface water level B 2010). For example, the concentration of substances in Nhue-Day Rivers is many times higher as standards—for instance, the content of Ammonium, COD and TSS respectively—exceeds 380 times, 5 times and 6 times the acceptable limits respectively.[4]

Domestic and industrial wastewater from industrial parks and craft villages in many urban areas is dumped directly into rivers without treatment. According to statistics, currently there are about 300 sources of environmental pollution at basins of the Nhue River, Day River, Sai Gon River, Dong Nai River and Cau River, with a total estimated volume of waste water being 712,532.48 cubic meters per day. Recently, some companies and enterprises discharged unqualified waste water into river basins. The Vedan Company discharged into the Thi Vai River causing serious pollution or[5] the Viet Tri Chemical Company discharged into the Hong River, causing severe pollution at the confluence.

The groundwater of Vietnam in general and in urban areas in particular, is abundant. However, groundwater in some urban areas is facing the risk of microbial, heavy metal contamination and salinity due to lack of planning in drilling wells and lack of adequate protection or saltwater intrusion.

According to environmental experts, major sources of water pollution in urban areas include: excessive exploitation and overuse of surface water, groundwater resources; domestic and industrial waste water; waste water leakage from landfills seeping into groundwater; and backward degraded water supply and drainage system.

Water pollution is the cause of many serious diseases such as: diarrhea caused by viruses, bacteria, bacilli, cholera, dysentery, typhoid, hepatitis A and parasites. Children may suffere from anemia, malnutrition, mortality. According to the Thanh Nhan Hospital in 2007 for example, the incidence of diarrhea of inner-city children was 11.4 per cent. The infection among women at Thanh Tri district who are exposed to sewage is six times higher than at the Van Phuc commune (suburban).

Air Pollution

According to estimates by the World Health Organization, annually there are about 2 million deaths due to air pollution; the number of deaths caused by lung infection, cardiovascular, respiratory, or even cancer is even more or have no accurate statistics. Sources of air pollution are mainly traffic, industrial activities, cooking with wood, coal, oil in households, and synthetic dust due to mining, metal refining, etc.

In the urban areas of India, the problem of indoor air pollution is emerging, especially in slums. This causes lung diseases among human beings. According to surveys of the Chest Research Fund and the Royal College of London, there are about 700 million people in India suffering from indoor air pollution, especially women and children as a result of the habit of using wood, straw, or cattle manure for cooking. In fact, cooking fuel of households is determined by their economic status; the poor often use utilized fuels for cooking. This means that they have to bear a high risk of environmental pollution.[6]

As we know, emissions such as carbon dioxide, nitrogen dioxide, sulfur dioxide etc. are compounds that cause greenhouse effect and global climate change and also the main cause of pollution in India. Most cities and urban areas in this country have air environment indicators that have exceeded permissible quality standards and their levels are different from city to city.[7] Vehicular traffic is considered as the largest source of air pollution in India, accounting for 70 per cent of polluting emissions. The fact that India has replaced internal combustion engines in cars also increases air pollution because it generates more than 30 per cent of methane emissions compared to previous engines. According to a recent study, emission from traffic vehicles has increased 84 times compared to 1990. This is understandable because the number of cars used by Indians has doubled from 7 million units in 2004 to 14 million units in 2010 and 100 million units in 2012[8]. Meanwhile, the government is finding it very difficult to ask people not to use private cars to go to work because it is seen as violating individual freedom. For example, in Mumbai, air pollution reaches alarming levels. The concentration of total dust and suspended dust is multiple times higher than permissible quality standards; odour, smoke and pollution from vehicles has exceeded warning levels, and the phenomenon of chemical fog, acid rain, etc. are commonplace.

Industrial activities also have a significant adverse impact on the air and environment in urban areas. In 2010-2011, the Indian government had to close 639 facilities seen to be causing serious air pollution; but this was only a very small number because the fact was that the number of manufacturing facilities that have not followed emission quality standards, was many times higher than that number. It is known that the disasters occurring in Bhopal, Madhya Pradesh, in which the leakage of methyl isocyanine affected 500,000 people, of which 2,259 people were killed immediately, 10,000 people died within 72 hours, and 25,000 people died due to poisoning a few years later. In 2010, chlorine emitted from Sewri Industrial Park led to 76 people being hospitalized.

In India, air pollution, especially dust pollution, usually occurs in the early dry season because of the change of wind direction. In dry season, the wind can bring pollutant substants from country to country in general, from city to city in India in particular. Cities with the lowest air quality in India include Kolkata, Delhi, Mumbai, Chennai. In Delhi, the phenomenon of toxic fog was witnessed in 2011 whose cause was supposed to be various types of vehicles using of both gasoline and diesel. Air pollution can adversely affect health, even threaten human life, especially among young children and the elderly; destroy historical sites, lead to a decline in biodiversity, etc. and this will be more serious if the Indian government does not reduce the birth rate and improve the living standards of its people.

In Vietnam, air pollution becomes a pressing issue for the environment in urban areas, industrial parks, and craft villages. Air pollutant compounds include SO_2, NO_2, CO, H_2S, suspended dust, lead, benzene, etc.

According to statistics of the Vietnam Environment Administration, most urban areas in Vietnam suffer from dust contamination, even serious pollution in some areas. In big cities such as Hanoi, Hai Phong, and Ho Chi Minh City, the concentration of dust is five times higher than permissible quality standards (No. 05/2013). This concentration can be high near roads, especially construction sites; the dust concentrations may exceed permissible quality limits by 10 to 20 times. Dust from traffic accounts for 80 per cent of the total dust concentration in the air. Estimated economic loss due to air pollution in Hanoi is around 1 billion VND per day not taking into account the damage to surrounding areas and flora and fauna[9].

Although the average concentration of SO_2, NO_2, CO_2, Pb in urban areas in Vietnam is now lower, but in future, this will also be the problem. Approximately 90 per cent of total emissions are exhausted from industrial and handicraft activities in urban areas. SO_2 emission from vehicles and living conditions accounts for only 1-2 per cent. At some major intersections in urban areas, the concentration of CO_2, NO_2 is several times higher than permissible quality standards.

It could be said that the major sources of air pollutants in urban areas are industrial and handicraft production activities; transport and traffic, infrastructure and other activites of community. In large urban areas, 70-90 per cent of the emissions are caused by transport, 10-30 per cent are due to industrial production, construction activities, and living conditions.

Air pollution is the cause of many respiratory and infectious diseases due to bacteria and viruses, like asthma, tuberculosis, allergies and bronchitis. According to investigations in the project for improving air quality in the incidence of diseases caused by air pollution among people living adjacent to industrial parks, the rate of people suffering from respiratory infection in Thuong Dinh was 36.1 per cent while in other areas it was 13.1 per cent. The percentage of people suffering from eye symptoms was 28.5 per cent and 16.1 per cent respectively. In 2003, air pollution was the cause of 35.7 per cent of respiratory infection cases and 22 per cent of chronic pneumonia cases.[10]

Municipal Solid Waste

In developing countries like India, government always pays attention to the disposal of municipal solid waste; however, with an urban population of 330 million currently and expected to be 600 million by 2030, this will be a big challenge for natural environment. A major challenge for India in the short-term as well as in the future, is how to manage the amount of municipal solid waste and ensure sustainable living conditions for people. According to estimates by the Energy Research Institute of India, with 5000 cities and towns at present, annually, there will be 40 million tons of waste to be collected and treated; in 2047 this figure will be 260 million tons. Municipal solid waste sources come from households and offices, and do not include waste from industrial and agricultural areas[11].

Nylon, plastic bags are considered the main source of municipal solid waste in India. It should be noted that this waste is discharged directly into ponds and rivers causing serious pollution. For instance, the Yamuna River in Delhi receives a large volume of solid waste on a daily basis, its water gradually turns black, stinks instead of the clear blue water. In India, only the central government is responsible for solid waste management leading to rapid increase of the waste volume. In other words, the continued lack of people's role, involvement, and responsibility in collection and treatment, will certainly not solve this problem.

Besides, the issue of managing hazardous waste is also an important problem in India currently. With a population of over 1 billion people, most of them are living in crowded cities, towns; known as the world's "navel of technology", this country receives a large volume of hazardous waste. According to 2010 statistics, India generated about 7.2 million tonnes of industrial hazardous waste, 4,000 tonnes of electronic waste, 1.5 milion tonnes of plastic waste, 1.7 million tonnes of medical waste, 48 million tonnes of minicipa; waste[12]. Also, India is one of largest waste importing countries in the world. In 2009, India imported 6.1 million tonnes of harzadous waste. It imports 50.000 tonnes everyday[13]. However, in order to control the pollution, India must not import any waste from abroad.

In Vietnam, according to an assessment of the Ministry of Natural Resources and Environment, the amount of solid waste generated in urban areas is growing with increasing toxicity, while management is unable to meet requirements. The average annual rate of solid waste generation increases by 10 per cent.[14] In 2002, the average amount of municipal solid waste generated from domestic activities in larger urban areas was between 0.6 and 0.9 kilograms per person and between 0.4 and 0.5 kilograms per person in smaller urban areas.[15]

By 2004, this rate increased to 0.9-1.2 kilograms per person and 0.5 -0.65 kilograms per person. In 2008, it reached 1.45 kilograms per person and 0.4 kilograms per person respectively. According to the report on the environmental status in 2010 (part of solid waste), most types of solid waste were generated from urban areas.

Up to 60-70 per cent of solid waste is generated from the households. As predicted by scientists, the total amount of household solid waste in cities will continue to grow from 10 to 16 per cent per year. This growth rate in large urban areas is higher than in smaller areas.[16]

Hazardous solid waste in urban areas is mainly generated from medical and household solid waste; a small number is generated from the import of outdated, broken electronic items from abroad.

Table 9.1: Situation of Solid Waste Generation for the Period of 2004-2010

Types of Solid Waste	*Unit*	*In 2003*	*In 2008*
Total amount of solid waste	ton/year	15,459,000	27,868,000
Municipal solid waste	ton/year	6,400,000	12,802,000
Industrial solid waste	ton/year	2,638,400	4,786,000
Medical solid waste	ton/year	21,500	179,000
Rural solid waste	ton/year	6,400,000	9,078,000
Craft-village solid waste	ton/year	774,000	1,023,000

Source: Report on Vietnam Environmental Status in 2004—Solid Waste, Urban-Rural Environmental Planning and Research Center, Ministry of Construction, 2010.

According to statistics, the volume of hazardous medical solid waste in Hanoi is approximately 8 tons per day.[17] The total amount of hazardous solid waste in the area is 300 tons per year; 70 per cent of medical solid waste is concentrated in cities and towns.

Meanwhile, the collection and transportation of municipal solid waste does not meet the demand—the collection rate has not increased due to limitations on human resources and low awareness among people about maintaining sanitation. Indiscriminate garbage and unclassified solid waste dumping prior to transporting them to landfills, is the main cause of environmental pollution.

Solid waste is the main cause for the adverse impact on soil, water, air environment and public health. Clinical solid waste is one of the causes of disease infection and adverse impact on living environment of communities. Unpleasant odours are created at landfills, garbage transfers if solid waste is not transported in time. Solid waste can alter physical and chemical properties of water, disturbing operation of microorganisms in water. On the ground, they pollute soil, destroy soil biota.

Comparison, Assessment and Conclusion

In terms of a qualitative perspective, both Vietnam and India are facingserious environmental pollution in urban areas, such as air pollution, water pollution, and solid waste. Transportation, living standards, industrial production and small and medium production networks are main causes of environmental pollution. And in quantitative terms, despite lack of details in numbers and figures, the above analysis shows that the pollution in India is more serious than in Vietnam. It is a result of higher population pressure and economic development in the urban areas of India than Vietnam.

Emission, waste water and non-treatment of solid waste discharge directly into the environment without treatment are main causes of environment pollution. In addition, the rapid ubanization, poor infrastructure not able to keep up with the standards of urbanization, makes the problem of sanitation in urban environments far more serious. The situation in slums—of poor housing, outdated water supply and drainage systems—makes people's life difficult and unhygienic. This is true for both Vietnam and India.

In addition to having low awareness about collection of solid waste and environment protection, bad habits among people in terms of culture and lifestyle in urban areas of Vietnam and India, makes the system of collection and treatment of waste, ineffective. Therefore, urban environment pollution will continue to be a big challenge for both India and Vietnam during their respective industrialization processes.

NOTES

1. Central Pollution Control Board, (2008), *Evaluation of Operation and Maintenance of Sewage Treatment Plants in the India*, Ministry of Environment & Forests.
2. *Environmental Issues in India, (2013),* URL: http://en.wikipedia.org/wiki/Environmental_issues_in_India, (accessed on July 23, 2012).
3. Central Pollution Control Board, (2005), *Status of Sewage Treatment in the India*, Ministry of Environment & Forests, Govt of India.
4. Ministry of Natural Resouces and Environment of Vietnam, (2010), *The national report of environment status*, Hanoi, pp. 80.
5. Thanh Nhat, *Vedan Company kill Thi Vai river,* URL: http://vnexpress.net/tin-tuc/thoi-su/vedan-la-thu-pham-giet-song-thi-vai-2150486.html, (accessed on February 12, 2012).

6. ICMR, 2001, *India Air Pollution in India–A Major Environmental and Public Health Concern,* http://icmr.nic.in/bumay01.pdf, (accessed on October 30, 2012).
7. Centre for Science and Environment, *State of Air Pollution in Indian Cities,* http://www.cseindia.org/node/207 (accessed on January 15, 2013).
8. Durgesh Nandan, (2013), *India have 30% weaker lungs than Europeans,* The Time of India.
9. Ministry of Natural Resouces and Environment of Vietnam, (2010), *The national report of environment status*, Hanoi, pp. 80-150.
10. *According to statistics of the World Health Organization in 2004.*
11. Ganguly *et al.* (2001), *Indoor Air Pollution in India – a Major Environmental and Public Health Concern,* Indian Council of Medical Research, New Delhi.
12. Agnihotri, (2011), *E-waste in India,* Reseach Unit Rajya Sabha Secretariat, New Delhi, p. 4.
13. Agnihotri, (2011), *E-waste in India,* Reseach Unit Rajya Sabha Secretariat, New Delhi, pp. 32-33.
14. Ministry of Natural Resouces and Environment of Vietnam, (2011), *The national report of environment status: Solid waste*, Hanoi, pp. 16.
15. Ministry of Natural Resouces and Environment of Vietnam, (2011), *The national report of environment status: Solid waste*, Hanoi, pp. 8.
16. Ministry of Natural Resouces and Environment of Vietnam, (2011), *The national report of environment status: Solid waste*, Hanoi, pp. 15.
17. Ministry of Natural Resouces and Environment of Vietnam, (2010), *The national report of environment status*, Hanoi, pp. 113.

REFERENCES

Agnihotri, *E-waste in India,* Reseach Unit Rajya Sabha Secretariat, New Delhi, 2011.

Central Pollution Control Board, *Status of Sewage Treatment in the India*, Ministry of Environment & Forests, Govt of India, 2005.

Central Pollution Control Board, *Evaluation of Operation and Maintenance of Sewage Treatment Plants in the India*, Ministry of Environment & Forests, 2008.

Durgesh Nandan, *India have 30% weaker lungs than Europeans,* The Time of India, 2013.

Ganguly *et al.*, *Indoor Air Pollution in India—a Major Environmental and Public Health Concern,* Indian Council of Medical Research, New Delhi, 2001.

Le Huong, (Chief author) (2006), *Human Factor in the State Management on Environment,* Social Sciences Publishing House, Hanoi, 2006.

Le Van Khoa, Nguyen Ngoc Sinh, Nguyen Tien Dung, (2001), *Environmental Strategy and Policy,* Publishing House of Hanoi National University, 2001.

Luu Duc Hai, and Nguyen Ngoc Sinh (2005), *Environmental Management for Sustainable Development,* Publishing House of Hanoi National University, 2005.

Ministry of Natural Resouces and Environment of Vietnam, *The national report of environment status*, Hanoi, 2010.

Ministry of Natural Resouces and Environment of Vietnam, *The national report of environment status: Solid waste*, Hanoi, 2011.

Nguyen Ngoc Tuan (Chief author), *Economic, Social and Environmental Issues of Peri-urban Areas in the Process of Sustainable Development*, Social Sciences Publishing House, Hanoi, 2003.

Nguyen Thi Ngoc, and Pham Thanh Tung, "Status of water and air environmental at Hai Ba Trung District," *Journal of Human Geography,* No. 3, 2005, pp. 22-28, Hanoi, 2005.

Vietnam Environment Administration, Department of Environmental Protection, *Report on National Environmental Situation in 2010,* Hanoi. 2010.

Centre for Science and Environment, *State of Air Pollution in Indian Cities,* http://www.cseindia.org/node/207 accession date January 15, 2013.

ICMR, *India Air Pollution in India—a Major Environmental and Public Health Concern,* http://icmr.nic.in/bumay01.pdf, accession date October 30, 2012.

10

Appraisal of Indira Gandhi's Religiosity

A Vietnamese Perspective

Le Thi Hang Nga

Introduction

The idea of writing about Indira Gandhi's spirituality came to my mind when I read Pupul Jayakar's biography of Indira Gandhi. Until then, Indira Gandhi and Nehru family was often thought of as a family which strongly upheld the secular tradition of India. But it was quite surprising to know about some of Indira Gandhi's religious activities. So, a question came to mind "Was Indira Gandhi religious?" In writing this paper, I try to answer this query.

This paper will try to answer this question with reference to Indira Gandhi's special relationship with Jiddu Krishnamurti, a great philosopher of her time. The paper is divided into three sections: (1) the concept of religiosity and spirituality; (2) Indira Gandhi's family tradition, and (3) Indira Gandhi's religiosity. The paper argues that Indira Gandhi was *spiritual but not religious in its narrow sense.* She rejected traditional organized religion as the sole or most valuable means of furthering spiritual growth; she emphasized the need to return to roots (in case of India the need to return to the roots of Indian thought); she believed that "the light is within you" and we need to find a way to discover it. In other words, Indira Gandhi represented India's mix of tradition and modernity.

Indira Gandhi (1917-1984) was the fourth Prime Minister of India and was perhaps the only woman in world history to have held the position of Prime Minister for three terms.

Being a woman, the accession of Indira Gandhi to the highest position in the world's most populous democracy was especially significant for Indian women, who had been traditionally seen to be subservient to men. As a Prime Minister of a secular country, Indira Gandhi was strongly influenced by her secular father Jawaharlal Nehru. In fact, the term "secular" was added to the Preamble of the Indian Constitution in 1976, during Indira Gandhi's prime ministership. Her biographer, Pupul Jayakar wrote in her biography "Unlike her mother, she was never a devotee, could not surrender herself to god or man. Krishna as a divinity played no role in her life".[1]

However, as it turned out in the last phase of Indira Gandhi's life and as her close relationship with Jiddu Krishnamurti—a great Indian philosopher of his times[2]-unfolded, it is difficult to say that Indira Gandhi was not religious through out her life. In 1971, after her victory over a war with Pakistan, Indira Gandhi was likened to Durga, the Invincible Goddess of Indian mythology. Between 1979 and 1983, as the threat to Sanjay (Indira's second son) increased Indira Gandhi agreed to perform Lakshachandi Path, a ritual where a hundred thousand verses were recited to invoke the primordial power and energy of Chandi, the all-encompassing Mother. The yagna, the oblations to fire, and the recitation of the verses were also conducted regularly. Indira Gandhi is also said to have been in contact with Jiddu Krishnamurti, Lakshmanjoo, one the last exponents of Kashmir Shaivism and sought the presence of Anandamayee Ma.

So, a relevant question which might be asked about Indira Gandhi's life is that "*Was Indira Gandhi religious?*"

The Concept of Religiosity and Spirituality

It is important to remind ourselves of the implications denoted by the concept of religiosity and spirituality. *Religiosity*, in its broadest sense, is a comprehensive sociological term used to refer to the numerous aspects of religious activity, dedication, and belief (religious doctrine). *Spirituality* is a word used in an abundance of contexts that means different things for different people at different times in different cultures. Although expressed through religions, art, nature and the built environment for centuries, recent expressions of spirituality have become more varied and diffuse.

John Swinton recognizes that spirituality has broadened in meaning into "a more diffused human need that can be met quite apart from institutionalized religious structures". He defines "Spirituality is that aspect of human existence that gives it its "humanness". It concerns the structures of significance that give meaning and direction to a person's life and helps them deal with the vicissitudes of existence. As such it includes such vital dimensions as the quest for meaning, purpose, self-transcending knowledge, meaningful relationships, love and commitments, as well as "for some" a sense of the Holy amongst us".[3]

Historically, the words *religious* and *spiritual* have been used synonymously to describe all the various aspects of the concept of religion. Gradually, the word *spiritual* came to be associated with the private realm of thought and experience while the word *religious* came to be connected with the public realm of membership in a religious institution with official denominational doctrines. By this definition, it could be presumed that Indira Gandhi is most of the time spiritual and sometimes religious.

The concept of spirituality is inclusive and affects everybody. It overlaps with that of religion, but unlike spirituality, religion is potentially divisive and adopted only by some. According to Bernard Spilka, most contemporary understandings of spirituality fall into one of three categories: (1) a God-oriented spirituality where thought and practice are premised in theologies, either broadly or narrowly conceived; (2) a world-oriented spirituality stressing one's relationship with ecology or nature; or (3) a humanistic (or people-oriented) spirituality stressing human achievement or potential. Thus spirituality should be viewed as a multi-dimensional construct. Dominique LaPierre identifies the following components of spirituality: (1) a search for meaning in life; (2) an encounter with transcendence; (3) a sense of community; (4) a search for ultimate truth, or highest value; (5) a respect and appreciation for the mystery of creation; and (6) a personal transformation.[4]

Indira Gandhi's Family Tradition

In order to understand Indira Gandhi's spirituality, it is important to have a brief overview of her family tradition.

Indira Gandhi was born in an aristocratic family on 19 November 1917 in Allahabad, India. Her father, Jawaharlal Nehru was a lawyer, leader of the Indian Nationalist Movement and also the first Prime Minister of India. Nehru played an important role in Indira Gandhi's life. Indira served Nehru as his hostess after her mother's death. In return, Nehru served as Indira's primary inspiration. In her words: "*My father's three books—Glimpses of World History, An Autobiography and The Discovery of India—have been my companions through life. It is difficult to be detached about them.*" One of the most important legacies of Nehru is secularism and his distaste with the conflicts among various religious communities. According to Nehru, "Religion as practiced in India has...not only broken our backs but stunted...all originality of thought and mind and...we must get rid of this terrible burden".

Influenced by her father's secular tradition, Indira Gandhi continued to uphold the values of secularism during her time. This is reflected in the fact that in 1976, when she was Prime Minister, the term "secular" was added to the Preamble of the Indian Constitution. This is also reflected in the fact that in the last year of her life, a few days after Operation Blue Star in June, 1984 which aroused hatred among the Sikh community against her leadership, in a secret meeting held at the Prime Minister's office, it was decided not to post any Sikh guards at the Prime Minister's house or office. But when this reached Indira Gandhi, she had refused it by saying: "Aren't we secular?"

Apart from her father, Indira Gandhi was also influenced by her mother, Kamala. Unlike Nehru, Kamala was a religious lady. She was a Kashmiri Brahman and daughter of a well-to-do businessman of Delhi, and had been reared in an orthodox Hindu home, completely insulated from Western influences. She had had little formal education and spoke no English. According to Katherine Frank, Indira Gandhi is a product, psychologically speaking, of Nehru and Kamala. If Indira has Nehru's vision of India civilizationally and culturally, she has Kamla's religiosity and spirituality.[5]

Influences on Indira Gandhi also came from Anand Bhawan, the joint family house where she spent her childhood. Anand Bhawan or "Abode of Happiness" was the splendid villa of Motilal Nehru. The meeting of Western and Eastern cultures within Anand Bhawan gave to the Nehru children—including Indira Gandhi—an early awareness of two sharply divided worlds. Although Motilal and Swarup Rani, (parents of Jawaharlal Nehru) were both Brahmans from Kashmir, Motilal, an affluent attorney, turned his face toward the West with the same intensity that his wife clung to the religious mores of her conservative Hindu upbringing. Swarup Rani exemplified the complacent older Indian women. The focal point of her existence was her husband and her children. Swarup Rani was married at fourteen and possessed of the unshaken loyalty of the Indian wife to her husband. At Anand Bhawan, she found sanctuary in Hindu quarters with their own cuisine, shared with her sister-a woman widowed at sixteen and forced thereafter to wear white—the colour of sacrificial service to others. Spending hours with the Nehru children, she imbued their minds with "the beautiful and terrible myths and legends" of their native land.

But Anand Bhawan was an essentially Westernized establishment with swimming pools, tennis courts, stables of horses, and European foods—a fitting setting for Motilal, a handsome man with a forceful personality, trenchant wit, and profound love of family. With the advent of the national struggle for independence, Anand Bhawan gradually turned into "Swaraj Bhawan" with the occasional visits of intellectuals and political leaders. Perhaps, this explains why Indira Gandhi was both modern and traditional, both secular and spiritual in her thought and action.

Indira Gandhi's Religiosity

What did Indira say about religion? It is difficult to trace Indira's view on religion as she hardly spoke on the subject. But it seems that she was more concerned with the philosophical aspect of religion and the spiritual development of the individual than the actual practices of religion. She said "most people see religion not as a basic philosophy or the essence of life but as the mantras that they may have learnt to utter at a given time...People must go back to the very roots, to the source of faith. Our philosophy says that the divine is in each one; there is light and strength in each one of us. We have to find a way of discovering the energy that is within us."[6]

Indira Gandhi's turn to spirituality was a slow process. It was due to the political compulsions (probably from 1975 onwards), or perhaps, the trauma of defeat and the sudden and violent death of Sanjay, which led Indira to religion. After 1978, Indira Gandhi began to display her religiosity by talking to priests and holy men more often. She was also seen at temples around India. Also from here, most public functions began to acquire a Hindu aura with lamps being lit at the start of each event, marigold garlands for every important guest and often an invocation in Sanskrit. Katherine Frank even went to the extent of saying that "though she (Indira) presented a secular faśade and claimed to have only the vaguest of spiritual beliefs, Indira had always been superstitious—a legacy no doubt of her grandmother Swarup Rani Nehru, as well as her mother. Indira had irritated Nehru, for example, by refusing to move to Teen Murti House until the exact auspicious time and date".[7]

Other events which reflected Indira Gandhi's turn to spirituality were that in 1980, at the age of 62, Indira Gandhi was sworn in as Prime Minister for the third time. At this inauguration, there was mention of God in her oath: "I, Indira Gandhi, swear in the name of God that I will bear true faith and allegiance to the Constitution of India..." If in 1966, she had sworn on the Constitution of India, in 1980 God found place in her pledge.[8]

Indira Gandhi's spirituality also showed during the time she was in jail in 1978. She planned her day with meticulous discipline; she woke up at 5 in the morning, did her morning yogic breathing, drank cold milk brought to her the previous evening by her daughter-in-law Sonia, and went back to bed till 7 o'clock. She then had a bath, meditated for a while and then read one of the six books she was permitted.

In November 1982, Indira's attention turned to Shakti, the primordial female principle as energy, which creates, sustains and destroys... Indira started loving to listen to the chanting of the Sapta Sati (the song in glory of the Goddess). When she heard it, she felt "It is like thunder; it fills the ears, the heart; it pervades".[9] In her letter to Pupul "you know how much I prefer the small primitive temples to the rather ostentatious and more commercialized ones. This afternoon the Maharani took me to Tripur Sundari in her constituency in Udaipur. I went reluctantly as I wasn't sure what she was up to. As I entered (the temple), I felt a close affinity, as if I were with a living person, an old friend..."[10]

Indira Gandhi's spirituality is also manifested in her experience of transcendental feeling. Indira recalled speaking of a day in her life when she felt an overwhelming surge of joy. It had no cause, but the explosion was of such intensity that she felt the earth would open and swallow her up. The ecstasy had transformed her face, and people commented that she looked radiant.

Indira Gandhi's spirituality is also reflected in her thoughts on death. She said she had never been afraid of dying at any age. "I have felt it as a natural process, a part of life. One lives a certain number of years, and then you die". She spoke of a need to return to roots; of Indian thought that maintained "light is within you" and the need to find a way to discover it. On 30 October, 1984, one day before her assassination, Indira Gandhi spoke to the youth of India: "I am here today, I may not be here tomorrow. But the responsibility to look after national interest is on the shoulder of every citizen of India... I do not care whether I live or die. I have lived a long life and I am proud that I spend the whole of my life in the service of my people. I am only proud of this and nothing else. I shall continue to serve until my last breath and when I die, I can say that every drop of my blood will invigorate India and strengthen it." When Andrew Neil questioned Indira as to what would happen to India after she was gone. She replied: "India has lived a long, long time—thousands of years—and my 66 years hardly count. India will survive and India will always find its feet. It has been through tremendous vicissitudes in its long history and it has come through."[11]

Indira Gandhi and Krishnamurti

Indira Gandhi's spirituality is reflected vividly in her special relationship with Jiddu Krishnamurti. Indira's first meeting with Krishnaji was at dinner at Pupul Jayakar's house in the late 1950s and since then Pupul became the bridge connecting Indira with Krishnamurti. Indira appeared shy and hesitant to speak, but later wrote to Pupul that she was "very glad of the opportunity of meeting Krishnaji again" that "his views are always stimulating."[12] Since then, every time Krishnaji returned to India from the United States, they would find time to meet each other. Apart from meetings, they also exchanged letters quite often.

During the Emergency in 1975-77, Krishnaji wished to return to India but was hesitant because of the government's censorship. But Indira said "he is most welcome to come to India and he can speak freely". During Krishnaji's trip to India in October 1976, Indira also expressed her desire to speak with him and was with him for quite some time at Pupul's place. During the dinner, Krishnaji did not talk to Indira. He sensed that she was vulnerable, and did not wish to intrude.

Krishnaji and Indira seemed to have a special connection. "Indira spent over an hour with Krishnaji. She came out of the room visibly moved, and tears were streaming down her face.... During the months Krishnaji was in India, he held Indira in his consciousness. He had been deeply touched by her ability to listen and her refusal to react or defend herself. For Krishnaji, Indira was possibly the only person in her position who was prepared to listen.

Indira did not get emotional easily but when she came to see Krishnaji at 1 King George's Avenue in November 1976, she could not hold back. "I have not cried like that for years". For Indira, "sorrow does not bring tears. But when I am deeply moved, especially by great beauty, I weep." Indira had wept when she met Kamakoti Sankaracharya of Kancheepuram, a great religious teacher of Tamil Nadu, South India. She had also cried when she met Krishnaji in November 1976.[13]

During the conversation between Krishnaji and Indira in November 1976, they spoke of the events in India over the last few months, and Indira had said, "I am riding the back of a tiger, but I do not know how to get off its back." Krishnaji replied, "If you are more intelligent than the tiger, you will know how to deal with the tiger." She had asked him what she should do. He refused to tell her, but said that she should look at the conflicts, the actions, the wrongs as one problem, and then act without motive. He said he did not know the facts, but that she should act rightly, without fear of consequence.[14]

Later, Indira Gandhi said that it was on October 28 1976, the day she met Krishnaji for the second time, a frail movement had awakened in her, suggesting an end to Emergency, whatever the consequences. She had contemplated on this feeling, talked to a few people close to her, and finally took the decision to end Emergency and call for elections.

Krishnaji said that before he left India in February 1977, he had a sudden perception in which he foresaw Indira's defeat in the election. He also said that Indira would face travail, tribulation and violence in the years ahead.

Krishnaji returned to India in early November 1978. He went to Rishi Valley during this trip and Indira wanted to visit Rishi Valley and hoped to meet Krishnaji. So in December 1978 Indira visited Rishi Valley with Rajiv and Sonia and their children Rahul and Priyanka. Krishnaji was puzzled that a prime minister would come such a long distance to visit him and see the valley. He spoke of the special quality of the feelings he had for her.

Krishnaji's next visit to India was on October 26 1981. The day after his arrival, he began to enquire about Indira. He had forebodings about her. There was increasing corruption and violence in India, and the violence would accelerate. Krishnaji was apprehensive if Indira could act and control it as for him, Indira was very "vulnerable". During these years, Krishnaji had been so concerned about Indira. He held her in his consciousness. He felt he could silently communicate with her.[15]

Indira had invited Krishnaji to tea, and was waiting for him on the porch. They were together for two hours. She said she "lost all track of time and had missed a meeting" due to her meeting with Krishnaji.[16]

Indira's letter to Krishnaji in July 1982 said "...my deep appreciation of your concern and I am deeply in need of it just now. This is a depressing time... The world needs your spirit of compassion and direction to look within themselves and the courage to act accordingly."[17]

By early November 1982, Krishnaji was back in New Delhi. Indira and Krishnaji were waiting to meet each other again. During this time, Indira "had not been able to sleep and was waking between two to three every morning, with a feeling of great uneasiness. There were rumours in Delhi that her opponents had been indulging in all manner of plots to destroy her. For three nights she had dreamed of an old, hideous hag who wished to harm her but could not succeed, for a luminous being with a beard was protecting her."[18]

After that, Indira wrote to him, questioning him on the nature of truth and reality. It was clear that her inner inquiry that had been dormant within Indira for years was reawakening.

For Indira, 1983 was a year of destiny. She was to play a vital role on the world stage; but within India, storms were gathering. As Indira's horizons extended, the burdens and responsibilities increased; and with it came extraordinary demands on her time and energy. To meet this challenge, from June 1983, she had imposed a rigorous discipline on her body, eating frugally to strip herself of every extra ounce. Her energy was legendary—her work day stretched to over 18 hours.

Indira's letter to Krishnaji dated December 12, 1983 wrote: "...I had received your message and how much your thoughts mean to me... there are few people to whom one can talk and with you one does not need to talk. I treasure our brief meetings"

Krishnaji was staying at Sterling Apartments, Peddar Road, Bombay, where Indira came to see him on the evening of February 13. She spent a little over an hour with him. He came down in the lift to see her to her car, and held her two hands as they parted. This was the last time they were to meet.

Conclusion

Beginning with a query "Was Indira Gandhi religious?" a satisfactory answer to this question was not available. This paper is hopefully just the beginning of a deeper research on Indira Gandhi's spiritual life. The term religiosity is not suitable to describe Indira Gandhi and the so-called religious activities of Indira Gandhi in the latter phase of her life could be explained as a trend towards the spiritual route.

Was Indira Gandhi religious? Yes and no. Was Indira Gandhi spiritual? Yes. We can safely say that Indira Gandhi was spiritual but not religious in its narrow sense. She might reject traditional organized religion as the sole or most valuable means of furthering spiritual growth; she emphasized the need to return to roots (in case of India the need to return to the roots of Indian thought); she believed that "light is within you" and we need to find a way to discover it. She is a strong and practical politician, but at the same time, deep inside her flow the course of Indian tradition. The best way to conclude about Indira Gandhi's spirituality is to quote her own words. She once said: "*My father loved rivers, but I am a daughter of the Himalayas and I have told my sons that my remains should be scattered on the snow-tipped Himalayas*".[19]

REFERENCES

1. Pupul Jayakar, *Indira Gandhi, A Biography,* Penguin Books, 1995, p. 470.
2. J. Krishnamurti (1895-1986) was born into a Telugu Brahmin family in Madras Presidency of British India (modern day Andra Pradesh). He is regarded by many as the most significant voice of our times and as one who has had a most profound impact on human consciousness. Sage, philosopher and thinker, Krishnamurti illumined the lives of millions the world over. It has been estimated that he talked to more people than any other person in recorded history.
3. Quoted from Dr. Deborah Cornah, *The impact of Spirituality on Mental Health*, Mental Health Foundation, 2006, p. 6.
4. Peter C. Hill, Kenneth I. Pargament, Ralph W. Hood, Jr., Michael E. Mccullough, James P. Swyers, David B. Larson and Brian J. Zinnbauer, Conceptualizing Religion and Spirituality: Points of Commonality, Points of Departure, *Journal for the Theory of Social Behavior* 30:1, 2000, p. 57.
5. Katherine Frank, *Indira: The Life of Indira Nehru Gandhi,* Harper Collins Publishers, London, 2001.
6. Pupul Jayakar, *Indira Gandhi, A Biography*, Penguin Books, 1995, p. 478.
7. Meghnad Desai, *Rediscovery of India*, Penguin Books, 2011.
8. Pupul Jayakar, no. 6, p. 399.
9. *Ibid.*, p. 443.
10. *Ibid.*, p. 443.
11. *Ibid.*, p. 467.
12. Pupul Jayakar, *J. Krishnamurti, A Biography*, Penguin Books, 1986, p. 339.
13. *Ibid.*, p. 345.
14. *Ibid.*, p. 346.
15. *Ibid.*, p. 357.
16. *Ibid.*, p. 357
17. *Ibid.*, p. 361.
18. *Ibid.*, p. 362.
19. *Ibid.*, p. 367.

Contributors

Huynh Thanh Loan (PhD. Candidate), Deputy Head, Department of International Relations, Institute for Indian and Southwest Asian Studies, VASS.

Ishani Naskar (Dr.), Associate Professor, Department of Political Science, Rabindra Bharati University.

Le Thi Hang Nga, Deputy Head, Department of Social and Historical Studies, Institute for Indian and Southwest Asian Studies, VASS.

Ngo Minh Duc, Fellow, Department of Geo-Economy, Institute of Geography and Humanities, VASS.

Ngo Xuan Binh (Prof. Dr.), Director-General, Institute for Indian and Southwest Asian Studies, Vietnam Academy of Social Sciences, Hanoi.

Nguyen Ngoc Quynh (Dr.), Vice Director, Department of Scientific Management, Vietnam Academy of Social Sciences (VASS).

Nguyen Thi Ngoc (Dr.) Research Fellow, Department of Environment and Sustainable Development, Institute of Western Studies.

Rabindra Sen (Prof. Dr.), Professor, Department of International Relations, Jadavpur University.

Subhadeep Bhattacharya, Fellow, Maulana Abul Kalam Azad Institute of Asian Studies (MAKAIAS), PhD. candidate, Department of History, University of Calcutta.

Swapna Bhattacharya Chakraborti (Prof. Dr.), Professor, Department of South & South East Asian Studies, University of Calcutta, Visiting Faculty, Institute of Foreign Policy Studies, University of Calcutta.

Tridib Chakraborti (Prof. Dr.), Professor, Department of International Relations, Jadavpur University.

Index